Fashion and Music

This book is dedicated to my sister Caroline,
with whom I have had more obsessive
conversations about music than any other person.

Fashion and Music

Janice Miller

BERG

Oxford · New York

English edition
First published in 2011 by
Berg
Editorial offices:
1st Floor, Angel Court, 81 St Clements Street, Oxford OX4 1AW, UK
175 Fifth Avenue, New York, NY 10010, USA

Berg is the imprint of Bloomsbury Publishing Plc.

Library of Congress Cataloging-in-Publication Data

A catalogue record for this book is available from the Library of Congress.

British Library Cataloguing-in-Publication Data

A catalogue record for this book is available from the British Library.

ISBN   978 1 84788 414 5 (Cloth)
        978 1 84788 413 8 (Paper)
e-ISBN 978 1 84788 415 2 (Institutional)
        978 0 85785 115 4 (Individual)

Typeset by Apex Publishing, LLC, Madison, WI, USA
Printed in the UK by the MPG Books Group

www.bergpublishers.com

Contents

Contents

Illustrations

Acknowledgements

I owe a great debt of gratitude to Pamela Church Gibson for all her help and encouragement throughout the development of this volume. I would have been lost without her. Thanks also go to our head of department, Adam Briggs.

It is unfortunately impossible for me to mention by name the many colleagues from London College of Fashion (LCF) who have, in myriad ways, provided support throughout the production of this book. However, for their friendship, Sina Shamsavari, Tony Sullivan, Agnès Rocamora and Rachel Lifter, as well as Jane Tynan at Central St. Martins College of Art and Design, deserve special mention. I should also note that the University of the Arts London sabbatical scheme funded invaluable time away from teaching to work on this volume.

The work contained in this book has grown out of several years teaching on the unit Music and Fashion at LCF. As such, the enthusiastic contributions of many students in seminars on these courses and, more recently, discussions with the first-year Foundation Degree Tailoring students have all fed my imagination.

For all their unfailing love and support, I must also mention my parents, Eric and Eileen Miller, as well as Steven Lock, Grace Townend, Sarah-Jane Simpson and Miranda Gavin. Also offering assistance in various ways at different times: Matthew Bernard, Simon Bird, Liam Gavin, Sarah Huxford, Eileen Morgan, Sean and Lucie Morgan, Claire Thomas, Joshua Thomas and Harrison Thomas. Finally, my thanks go to Julia Hall and Anna Wright at Berg for patiently guiding me through the production of this book.

Introduction: Fashion, Identity, Authenticity and Music

The relationship between fashion and music is embedded in and emphasized by the sharing of language. Innumerable songs from David Bowie's 'Queen Bitch' through ZZ Top's 'Sharp Dressed Man' to Estelle's 'American Boy' name fashion brands, fashion looks or engage, one way or another, with the act of dressing up. In the fashion media, the vocabulary of music is ubiquitous. To describe someone as 'rockin' the look' has become a recurrent phrase of approval for an individual look or an individual's style. In similar vein, 'rock chic' has become a perennial fashion staple. Most recently, in 2009, it was credited with putting the 'once dusty Parisian house of Balmain' (see Quick 2009) back on the fashion map thanks to the concurrent injection of some new, young talent in creative director Christophe Decarnin.

Rock chic shares some of the characteristics of another enduring style, the 'rock chick' look, epitomized in the contemporary period by fashion model Kate Moss. This look owes a greater debt to the likes of Anita Pallenberg and Marianne Faithfull and is thus defined not by those making music so much as those living the lifestyle vicariously: fans, girlfriends or groupies. In all cases, black garments, leather, studs, just-out-of-bed hair and smoky eyes are de rigueur.

Clearly, then, music has qualities that offer something to the fashion industry at large. An investigation of what this might be is the focus of chapter 1. It is clear from the start that this must have something to do with rock music's underground credentials and, in particular, the notion of rock as something powerful and dangerous. Chapter 1 argues that such concepts resonate through all forms of music no matter the genre, where a sense of authentic expression becomes intrinsic to music's worth. No matter how manufactured some music performances may be, the desire of both audience and performer to be involved in something with genuine integrity is always present. This mood is identifiable in British *X Factor* 2008 winner Alexandra Burke's assertion that, though she did not write her own songs in a career obviously manufactured by reality television, she would not sing a song that did not resonate with her personally (see BBC 2010). The ability to communicate a story with honesty and sincerity is clearly an important part of how she sees her relationship to her audience. Chapter 1 explores the possibility that such notions of truthfulness and authenticity in music performance have a pervasiveness that, in turn, adds value when placed in association with fashion.

Thus, the correlation between music and fashion informs not only the creative activities that are part and parcel of these industries, but also the interests of both the existing audiences for specific brands or stars and the tastes and habits of consumers more generally. As Patrizia Calefato has argued, 'Fashion and music are two intimately connected forms of worldliness, two social practices that go hand in hand, sustaining one another in the medium of mass communication and drawing on a common sensibility which translates into taste' (2004: 117). Consequently, this relationship plays a significant role in the marketing mystique that surrounds both industries. The part that crossovers between music and fashion play in branding products is the ultimate focus for chapter 1. This is underpinned by a clear understanding that the ability to be active and successful in both the music and fashion markets seems increasingly to be a requirement for music stars—particularly women.

Of course, the influence of music across a variety of industries also offers opportunities for audiences. Inevitably, the fashion ranges produced by increasing numbers of music stars have significance for a contemporary understanding of music fandom because fashion and style present a means by which fans can create cultures and communities and make visible their fan identities. The role of the fashioned body and of clothing itself in making fan cultures material is the focus of chapter 2. Here, the work of clothing in making identities which are informed by fandom is the overarching theme. This is framed by more general ideas about the fan as a cultural figure and, in particular, debates around active fandom. Such discussions are always contextualized by the recognition that fandom has been understood to be a product of industrialized, consumer cultures. Thus, the role that fashion might play in developing an individual's sense of self, his or her skills and social lives informed by fan identities, is considered in relation to a number of fan communities.

More specifically, youth markets and the significance of new media environments for the development of fan identities for this age group offer ways to understand the privileged role of the body and fashion in such youth fan cultures. However, whilst youth fan cultures may have a strong presence online, where fashion is central, such positions are not exclusive to the young. Ultimately in this chapter, fashion and clothing are seen to work in two different ways in fan cultures, as both acts of iteration *through* a variety of fan bodies and communities alongside a commemoration *of* star bodies.

Identifying the role that fashion and music play in the marketing of both industries in these earlier chapters does not aim to undermine the contribution of music and the creative acts of musicians to the making of fundamental, cultural and social change. Throughout its history, music has been seen as a locus for alternative views of the world and, more particularly, a place where challenges can be made to the ways in which bodies are expected to be shaped, formed and adorned. Chapters 3 and 4 examine fashioned styles that seem to go hand in hand with different types of music. These chapters argue that such examples demonstrate the crucial role that a melding of the embodied, the musical and the lyrical, can play in the creation of cohesive and coherent music performances. In particular, the way in which types of gender identity are carved out in relation to both the content of music and its audience is central to the discussions here.

Chapter 3 takes a particular style identifiable in the look of a number of female performers as a starting point for an analysis of femininity and music. The idea that female musicians work within a context that, like many areas of cultural and social life, carries expectations about how women's bodies should both look and work presents an opportunity to, in turn, consider how some forms of embodiment can be understood to resist such limitations.

The chapter is framed by a tacit understanding that the particular witchy look placed in focus here might reflect music content that is often concerned with telling stories of women's lives. The chapter argues that female bodies formed towards heterosexual desire in the conventional way—the aim of much mainstream fashion—would fail to tell these stories coherently to what is often an audience made up of significant numbers of women. Equally, it acknowledges that to fail to conform has often resulted in ridicule from the press and a failure to achieve the kind of mainstream success that ensures career longevity. Thus, the chapter argues that the witchy look can be understood to be a resolution found in ambiguity and suggests that this style of dress can be seen to symbolically negotiate these competing agendas whilst accessing empowered identities and portraying alternative femininities.

Multiple masculinities are core to chapter 4, as is the notion that a look can speak of a whole type of music performance and its market. The suit as an archetypal garment around which a variety of different masculinities are formed in music is central to this discussion. In particular, the chapter comes to focus on the uniformity that the suit has offered to manufactured pop bands. Here, the link between the suit—and ultimately in this chapter, the white suit—and thus a specifically respectable and innocent construction of masculinity is connected to the perceived needs and aspirations of a young female audience. Equally important, the chapter argues that the uniformity of style embodied by these bands can be seen as a manifestation of the contemporary boyband's position within the increasing industrialization of popular music that is part and parcel of the postmodern condition.

Gender continues to be significant in chapter 5, which analyses the implications of ageing to the music performer and the role that fashion plays in working this process through. Inevitably, just as much of the existing debate around ageing acknowledges that women and men are subject to different pressures in this regard, so this chapter is framed by similar concerns of gender difference. At the same time, it also acknowledges that ageing can be a fraught process for many people, requiring seismic shifts in self-identity. In order to be deemed as one who is ageing successfully and in turn to enjoy the esteem that comes with such judgements, the ability to respond to these shifts has become a contemporary imperative.

As objects of desire and thus open to a great deal of scrutiny, stars arguably endure more pressure than the rest of us in this regard. In music, this is amplified as a consequence of some long-held cultural values that make a prevailing connection between youth and music. These values primarily oscillate around the idea that sex, rebellion, spectacular bodies and subcultural resistance are the preserve of the young. Thus, this chapter argues that the pressures on music stars as they age are greater but also helps demonstrate how the products of consumer culture suggest methods of resolution and the means to construct age-appropriate identities as attitudes to life-stage shifts. At the same time, the treatment of older stars by the press and by audiences also makes clear the pitfalls for those who are too fervent in their age-defying activities. Since ageing is rarely conceptualized as anything other than a condition of the body (rather than the inner-self), fashion and bodily maintenance of all kinds offer the primary means by which this ageing process is worked through whilst also acting as a marker by which the success of such strategies is measured.

The notion of subcultural, symbolic resistance is a central tenet of chapter 6, which focuses on the ways in which music and fashion come together to symbolize issues of ethnic and national identities. Specifically, the chapter focuses first on the music of the Black Atlantic. It gives both an overview of the existing in-depth work which has demonstrated the style synonymous with hip-hop and rap music to be a symbolic resistance to the marginalization of black masculinity. It then moves forward to look at the way in which many black hip-hop artists have become an integral part of the fashion industry through their own ranges or via association with long-standing fashion houses. The chapter argues that music and fashion have acted as a way for these artists to access the American Dream of success, choice and fiscal reward. It contends that attached to this is an authenticity which differs from values held elsewhere in music. This difference occurs because it is not being on the margins, but instead enjoying the ability to access some quite conventional areas of cultural life, that signals success and authenticity for groups who were previously denied full access to such experiences.

Secondly, the chapter examines the way in which ideas of national identity as embodied in music often reverberate with issues of social class. Here, in particular, the idea of Americana as an identity construct which runs through the history of popular music is core to the analysis. Thus, the chapter is ultimately shaped by American identities. Here, both the resolute necessity for performers like Bruce Springsteen to articulate a particular sense of Americanness appropriate to a classed identity and the 'double consciousness'—to use Gilroy's (1993) term—of African American performers is made visible through fashion and dress.

Similarly, music and fashion have offered the means by which queer performers could put their identities into mainstream circulation. Strategies of camp have long been a way to make queer identities material through performances that contravene the requirements of conventional behaviour. Chapter 7 argues that music has opened up a unique space for such identity articulations. Here, queer performers dress bodies in unconventional ways and in some cases display what can be argued to be unconventional bodies in themselves, thus marking out queer culture.

The ways in which queer female performers can be seen to shape identities in response to notions of femininity, attitudes to bodies and modes of embodiment are of particular focus here. Ultimately, this analysis leads towards a discussion of how such representations have an impact on the mainstream and ends by evaluating the likelihood that the co-option of some queer female performers—notably Beth Ditto—by the fashion industry might initiate a change in attitudes to bodies and body size. It does not come to the most optimistic of conclusions.

The examples discussed in this book are few amongst many. After all, in the public consciousness the relationship between fashion and music is everywhere. At the level of both representation and industry, their convergence can create new meanings with implications for our understanding of how contemporary social life works. As Noel McLoughlin argues, 'The meaning of dress will be inflected, altered, amplified and contradicted by the musical and performing conventions and associations within which they are placed' (2000: 271). Yet any interrogation of this relationship in academic terms has been severely limited. Whilst implicit in some discussions on music and on fashion separately may be tacit references to style in music and music in fashion, these often relate only to certain music performances (see for example Breward 1999 and the analysis of the music hall audience); certain performers, like David Bowie and Madonna (see for example Auslander 2006; Fiske 1989); and certain subcultures (see Cohen 2002; Hebdige 1979; Muggleton 2000; Thornton 2005).

In one of the only essays to explicitly interrogate the links between music and fashion, McLoughlin (2000) identifies an emphasis on authenticity within the music industry, communities of musicians and their audience as significant to this silence. He argues that such attitudes have carried over into the study of popular music as a theoretical subject. As he notes, 'Rock ideology and popular music studies has colluded together in treating clothes and fashion as the "gloss" on a performing pop culture that has valued the organic, the natural and the spontaneous' (McLoughlin 2000: 267).

Further, he also implicates issues of gender here. He argues that the historical linkage between dress and the feminine (see Craik 1994; Church Gibson 2006; Davis 1992; Entwistle 2000; Hollander 1994; Wilson 1985) places fashion at odds with the masculine conventions of many forms of music. Here, he indicates that within popular music studies there is a dominance of male writers with an imperative to ensure the 'serious' in the study of popular culture. This, he argues, may account for an emphasis on perspectives that tend not to include forms of engagement whose origins lie firmly in the feminine realm; fashion being one example, pop music, in its most pop sense, another. As Marc Brennan writes, 'Music's perceived abilities to appeal to the subconscious, incite political beliefs, or reveal social injustices results in limited ways of understanding the attraction of music which shares none of these aims' (2007: 182–3). Lawrence Grossberg (1999) goes further, suggesting that in popular music studies, there has been a tendency to be too emotionally attached to the field of study, which has limited the development of the subject and contributed to its failure to reach into all aspects of music performance.

Thus, notions of authenticity, gender identities, disciplinary developments and political ideologies have all contributed to a lack of discussion of the correlation between music and fashion within popular music studies. However, writers like McLoughlin (2000) do not account for the lack of explicit focus on fashion and music from those working within fashion studies. The work of writers such as Entwistle (2000), Breward (1999), Craik (1994) and Wilson (1985) has explored the part that fashion plays in articulating key facets of individual identity—class, gender, sexuality, age, taste and race—to demonstrate clothing's symbolic as well as practical function. As fashionable dress is all about seasonal change, so such study has shown it to be a constantly shifting, but often emphatic marker, of either integration into social groups or the resistance to and marking out of difference from those to which we do not belong. What such work has most importantly established is that the clothed body—fashionable or not—speaks a nuanced language. Fashion theory uncovers, acknowledges and to a greater degree celebrates the creative artifice of dressing and shaping the human body. Like much work in fashion studies, this book does not attempt to separate fashion from the body but instead sees the two as intertwined in identity making, understanding the body itself as just as open to shifts in fashion as the clothes which cover it. Despite some perceived political tensions, in the last 30 years, fashion has become a focus of inquiry within the frameworks of subjects such as sociology and cultural studies, going beyond a simple descriptive fashion history towards a more revealing analysis of the meanings of the fashioned body, but this has failed to reflect the significant role of music to fashioned identity.

MUSIC STYLES: A WORD ABOUT GENRE

One of the challenges for anyone wishing to discuss music is the problem of categorization and organization around ideas of genre; the decision about where to place any music performance within definitions of genre can shape a variety of perceptions about what is expected of it. This, is turn, affects how a range of gestures which make up the whole performance are interpreted and understood. Thus, genres are packages of meaning that have attributed to them traditions, behaviours, forms of presentation, poses, gestures and technologies that help identify the context within which music experiences are judged, valued, categorized and understood (see Gilbert and Pearson 1999).

Tackling any discussion of music is thus to navigate, to some degree, the complex terrain of genre. Music is primarily understood in the popular consciousness as an art form closely linked to the emotions of those producing it, listening to it and writing about it (see Sennett 2003; Frith 1996). As such, it is also closely linked to social interactions and articulations of identity and taste; 'a musical style creates, and is created by social identity' (Moore 2001: 193). This means that the genre any particular piece of music or performance belongs to is also an articulation of particular histories, identities and patterns of taste for not only the performer but also the audience.

At the same time, to become bound by such ideas or to attempt to resolve them in a book of this kind would be an unnecessary distraction. If those writing about and making music find it hard to categorize it cleanly, it is well beyond the scope of this book. Indeed, in postmodernity, fixed notions of genre are hard to apply because music experiences often, in fact, 'cut right across styles such that there will be genres that intersect both rock *and* other styles of music' (Moore 2001: 3). Notions of genre or, certainly, music type matter in this volume, when they play a part in connecting audience to performer (see Frith and McRobbie 1990; Longhurst 1995) and when fashion and style are involved in making this connection. Thus to traverse the complex problem of genre in this book, it is most often patterns of fashioned style rather than music style that lead me to categorize different performers and performances together. Other methods would undoubtedly produce other results. The discussion here is best served by an acknowledgement that there is a set of core values shared by most musics, focused on concepts of 'spectacle and emotion, presence and absence, belonging and difference' (Frith 1996: 276).

These themes are core to the spirit of the analysis in this book. The focus here is very much on the visual aspects of style. While the role of intermediaries like stylists, art directors and managers may be central to how these looks come into being, this book most often takes them at face value: how and who created them is beyond its scope. As Noel McLoughlin argues, even in film studies, where fashion and costume enjoy a great deal more attention, 'the labour of the technical' has been privileged 'over fashion labour and the development of a semiotics of dress' (2000: 281). There is certainly an increasing need to rebalance this, and such aims inspire some of the methods employed in this volume.

My way of navigating these challenges in this book is to take a case study approach that melds key themes in fashion and cultural studies: gender, consumer culture, sexuality, ethnicity and national identities and fan cultures, with visual texts and styles and examples of music media and performances. This is somewhat in the spirit of the 'Visual Cultural Studies' model of visual analysis proposed by Lister and Wells (2000). This method of analysis is non-prescriptive and draws in a variety of methods and materials here to build a picture of how the intertextual relationship between music and fashion can be understood to communicate. Thus, like much visual analysis, 'the relationship between images and words is always central' (Pink 2008: 131).

Equally in the spirit of cultural studies, this book is interested as much in the mainstream as it is in the underground. The significance of everyday, pervasive music performances to the fashion tastes of a wider audience is ripe for analysis. It is interesting that despite a commitment to establish the everyday as central to a meaningful analysis of culture, in the very limited discussions of music and fashion that can be found, there has been a tendency to focus on underground cultures that may be in some sense everyday, but which are far from the experience of most ordinary people. As Edgar, Sedgwick and Sedgwick argue, 'An emphasis on subcultures may serve to highlight the spectacular at the cost of ignoring the more mundane forms that are of concern to the majority of young people' (1999: 258). Equally, this has also threatened to discount anyone who is not young—a different form of elitism, but elitism nonetheless. Fashion and music are neither the preserve of the young nor the underground, as the following chapters aim to uncover.

Thus, this book is about the cultural significance of the relationship between fashion and music once it is in circulation: through performances both live and recorded, through images and through old and new media. In returning to textual analysis as its primary methodology, it does not contend that this is the best way to interrogate this relationship, but it does argue that it is a valid way. Fashion and music are both creative and industry, and as such they symbolize in a number of ways. There is much to be done to help us understand how this pervasive relationship shapes our cultural and social lives. Other approaches would reveal other new, interesting perspectives with which to understand this relationship—but this is a project for another time and another writer. This book merely aims to open up this dialogue.

Branding, Fashion and Music

In the film *Control* (2007), based on the biography of his wife, Deborah, the late Ian Curtis, lead singer of Joy Division, is portrayed as the embodiment of many of the most popular cultural myths about musicians. As a teenager growing up in an unremarkable suburban town in the 1970s, he writes songs and poems, smokes spliffs in his bedroom while listening to David Bowie and experiments with pills. He is something of an outsider—unusual, intellectual and creative. It is this which makes him vulnerable, interesting and attractive to Deborah, who becomes his long-standing girlfriend and later long-suffering wife.

He joins the band and balances their growing success with a job at the labour exchange. He marries young and, with a small child, is tied to the need to make a living the conventional way. He is good at his job, and sympathetic to his clients, but bored and unfulfilled. He wears the nondescript uniform of the clerical worker: dark trousers and a white shirt. The coat he wears to work, though, is a fashioned hint of a more unconventional life: a dark green parka, emblazoned with the word *hate* in white paint. As is often the case with film, his inner struggle is made visible through his clothing.

Ultimately, Curtis battles unsuccessfully with inner demons which create a complicated private life: he has a wife and a girlfriend, both of whom he finds it impossible to give up; he enjoys success with the band but finds fame difficult to cope with; he loves his daughter but is unable to commit to the dual role of father and rock star; he suffers from serious epileptic episodes and side effects from the drugs supposed to control it, compromising his physical and mental health. Unable to find any resolution and overtaken by circumstances which seem to be beyond his control, he eventually takes his own life.

Throughout, Ian Curtis is shown to be a special kind of person, with inherent gifts that bring with them an inevitable cost: the inability to fit into conventional social life. Curtis was thus shown throughout the film to fulfil many of the stereotypes of an artist. It is the notion of an inherent artistic character for the musician that creates, in the popular consciousness, an embedded social value for music performers. This shapes both how they are understood by their audiences, how they understand themselves and how, as cultural figures, they relate to a variety of facets of contemporary culture, including fashion.

This chapter explores the complexities of the triangulation of music, visual branding and fashion, considering some of the ways in which a codependency between the music and fashion industries has shaped a variety of aspects of contemporary consumer culture. It aims to establish that both music and fashion marketing are fed by a variety of practical and visual interrelationships in which fashion and style are core to a kind of intertextual taste-sharing between the two industries. It argues that popular music's relationship to style in the popular imagination means that interdependency between musicians and designers and between the music and fashion industries is a natural consequence of a consumer culture where, at the same time, the musician has come to be a powerful signifier of contemporary desires. The chapter argues that inherent in this relationship is 'the attraction of the romantic bohemian lifestyle with the artist presented as an expressive rebel and stylistic hero [which is such a] strong theme, particularly with respect to popular and rock music' (Featherstone 2007: 25).

MUSICIANS, CREATIVITY AND THE ARTIST

A kind of special status for creative people is part of a set of characteristics constructed in the nineteenth century by the writers, poets, composers and painters that Raymond Williams (1971) labels the 'Romantic Artists'. Williams argues that a certain mystique and an almost stereotypical artistic personality were created by and around sets of individuals as a method of resistance to encroaching industrialization.

In this mid-nineteenth-century period, the middle classes became the dominant group within many industrializing societies, particularly Europe and America. This class group carried a set of ideals informed by a work ethic and increasingly business-oriented values, often owning the means of production of goods and services. Thus, it is here that the figure of the self-made, affluent man was conceptualized.

The middle classes were thus largely defined by their wealth and their ability to control many of the means of accruing further wealth. Consequently, the adoption of an affluent lifestyle driven by earned money and the demonstration of this earning power became an aspiration. It is in this moment that we see the development of what we understand today as a contemporary consumer society, a notion we will return to later in this chapter. This was driven by the new dominant class' desire for increased financial success, demonstrated by the ability to access goods and services.

In the face of what was essentially a new middle-class customer base for their work—which contrasted with the previous patronage many artists enjoyed from members of the aristocratic classes who funded the work of individual artists and writers, indulging and trusting in their abilities beyond any sense of their fashionability—creative individuals sought to 'generalize their skills into the common property of the imaginative truth' (Williams 1971: 57). The aim was to keep cultural forms as something not easily absorbed into consumer culture: an attempt to make artistic and creative outputs something that could not be reduced to basic financial worth and market forces. In doing so, the creative focus centred on human concerns: love, relationships, nature and a search for truth, providing a contrast to the developing machine age. As such, this special status was an attempt to establish 'whether culture could be saved from commercialism by isolating it' (156). It also aimed to maintain freedom from the tyranny of consumer-led markets for those making creative works and a sense of a possible alternative social order, one not driven by mere money-making (Williams 1971).

Focusing on a later period, Brian Longhurst discusses the jazz musicians who, working in America in the 1920s and 1930s, navigated a path in which 'the musician wished to follow his/her artistic sensibility and expression, but was in danger of being forced along the lines of commercialism by the dictates of the "square"' (1995: 58). This encoding was designed to construct a perceptible separation between market, the masses and creative endeavour as a way of, in part, marking out the boundaries between good and bad and, in relation to this, authentic and inauthentic music.

MUSIC, MUSICIANS AND THE BOHEMIAN LIFESTYLE

Most importantly for this chapter, however, such historical moments marked out the musician as someone whose role carried with it expectations defined in the greater part by a particular idea of lifestyle, perhaps best understood as bohemian. The history of the notion of bohemianism is explored in the work of Elizabeth Wilson (1999, 2003), who identifies the emergence of the bohemian figure from the kinds of developing commercial conditions that Williams (1971) also describes. Importantly, for Wilson, this moment saw a shift of emphasis for the creative elite from the production of work as a marker of artistic status towards the increased prominence of a particular identity or personality and way of living as the defining factor.

For Wilson, bohemian life was most importantly 'safely transient, part of the irresponsibility of youth' (1999: 15); it 'became a subculture because its writers, painters, musicians and composers, performers, journalists and intellectuals congregated in bohemian cafes and salons and saw themselves as different' (12) and was primarily driven by class struggles which pitted the bohemian (often in the nineteenth-century period, the bohemian world was made up of the convergence of working-class, underclass and aristocratic individuals) against the new and strengthening dominant bourgeoisie.

Thus, to be bohemian was to reject the ideals of middle-class, bourgeois life, with its emphasis on financial success, and instead to 'dramatize' poverty (Wilson 1999: 13). This led those seeking to define themselves as bohemian to go 'in search of new material seek[ing] extreme, even dangerous forms of experience, hence the centrality of Bohemia to excess of all kinds: alcoholism, drugs, erotic deviance, political extremism, blasphemy and madness' (13). Ultimately, this aimed to provide a way to live a life that contravened bourgeois ideals and moralities.

In contemporary terms, Wilson acknowledges that the true bohemian is becoming harder to locate as 'art itself [becomes] something of a metropolitan mass pursuit' (1999: 22) and is, as such, absorbed into mainstream, middle-class lifestyles. Nonetheless, she argues the bohemian ethos lives on in areas of contemporary cultural life, where 'above all there are bohemian personalities . . . used to describe glamorous personalities just outside the mainstream of Hollywood or the rock industry' (24).

Clearly, though what constitutes the bohemian may vary greatly between different facets of the cultural landscape and different historical moments, the bohemian remains a continuing cultural trope. Thus, while 'many contemporary stars are extremely wealthy [this] does not detract from the similarities of the role and persona: genius, talent, excess, erotic transgression and self destruction are the common ingredients' (Wilson 1999: 23) which bind this identity together. As Wilson notes, 'Kurt Cobain and Michael Hutchence are two more recent examples of the way in which the bohemian dedication to excess as a necessary concomant of artistic endeavour and "genius" led to tragedies' (23). Excess and tragedy have thus become essential parts of the authentic, artistic, bohemian lifestyle, and musicians have become the archetype of those who live it.

It seems that the notion of authenticity is core to the musician's identity, but it must be noted that for many thinkers this is no more than a myth, since 'it may derive from a particular set of cultural tastes and values, rather than from a considered analysis of popular music' (Strinati 1995: 43). In turn, we 'might be prompted to ask if there is any such thing as an authentic popular culture' (43) anyway. Mere illusion or not, authenticity has been demonstrated by many writers to be key to a cultural understanding of the musician. The musician's lure as a seductive force is modelled on 'the criteria of originality, roots, community and authenticity [which] can be deployed as marketing strategies to appeal to particular segments of the audience for pop music' (43).

It seems to matter little what kind of music an artiste makes. Whilst different music genres are often imbued with more or less authenticity in the way in which they are valued and written about, this is a slippery notion. As we saw in the introduction, what is seen as authenticity in one case may not be in another. Miranda Sawyer noted in the *Observer Music Monthly's* art issue that authorship is an important part of music participation, establishing a sense of authentic engagement where 'Post-Beatles, even the most manufactured of pop stars will claim a writing credit on their hits . . . pop music is meant to be genuine, an expression of the singer's innermost soul' (2009). At the same time, of course, it has to be remembered that it is in songwriting credits that the most money lies, which may play an equivalent role in the desire for accreditation in some cases. Yet the nebulous idea of music as authentic expression is held dear.

Importantly, like other public figures, musicians enact a 'star personality' (see Frith 1996: 212). Whilst much of the analysis of celebrity culture has largely left them alone because of their perceived authenticity, they are, like many public figures, privileged a 'glamorous status which bourgeois society liberally grants its spiritual representatives (so long as they remain harmless)' (Barthes 2000: 29). This notion of the glamour of public life is made even more powerful when coupled with the historical figuration of the musician with a bohemian status. Consequently, this has made musicians seductive figures for the consumer culture that, ironically, so many of their kind fought so hard to resist.

Thus, the musician is an extremely fruitful marketing tool with a contemporary reach far beyond the music industry itself. Consequently, since the musician's identity is historically required and understood to be an artistic, creative and bohemian one, this notion has become the marker against which all musicians carve out their professional identities. Most importantly for this chapter, this in turn creates the right conditions to invite clear links between the fashion and music industries in contemporary consumer culture.

MUSICIANS AND FASHION PROMOTION

In 2008, Rolling Stones guitarist Keith Richards was photographed by Annie Leibovitz for an advertising campaign for Louis Vuitton with the tagline 'Some journeys cannot be put into words. New York. 3 A.M. Blues in C'. Richards's custom-made, Louis Vuitton–branded guitar case and customized hotel room—skull-emblazoned scarves draped over lamps in a rather ordinary but luxurious room—reinforced his rock-and-roll lifestyle; forever on the road, making rudimentary attempts to feel at home. There is a glass of some kind of orange fluid on the side table: perhaps a vodka and juice, but maybe, one is more tempted to think, a soluble vitamin—this might, like the magnifying glass on top of the book on his bed, reinforce his age and its attendant physical vulnerability. The cup of tea on another table reinforced his Britishness, perhaps; this particular national identity is, after all, a stereotypical one for the ageing rock star.

Crucially, it was made very clear that despite the fact that Richards was modelling for a high-end fashion brand, this was not Keith selling out. The press release that accompanied the ad was very careful to point out that he received no fee and that a donation was made on his behalf to Al Gore's 'Climate Project' (see *Daily Mail* 2008). As such, his integrity and status as an individual outside the system remain intact, but also, as the only ad campaign Richards has ever taken part in, Louis Vuitton absorbs some of his bohemian danger, integrity and style.

Ultimately, such images are, of course, designed to promote and sell Louis Vuitton's products. In contemporary consumer culture, the promotional image has become almost as important, if not more so, than the objects it promotes. Perhaps more accurately, the bags which Louis Vuitton makes and sells clearly have a function that goes beyond their usefulness as vessels for carrying belongings. This very fact makes them an example of what Guy Julier (2000) would call 'high design'—status symbols whose function as part of cultural and social life overrides their physical function. But also, as Barker argues, 'The moment of consumption marks one of the processes by which we are formed as persons' (2000: 11), and the act of consuming a particular brand, or an object advertised by a particular public figure, becomes a way of accruing meaning for one's self and of communicating this to others. Thus, the added-value function of Louis Vuitton as a brand lies in its use of particular performers who create a link between this brand identity and a lifestyle that is thus offered as a possibility—however imaginary and aspirational—to consumers.

MUSIC, IDENTITIES AND CONSUMER CULTURE

When consumption happens, when a consumer acquires a product that they feel has the potential to augment their social life, then they operate within consumer culture. In modernity, consumer culture became the primary means through which individuals marked themselves out in a social context where people were becoming, otherwise, more and more anonymous. Consumer culture was the result of the gradual industrialization of manufacture and, in relation to this, the move of larger communities of people into cities, where many encounters with others were unspoken. This brought about an increasingly pressing need to mark oneself out. Here people came to be defined not by who they were born to be, their ancestry or what they did for a living, but instead by the choices they made in their self-presentation and in relation to consumer culture (see for example Bocock 1993; Slater 1997).

Social identity became something that was created out of the goods acquired by the individual, allowing this identity to be enacted to those around them. This social identity is something we work on throughout our lives, what Giddens (1991) and Barker (2000) term 'an identity project [which involves] building on what we think we are now in the light of our past and present circumstances, together with what we think we would like to be, the trajectory of our hoped-for future' (Barker 2000: 167)

One of the ways we envisage what this future might or should be is through the kinds of images that promote goods to us as objects of desire. These function to 'provide consumers with images of goods and services that might be acquired and incorporated as meaningful components of their expressive style' (Jansson 2002: 14). As such, they function as more than promotional tools and demonstrate that 'trade in symbols and experiences has proved to be a vast and profitable arena for business' (Holt 2006: 299). In the case of the Louis Vuitton advertisement, the power of such images is intended to lie with the inclusion of particular kinds of people: those who are famous and, as a result, wealthy, glamorous and aspirational. As such, the use of well-known figures in promotion and advertising has embedded meanings that relate to each individual star's cultural image (see Williamson 1978; also Dyer 1979).

Consequently, the use of particular types of stars is key to the symbolism of such images. Music stars, in particular, carry connotations of their symbolic value as bohemian outsiders. As Elizabeth Wilson has noted, mainstream culture has always been keen to co-opt some of the most appealing aspects of bohemian life as 'romantic and picturesque' (1999: 15). Such co-option into marketing imagery, in turn, offers consumers a model to symbolically escape the very system of mainstream behaviour and consumer culture of which such images and consumer experiences are in fact part and parcel. Thus, as the bohemian has become just another possible marker of lifestyle for consumers to buy into, so the danger of the bohemian figure has become more a symbolic fantasy than a tangible reality; in fact, 'the market has used bohemian glamour for profit' (20).

FASHION, MUSIC AND THE CONTROL OF BRAND IMAGE

While it might seem that as a fashion brand, Louis Vuitton has shown an almost avaricious desire to ally itself with musicians of a range of ages and genres with much to gain from such associations, it has also demonstrated almost as keen a desire to hold the controlling hand in these relationships. In

2009, both Sean Combs Bad Boy Records and Sony BMG have had to pay for infringements of copyright after products appeared unendorsed by companies in videos and lyrics for little-known girl band Danity Kane and other artists, including Britney Spears (see Odell 2009). When such legal processes are called into action, we see a demonstration of the way in which brand identity is something that individual companies hold very dear, undoubtedly because 'as poignant symbols marking out where capitalism meets consumerism, it is hardly surprising that brands often stand accused as the capitalist's weapon of choice to prey upon anxieties and concoct false desires' (Holt 2006: 300). Therefore, the blend of desire and desirability essential to branding is far from foolproof, and it would be a mistake not to acknowledge the relationship of the individual to advertised goods and consumer culture as deeply complex. As such, companies attempt to carefully manage their brand images. After all, no brand ever has complete control over how its social life will be shaped once it has been consumed because 'meanings produced at the level of production are available to be worked on at the level of consumption but do not determine them' (Barker 2000: 54).

MUSIC AND THE MARKET APPEAL OF THE BOHEMIAN LIFESTYLE

The use of the musician in promotional fashion imagery of this kind can be argued as offering a symbolic means of escape to the consumer: a fantasy of a lifestyle they may never access in reality. But it might also be argued that the perceived authenticity of bohemian life is attractive not just to the individual. Fashion as both a cultural and industrial entity is criticized for a number of factors which centre on the perceived glut of superficial characteristics it is seen to possess. The very title and activity of fashion has been hard for theorists to pin down. It has been 'characterized as a social, economic and aesthetic force, and more often than not, all three at the same time' (Finkelstein 1996: 6) Often these agendas compete and provide something of an identity crisis for those making, consuming and writing about fashion. While writers such as Wilson (1985), Church Gibson (2006), Entwistle (2000) and Breward (1999) have established fashion's potential as a site of meaningful engagement for the individual, more often it is charged with being little more than a distracting smokescreen to real life.

For example, Joanna Finkelstein argues that 'fashion is often considered one of those social forces which keeps us ever attentive to the present in one of the worst possible ways; that is as a source of novelty, distraction, and self absorption' (1996: 4). It is certainly one of the most archetypal demonstrations of consumer culture at work. As such, we might argue that the figure of the musician is attractive to fashion brands because it not only offers validation for the individual, but also serves an authenticating purpose for the fashion industry itself. As writers such as Elizabeth Wilson (1999) and Anne Hollander (1994) demonstrate, bohemian figures—artists, musicians and writers—managed, historically, to navigate a path in which they both fashioned a clearly constructed embodiment whilst also remaining faithful to a veneer of an authentic self. Still, consumer culture has, as Elizabeth Wilson notes, shown a greedy attraction to bohemian culture, where it has 'adapted the most challenging propositions of the bohemians and reconstituted sexual licence and hedonism as a new opium of the people' (24).

THE MISSHAPES: TASTEMAKERS IN NEW YORK

In New York, DJ trio The Misshapes have become an amalgamated fashion and music industry in their own right. Between 2003 and 2007, The Misshapes 'defined the downtown Manhattan club scene . . . eschewing glittery clothes and glow sticks for asymmetrical haircuts and monochromatic uniforms plucked straight from the runway' (Horne 2009). They ran parties from their downtown apartment, where partygoers' clothes were as near centre stage as the music played. Many well-known figures, from Yoko Ono to Madonna, attended these parties. The Misshapes, made up of two boys—Geordon Nicol and Greg Krelenstein—and one girl—Leigh Lezark—look like hyper-fashionable triplets; they are of similar height and have glossy black hair, thin frames and sun-shy pale skin. Their self-created 'phenomenon' status was certainly helped by both the old and new media with 'breathless stories in *Vogue* and the *New York Times* and on blogs like gawker.com' (Horne 2009).

The Misshapes are a very New York phenomenon, what Elizabeth Currid (2007) might describe as part of the 'Warhol Economy'. Currid (157) argues that it is the geographical nature of New York and its organization into different areas with different cultural identities that creates the right conditions for groups of individuals like The Misshapes to have an impact:

> The concentration of cultural producers, reviewers and institutions means that New York has developed itself as the type of place where prescience regarding trends or creative production has a greater chance of occurring, and as such, leading to an inextricable link between place, and generating value for cultural goods.

Thus, for Currid, these creative conditions are the lifeblood of New York, contributing to its regeneration and success as a global city. The Misshapes are an archetypal example of what can result from such conditions.

We might also understand The Misshapes to be an example of the way in which taste is established, defined and maintained by an elite group and how, in this context, it equates to social, cultural and economic power. This would seem to be a contemporary echo of an earlier courtly and later salon culture, and as such it is nothing new. The royal court was the place, in early European societies, where luxury and taste were defined, because 'painting, sculpture, literature, music, dance, drama and the applied arts could serve many purposes. But, in a courtly setting, they could convey specific messages about the nature and representation of power . . . and the forms of behaviour appropriate to a social milieu' (Vale 2001: 165). Those inhabiting the court are defined by their social position as privileged, upper class and aristocratic.

The move from court towards a salon culture represented the shift towards the affluent middle class as the dominant group who thus established good taste and aspiration but who as 'new wealth needed to be educated, and the choice, display and use of the variety of goods had to be cultivated' (Berg 2005: 41). This was the ultimate function of the salon.

Maxine Berg (2005: 40) examines the role of the salon in the establishment of luxury and taste as recreational, pleasurable activities in the eighteenth century, but, more importantly, she also makes links to the burgeoning consumer culture of this period:

> The salon, however might also become a platform for the exercise of taste along with the active promotion of commerce. The bluestocking Elizabeth Montagu, used her literary salon as a cultural display and an exercise in the 'right use of luxury' . . . she was recognized as an arbiter of literary and artistic taste and as a writer on aesthetics . . . She connected her power as a consumer to the promotion of British industry writing to her sister Sarah Scott in 1790 'I am going to the city end of the town this morning to bespeak 280 yards of white satin for the window curtains of my great home, and about 200 for the hangings. I think this order will make me very popular in Spitalfields.

In the case of The Misshapes' party, then, we might see similar forces at work. Simply by running a party and looking stylish, The Misshapes have achieved mythic status amongst the fashion set, providing runway music for a number of designers, including Henry Holland and Jeremy Scott, and giving advice to Vivienne Westwood on her New York store (Horyn 2006). At the end of the run of their parties on 8 September 2007, they produced The Misshapes style book—containing images of partygoers with no anchoring text—which cemented music and fashion together, published as it was in association with MTV (see Nicol 2007).

The Misshapes also found another space of influence in the virtual world. They owe a great deal of their success to new technologies and blogs, which spread the word about their parties fast. With their site www.misshapes.com, they extend their influence beyond their own physical space, listing the best up-and-coming cultural, music and fashion events, with their feature 'side-walking'. It includes images from festivals, parties and fashion shows centred on the fashionable style of the individuals inhabiting these spaces.

As the title of Elizabeth Currid's book *The Warhol Economy* (2007) clearly suggests, groups like The Misshapes are the children of Andy Warhol's vision-ary dalliances with celebrity culture, becoming famous overnight for develop-ing a 'scene' focused on art, fashion and the underground. In fact, they have perhaps adopted this past idea of the New York underground scene quite knowingly, a notion supported by the choice of name for Lezark's dog: Edie, named after Warhol's muse, Edie Sedgwick.

Thus, the power of The Misshapes lies both in their original underground status and in the drawing together of a variety of creative and cultural ideas which come to define taste. In turn, this establishes the objects and im-ages associated with this taste-making as desirable and aspirational to many areas of consumer culture and to consumer culture itself. It maybe, therefore, that the power of fashion and music in this context lies in their allegiance with one another but also with other cultural ideas. The Misshapes' success seems to be thanks to a number of factors, all of which can be located within the context of a particularly fondly held idea of a New York scene. Their geo-graphical location, their resonance with the past and, in particular, Warhol's Factory and their underground credentials all contribute to their appeal and mystique.

Consequently, The Misshapes become a meaningful image for taste-making, for the music and fashion industries and, thus, also for consumer culture because they are part of what Jansson would term a 'web of significance' (2002: 9). This web of significance creates the conditions where 'when a particular object [or experience] is consumed, the object, as well as the practice is interpreted according to standards which are greatly influenced by media images, not just advertising, but also images created in other media texts' (19). Hence, it is the ideas that circulate around The Misshapes that play as great a part in establishing their importance as the reality of what they do.

BRANDING, FASHION AND POSTMODERNITY

In the advert for the Blason jewellery range designed in collaboration with Louis Vuitton, hip-hop star Pharrell Williams plays a central role. In the first frames it appears to be a music video—many of the right visual characteris-tics are in place, and this is the kind of context in which we would expect to encounter a music star. After a few seconds, however, it becomes clear from the lingering shots on particular pieces of jewellery that this is a filmed advertisement; an example of the 'blurring of genre boundaries between cultural products' (Barker 2000: 154). It is Williams's presence here that plays a fundamental role in blurring these boundaries.

In one minute and thirty seconds, the Blason advert demonstrates a double function: it both promotes Williams as a musician *and* a designer, remixing part of his band N.E.R.D.'s song 'Everyone Nose' alongside its promotion of Blason and Louis Vuitton. Music video is always advertising in that its function is the promotion of an artist and a song. Accordingly, the distinctions between music video and moving advertisements may not be as great as they first seem, but nonetheless, this advert reduces the clarity of definition between the two. Here, then, music video becomes advertising of a different kind, or perhaps more accurately, advertising becomes entertainment, what Pamela Odih might describe as 'branded entertainment' (2007: 199). As Douglas B. Holt has argued, 'brands work by moulding existing ideologies to serve the needs of capital' (2006: 301). Here, a music star and a form of visual entertainment already familiar to an audience create symbolic meaning for the brand by 'presuppos[ing] precisely the creativity of interpreting subjects' (Jansson 2002: 24), who will themselves imbue the product with the creative and authentic characteristics of music expression and the simple glamour of a star body but who will also, in turn, find it increasingly difficult to separate different types of visual material.

This kind of boundary blurring is often maintained to be a typical phenomenon of postmodern culture, fulfilling what David Harvey would identify as the kind of collage or montage typical of postmodernity. Here, 'cultural life is . . . viewed as a series of texts intersecting with other texts, producing more texts' (1990: 49). We will look in more detail at the notion of postmodernity in chapter 4, but most importantly here, it is argued to be the cultural manifestation of a late capitalist system of which consumer culture is an embedded part (see Jameson 1991). This kind of intersection of texts, or intertextuality, is a significant part of how visual culture is argued to operate within postmodernity and is defined by Chris Barker as 'citation of one text within another' (2000: 154). This means that images and texts are constantly borrowing from other texts, recycling and renewing symbols and, in turn, accruing meaning. It also means that audiences bring to the reading of such images references to other kinds of images, objects or cultural experiences to which the current image seems to relate. Consequently, how much an audience understands the meaning of an image or object depends to some extent on prior knowledge of 'the other text(s), which a reader requires knowledge of, so as to decode [it]' (Featherstone 2007: 193). Thus, in postmodernity, the past, other cultures, other images and objects and other cultural experiences can all come to be drawn into the creation of new images, experiences and objects; their meanings both create a shortcut for an audience's understanding of the messages to be conveyed while also often exploiting these associations.

MTV, MUSIC VIDEO AND POSTMODERN INTERTEXTUALITY

Mike Featherstone has suggested that 'MTV seems to exist in a timeless present with video artists ransacking film genres and art movements from different historical periods to blur boundaries and the sense of history' (2007: 68). Such intertextual borrowing always carries with it the danger that in repeating and making use of ideas at a fast pace, such meaning is emptied out, and 'theorists of the postmodern talk of an ideal-type channel hopping MTV viewer who flips through different images at such speed that she/he is unable to chain signifiers together into a meaningful narrative, he/she merely enjoys the multiphrenetic intensities and sensations of the surface of the images' (5).

Writing in 1998, John Fiske had high hopes for MTV and music video, seeing in its fragmentary structures and illogical and often nonsensical narratives 'the potential for a non-conventional, possibly oppositional audience' (1998: 167). Fiske both acknowledged that MTV 'foreground[ed] fashion' (170) as well as noted that music videos had an ambiguous relationship to market forces, both 'offending realism' and thus 'offending capitalism; [whilst] in boosting record sales . . . also maintain[ing] it' (169). Thus, the music video has an unclear status sharing characteristics of TV and film, advertising and art, potentially being all or none of these things almost at the same time. In fragmented postmodernity, music video is appropriately ambiguous and contradictory.

GWEN LOVES VIVIENNE: INTERTEXTUALITY, ADVERTISING AND THE MUSIC VIDEO

In the video for her song 'Rich Girl', Gwen Stefani embodies the symbols of a variety of cultural figures, from a geisha to a dandy pirate. The video and the clothes worn in it clearly look back to earlier times and across a variety of cultures. Echoing the lyrics of the song, the video draws heavily on the imagery of advertising campaigns for both John Galliano and Vivienne Westwood.

In particular, large portions of the video reverberate with the aesthetics of the advertising campaign for Vivienne Westwood's Spring/Summer 1998 collection, Tied to the Mast: on a ship with clearly staged storm clouds, Stefani inhabits an imaginary world, part eighteenth-century pirate, part 1980s punk pop. This is intercut with Stefani dressed in Galliano's nineteenth-century inspired geisha look from Autumn 1997. The video was directed, not insignificantly, by the fashion photographer David LaChapelle. Made in 2006, it harks back to a number of fashion eras and mixes them together in one visual product intended, primarily, to promote a song.

Here, we see music video not quoting, excerpting from, accumulating or repeating the imagery of film or TV, the usual media forms plundered and parodied in music video's disjointed narratives. Nor do we see advertising masked as music video. Instead, we see the aesthetics of fashion and, more particularly, fashion advertising reformulated into a narrative-less set of images that resonates with the kudos of fashion taste reinforcing Stefani's desire to be a true, individual leader and arbiter of fashion.

Being in the fashion forefront is, of course, central to the success of many female stars forming an important link between themselves and their audience (see Gledhill 1999; Stacey 1991). As such, references to Westwood here seem more than 'irrelevant cultural representations' (Chen 1998: 176). While postmodernist thought might encourage us to believe these images lack any kind of meaning beyond their own spectacular potential, can it be any coincidence that from punk through to Adam and the Ants, Bow Wow Wow and beyond, Westwood has enjoyed both subcultural and pop cool credentials? As a symbol within the intertextual landscape of this particular video, it is these credentials that Westwood's presence must be argued to offer to Stefani. Here, we see fashion taste and cultural relevance established and reinforced.

In this case study, we see two forms of intertextuality. On the one hand, visual symbols from other contexts are drawn together to create the video, and on the other, we see also an intersection of brand names and values. As Stefani promotes her song, so she also promotes her own fashion brand, L.A.M.B. (Love, Angel, Music, Baby). In drawing together previously existing brands, we might argue that this video demonstrates a 'co-op[tion] and reterritoriali[zation] by the capitalist machine' (Chen 1998: 178), where music video opens a space to promote more than just music. In making these links, Stefani's L.A.M.B. range can aim towards 'instantaneous impact' but with an inevitable 'parallel loss of depth' which for David Harvey (1990) is so characteristic of postmodern culture. Thus, this music video links the fashion and music industries together in 'a postmodern culture which celebrates consumerism, hedonism and style' (Strinati 1995: 236).

MUSIC AND FASHION, FASHION AND MUSIC

In the earlier part of this chapter, then, we saw some arguments as to why musicians might be useful allies for the fashion industry thanks to their status as bohemian individuals, an identity which offered a fantasy lifestyle to the consumer through consumer culture. In the Stefani example, we can see an explanation for why the music industry might need fashion. Will Straw (2002) argues that music is a fundamentally precarious product. This is because it is a cultural commodity rather than a necessity for life. As such, how successful any music-related product will be is hard to predict. Straw argues that in order to counteract this uncertainty, cultural industries often 'create a social demand' through 'a whole interlocking package of new products' (5–6).

It might be argued, then, that in making links to the fashion industry through a music product, 'Rich Girl' gives an impression of a more established familiarity for Stefani's solo career than this, her second single, deserved. In a context where 'the cultural commodity is a fragile entity, one whose success within a marketplace can never be determined or predicted in advance with anything approaching the levels of certainty common in other industries' (Straw 2002: 3), creating a contemporary circuit of shared meaning and, indeed, taste-making arguably establishes a greater sense of certainty and a greater chance of success for this product. This also, even more powerfully, extends to Stefani's fashion brand, L.A.M.B. Making links to more established fashion brands helps identify this as a desirable fashion brand with design worth not unlike that of the far more established and successful designers evoked in the song and video.

BACK IN JAPAN: GWEN STEFANI, SUBCULTURE
AND GLOBAL YOUTH MARKETS

Providing one last element to this intertextual, certainty-providing mix, Stefani's Harajuku dancers establish Japanese street culture value for both her music and her clothes. Here, we see contemporary subculture linked to past subculture with the significant inclusion of references to Vivienne Westwood. This kind of activity is common to the making of brand identities, as Celia Lury (2004: 42) argues:

> In such practices, the brand seeks to incorporate not only (aspects of) the consumer, but also (aspects of) the context of use or wider environment, inserting itself into activities and entities that exceed the individual consumer and are understood in terms of collectives such as fans, lifestyles and communities.

This is part and parcel of what Anne Allison argues to be the 'recognition that youth sells; that it sells to sell to youth; and that selling a particular iteration of youth sells something for Japan and something of Japan in all those global markets currently flooded with Japanese kids goods. That is, in the new buzz around Japanese cool, interest is paid both in the capitalization on the market to extend the attraction Japanese goods have for global consumers' (2009: 90). For Allison, the contemporary subcultural landscape in Japan has a close relationship to the kinds of symbolic resistance exhibited by the subcultural groups of the 1950s, 1960s and 1970s, which we look at in more detail in chapter 5.

Allison links the significance of subculture in this cultural context in part to 'the bursting of the bubble economy in 1991', which resulted in the 'growth of Japanese play industries' (2009: 90). This resulted in social upheaval because many cultural ideals of adult behaviour centred on a work ethic very much linked to an economy that was stable, successful and productive. The reduction of industrial production did not remove such ideals of behaviour overnight. In the resulting confusion about what they should be doing as they moved towards adulthood, and unable to find economic independence and stability because 'the economy renders youth socio-economically precarious', Allison argues that, in response, 'youth assume[d] a critical position', adopting instead essences of what she terms 'J-Cool', which 'refers somewhat imprecisely to everything from Japanese video games and vinyl toys, to the superflat aesthetics of Murakami Takashi and Harajuku fashion' (90). These cultural forms reflected 'an interminable childishness of flexible attachments, frenetic mobility and fictional role playing [all] at the very heart of J-Cool' (90). This is clearly embodied in Harajuku fashion (Figure 1), with its theatrical and colourful identities, many of which have their origins either in subcultures like goth and punk or in characterizations from children's stories and science fiction narratives: faeries, pixies and aliens.

This subcultural engagement has become something which the Japanese economy has identified as marketable globally (see Allison 2009) and which has equally offered the global appeal of what Sarah Thornton (2005) would term 'subcultural capital' to the marketing of Gwen Stefani's music. In formulating the notion of subcultural capital, Thornton develops her ideas from the work of Pierre Bourdieu (1984). Bourdieu examined how facets of identity and knowledge—what he termed 'cultural capital'—could operate as a currency to facilitate social and professional lives and could further, in focusing on facets of identity formation like social class and education, be transformed into economic capital.

For Thornton, 'Subcultural capital confers status' (2005: 186) of a different, unofficial kind. Both cultural and subcultural capital are ideas closely linked to social and peer esteem. Subcultural capital was a way for those

Figure 1   Harajuku girls, Japanese street culture. © Jarvis Gray, 2010, used under license from shutterstock.com

aligned with subcultural groups to 'affirm that they are not anonymous members of an undifferentiated mass' (185). Applied to a music brand, then, it might be argued this aims to confer similar meaning: to differentiate Stefani from her peers, to differentiate her products (an essential function of advertising; see Williamson 1978) and to imprint upon the audience her authenticity as musician and her status as fashion leader.

CONCLUSION

Thus, fashion and music share a powerful relationship at the level of industry. In the promotion of these industries, the adoption of the one by the other offers useful, but opposing, characteristics. These characteristics are formed by the way in which, as cultural activities, music and fashion are valued. Music has a powerful link to the search for authentic experiences: emotions, creativity, even lifestyle. Whilst long-held ideas of music and musicians' identities as authentic can be easily unpicked, they remain notions that are held dear. What constitutes this authenticity can be fluid, can vary between genres of music and is extremely subjective: what constitutes an authentic or underground experience for one individual may seem disappointingly manufactured and conventional to another. Nonetheless, this discourse pervades.

Conversely, fashion has long been charged with superficiality. This is written throughout fashion's history. Yet it is one of the most financially successful creative industries, with a power and reach that extends beyond itself. As such, it can be argued to offer an important level of certainty to the more precarious investments of the music industry. Indeed, the pressure on individual artists to be successful in many areas of cultural life has become pervasive. Ultimately, this is cultivated by financial imperatives emanating less from performers themselves than from those behind the scenes and is a condition of a postmodern culture always linked to the needs of capitalism.

Consequently, one of the most powerful links between music and fashion is their position as industries embedded within consumer culture. This is true whatever the mystique created around music, which might privilege less financially cynical concerns. This should not undermine the artistic, creative outputs of those working in music, but it remains the context within which their work is allowed to develop if they choose to become part of that industry. Just as opposites are often believed to attract, so in promotional culture the intertextual relationship between fashion and music can be employed to shore up precarious products. Thus, fashion and music are wedded together in consumer culture because of oppositional traits which may be nothing more than long-held, constructed ideas but which have an impact on the way fashion and music continue to be valued as areas of cultural life.

–2–

Fans, Music, Clothes and Consumption

In the video for the 1998 single 'Let Me Entertain You', Robbie Williams paid homage to the American rock band Kiss, celebrating, tongue in cheek, the excesses of their particular brand of glam, stadium rock. Wearing a spandex, studded cat suit, cut low to reveal his hairy chest, Williams mimicked one of the masculine stereotypes of rock music epitomized by the band. The 'cock rocker', to use Frith and McRobbie's (1990) term, embodies aggressive masculinity, and, in part, the presentation of this kind of gendered identity—promiscuous, arrogant and dominant—defines the kind of image portrayed by the band.

The video begins as Williams holds a white dove, about to bite off its head, before he changes his mind and releases it. Here, he re-presents the audience with not only one of the long-held characterizations of rock music, but also what is arguably one of its most recognizable stage looks, Kiss' painted, black and white, kabuki-inspired faces: mask like, reminiscent of animals, aliens, super heroes or villains (Figure 2). In painting his face, then, Williams makes his reference to this particular rock band absolutely clear. He never seems to have clearly declared himself a fan of the band—or of Gene Simmons, the lead singer, whom he particularly evokes here—but Simmons establishes something of a relationship between himself and the singer in the *Daily Mirror* newspaper, saying, 'Robbie lives right down the road from me in the Hollywood Hills. I thought his video was great and was the sincerest form of flattery' (see Callan 2004). Of course, like most of Williams's videos, this representation comes with a heavy dose of irony.

The band Kiss have enjoyed almost forty years in the public eye and an extremely lucrative career. They have enjoyed less critical acclaim. As Tim Clifford writes, 'They wanted to dress like comic-book superheroes and write football-terrace anthems like Slade. Out of such dumb genius, vast fortunes are made. Kiss were also one of the first—if not the first—bands to recognize their own brand value and exploit it to the full—from lunchboxes to wrestlers, dolls to caskets. This may not have endeared them to the critics, but it certainly made their bank managers happy' (2002). Kiss' longevity must demonstrate that though they may have failed to gain the approval of many music critics, they captured the imagination of legions of fans who have maintained a loyalty to the band over decades: for them, Kiss are the real deal. The Kiss

Figure 2   Gene Simmons look-alike with painted face. © Vince Clements, 2010, used under license from shutterstock.com

Army—as those belonging to the fan club are called—have created a strong fan culture around the band both online and off. 'Our audiences,' drummer Peter Criss once said, 'are a show in themselves' (Gross 1977).

Thus, what has arguably made Kiss successful, enjoying a long and financially lucrative career, is the power of their audience to maintain their status. This rests on the recognition of what Jason Toynbee describes as 'one banal but vitally important point to keep hold of . . . that musicians continue to believe in the possibility of getting across to an audience', but perhaps even more importantly in the case of this band, that 'audiences continue to believe in the possibility of being touched' (2006: 76). This reveals the inherent part the audience plays in creating any popular music performance since 'performance implies the existence of an audience for fan consumption and a process of interaction between performer and spectators' (Sandvoss 2005: 45). Therefore, whatever the position of critics to any particular performer or performance, or its critical validity, the relationship between performer and fan is always based on the premise that from their exchanges there is the potential for meaningful and emotive experiences.

FANDOM, INDUSTRIALIZATION AND CONSUMER CULTURE

For many writers who focus on fandom, this relationship is made manifest in the greater part by the engagement of fans with consumption and consumer culture. Perhaps even more accurately, it is through patterns of consumption that fan identities are marked out and made visible (see for example Sandvoss 2005; Hills 2002; Jenkins 1992; Toynbee 2006). This, therefore, suggests that contemporary notions of fandom may share a link to industrialized economies and thus to the cultures of consumerism which are formed in such economies. As John Fiske argues, 'Fandom is a common feature of popular culture in industrial societies. It selects from the repertoire of mass-produced and mass-distributed entertainment certain performers, narratives or genres and takes them into the culture of a self-selected fraction of people. They are then reworked into an intensely pleasurable, intensely signifying popular culture that is both similar to, yet significantly different from, the culture of more "normal" popular audiences' (1992: 30).

Here, then, Fiske suggests that it is the industrialization of societies that produces the right conditions for cultures of fandom. The gradual industrialization of many societies, initially in the West, but now more globally, was part and parcel of a number of social, cultural and economic changes. These came about as a result of changed ways of thinking during the period known as the enlightenment and the development of progressive scientific and technological ideas that occurred alongside this. These changes have come to be understood as *modernity*. Though this term is somewhat contested, for this chapter it is best understood to be 'the most conventional sociological understanding of modernity: industrialisation based on technology and science, rapid economic change, elite groups with vested interests, mass education, mass political movements, debunking of traditional values, changing in consumer patterns, growing individualism, nationalism and so on' (Chernilo 2007: 81–2).

For Don Slater, the shift in social structures and values brought about by modernity equated to a 'mass identity crisis' (1997: 85) that had an impact both collectively on communities and on the individuals inhabiting them. Modern industrialization provoked what Robert Bocock describes as 'a move away from productive work roles being central to people's lives to their sense of identity, to who they are' towards 'roles in family formations, in sexual partnerships of various kinds, in leisure time pursuits, in consumption in general, which have come to be seen as being more and more significant to people'

(1993: 4). Essentially, then, identities came to be marked out more and more by what people did outside their working lives—thus, in their leisure time.

At just the moment when this change in identity construction manifested itself, there was a greater need to communicate an identity. This was a result of the increasing urbanization of communities that is part and parcel of modernity. As production is industrialized, it becomes large scale and centralized. It is moved into factories, which create around them large, anonymous city communities. These processes resulted in a need on the part of the individual to seek out and define a self-identity publicly and nonverbally as a response to this kind of anonymity (see for example Meagher 2008).

Consumer culture grew from these conditions. Modernity caused the development of a new approach to products and marketplaces. The new technologies of modernism facilitated the increased pace of the production of goods with increasingly mechanized methods of manufacture. Ultimately, production increased with the simple aim to make more money for those owning the factories and companies which were the means of production.

Of course, production in itself does not serve this purpose, and fast production in itself does not make increasing amounts of money. It is at the point of purchase that the cycle of consumer culture is created. Here, consumers are encouraged to make purchases at an increased pace and beyond physical need. In order to keep this cycle in operation, new functions for goods were instilled in the collective psyche of the consumer; these functions related a great deal more to social lives than to physical necessity. Consequently, for many writers, consumer culture has become the place where identities and lives are played out and made tangible. As Don Slater argues, 'Consumer culture is largely mundane, yet that mundanity is where we live and breathe . . . "Consumer Culture" is therefore a story of struggles for the soul of everyday life' (1997: 4).

Thus, modernity both created the need to communicate identity but also made objects which offered meanings that served this purpose. In its relationship to everyday life, then, consumer culture is self-perpetuating—it grows from a sense of individual alienation, which in turn creates a desire for greater meaning and a defined identity. At the same time, it also provides a possible resolution: the products, services and experiences in which consumers are encouraged to search for such meaning. Thus, 'consumerism simultaneously exploits mass identity crisis by proffering its goods as solutions to the problems of identity, and in the process intensifies it by offering ever more plural values and ways of being. Consumer culture lives and breeds in the cultural deficits of modernity' (Slater 1997: 85). Fandom is in itself a possible form of resolution to this sense of lack. Like other forms of identity played out through consumer culture, fan identities are both a specific product of this crisis and also a response to it.

KISS: CLOTHES AND COMMUNITIES

Equally, like most identities, being a fan is as much about belonging to a group as it is about standing out. That fandom has often been understood as a culture (see Sandvoss 2005) should also suggest that fandom is considered a way for groups of people to mark out a cultural space for themselves which distinguishes them from other groups outside of this culture. Like many such identities, the fashioning of the body is central to the articulation of fan identities. Much of the expression of belonging for the Kiss Army focuses on the band's look. This is perhaps unsurprising since such painted faces remain—off stage, at least—both visually striking and transgressive, particularly on men. Thus, adopting the look is a powerful way to mark out community for this fan group.

The Kiss Kommunity—found on the band's official website, kissonline.com—offers fans the chance to chat and share ideas, videos and photos. Many of the visuals show fans mimicking the band, at gigs and festivals, costumed or, more often, with painted faces. At Kiss Fan Shop (kissfanshop.com n.d.), descriptions lead visitors through the costumes worn by the band during what they term here 'the make-up years' (1973–89), focusing in detail on what each band member wore on different tours. The site Kiss Costumes offers official band-endorsed replica costumes for the not inconsequential sum of between $189.99 and $499.99 for adult costumes (children's costumes are cheaper, at between around $50 and $70). These looks can be finished with accessories like wigs, masks, makeup, hats and boots, and the site 'can guarantee customer satisfaction because all of our costumes and accessories are approved by the band' (kisscostumes.com n.d.) Here, as in many other areas relating to music, the authenticity of these costumes is key to their market value and appeal.

If Kiss fans want to express their allegiance in slightly less spectacular ways, then the American designer Marc Ecko offers, at the time of writing, what is also at $29.99 a much cheaper option. For his Black Rhino range, Ecko has created a Kiss hoodie which pays homage to Gene Simmons and, in particular, 'his impossibly long tongue' (Kiss Fan Site n.d.), which is often suggestively displayed on stage and in images of the band. The black hoodie zips right to the top of the head, providing the requisite painted face mask, and a long tongue snakes down the body and curls over the torso. There is a Kiss logo on the back. This is part of a collection of similar limited-edition garments which pay tribute to other icons of kitsch popular culture, including Batman, the Joker, and Jason from *Friday the 13th*. Thus, these products are probably aimed at a dual audience: fans of ironic, popular culture kitsch and true fans of the band. This is an example of how fashionable goods have resonance with a variety of aspects of popular culture, including music, and, more particularly, how fan cultures are an embedded part of consumer culture.

This chapter considers the various ways in which fashion and clothing as significant sectors of this consumer culture shape articulations of fandom in relation to popular music. It evaluates a range of case studies that provide a three-fold analysis of the ways in which music fandom, fashion and consumption are linked in the contemporary period. First, the notion of the fan as mimic and the part fashion plays in such fan performances are considered. This is framed by an inherent understanding of both fashion and fandom's relationships to consumer culture and practices of consumption, but also the possibility consumers and fans might also, conversely, be understood to be creative and productive. Second, it focuses on the notion of the celebrity fashion brand, which is predicated on a star system which assumes audience identification. Here, more specifically, teen and preteen markets are a particular focus. Thirdly, it considers the notion of collectorship in relation to fashion and fandom. Inherent in this discussion is a consideration of the part taste and knowledge may play in fan identities, serving as currency with which individuals negotiate their social lives. These discussions are all framed by wider debates around fan cultures. From these wider debates, this chapter aims to draw out and establish clothing as one of the most powerful and public signifiers of fandom, suggesting that it forms a symbolic bridge between fandom and its object and that it is its close relationship to the body that give it such value.

THE FAN AS CULTURAL FIGURE: SOME DEBATES

As the example of Kiss testifies, it is the relationship between performer and fan that forms the very basis of the contemporary music industry. This relationship arguably has greater importance than the creation of music itself. In part, this is because, as Brian Longhurst argues, 'stars function as trademarks which generate sales for the music business and the culture industries more widely' (1995: 185). Here, Longhurst argues that music stars can be understood 'as brands', which has become 'a very important focus of musical meanings' (190). Whether this kind of brand identity is clear (as in the case of Kiss) or more covert, the relationship between music and its market, whatever that may be, defines the production and consumption of popular music.

For Peter Wicke, fan cultures have been a way of symbolically resolving the tensions in popular music between art, creativity and commercial success, a tension which frames much of this book. As he argues, 'If a relationship with a mass audience was not to be justified by crude market criteria, criteria were needed which could mediate between artistic demands and commercial success . . . So commercial success no longer implied conforming to the music market but rather the artistic realisation of what bound the rock community together' (1999: 106).

Thus, for Wicke, the very existence of a meaningful fan culture comes to signify and validate an authentic music experience. As Keith Negus argues, 'For a song to be fully realized, for it to have any social meaning, then its production has to be connected to consumption, to an audience for the song' (1996: 134). Consequently, it becomes clear that stars and fans have a symbiotic relationship in which the performer only exists as a performer because of the presence of an audience for his or her performance.

Stars and star industries, of which popular music is part, are reliant on fans. As such, fandom is an everyday phenomenon; most individuals surely must, at some point in their lives, at least, consider themselves to be fans. This suggests that fan identities are not unusual or marginal. Yet many of the key debates in relation to fandom note how the very notion of the fan carries with it a sense that this identity might signal a problem of the psyche. As Joli Jensen writes, 'The literature on fandom is haunted by images of deviance. The fan is consistently characterised (referencing the term's origins) as a potential fanatic. This means that fandom is seen as excessive, bordering on deranged behaviour' (1992: 9).

For Jensen, much writing about fandom has been preoccupied with such possibilities. Here, the figure of the fan has most often been understood in two ways: as a troubled, sick, needy or excessive individual, one who waivers on the borders of acceptable behaviour, the extreme version of which might be the stalker; or as a threatening mob, a danger to the rest of society, often framed by analysis of the sports and, in particular, the football fan (Jensen 1992). In more positive discussions of fandom, which we will look at in a moment, the protestations against such ideas are often so strong that they conversely seem to serve only to reinforce the fear that runs as an undercurrent to these debates; the enduring possibility that such identities may be pernicious in some way.

ACTIVE FANS

In contrast to such long-held and negative viewpoints, many writers (see Lewis 1992; Hills 2002; Sandvoss 2005; Fiske 1989, 1992) have seen fandom in more positive terms. Many of these more positive perspectives note the rather contradictory relationship of fan cultures to more mainstream forms of cultural engagement. This is because, in the making of fan identities, individuals are often drawing on the mainstream products of consumer culture. As John Fiske notes, 'Fandom . . . is a peculiar mix of cultural determinations. On the one hand it is an intensification of popular culture which is formed outside and often against official culture, on the other it expropriates and reworks certain values and characteristics of that official culture to which it is exposed' (Fiske 1992: 34). Matt Hills argues that this is 'an inescapable contradiction which fans live out' (2002: 29). Music and style both clearly form lucrative markets within this consumer culture, and much debate around both echoes with similar concerns: they are both creative and industry, and, as such, a great deal of analysis focuses on trying to resolve these contradictory characteristics. In an attempt to address this, many writers argue that the fan is an active and creative participant in cultural life and that 'the producers of today are frequently the consumers of yesterday. Through the experience of consuming music as a listener, many individuals are drawn into producing music of their own' (Laing 1990: 186).

Hills argues, however, that any attempt to resolve such contradictions is a mistake. For him, this represents a 'moral dualism which places "good" fandom in opposition to the "bad" consumer' (2002: 29). Hills argues that this approach 'colludes with "half" of the fan experience (anti-commercial ideology) by writing out or marginalising the other contradictory "half" (that of the commodity completist) . . . [producing] rigid assumptions that fandom and production are valuable, whereas consumption is somehow secondary and lacks value, [ideas which] still need to be contested' (30). For Hills, then, fan expression is important to individual fans and to our understanding of how fan cultures work, no matter how it is played out. Thus, echoing many writers on consumer culture and fashion (see Wilson 1985; Church Gibson 2006), consumption is, for Hills (2002), as legitimate a form of creativity for this group as production itself.

THE BODY IN FAN CULTURES

Importantly for this chapter, fan identity is often played out through the body, and yet, as Matt Hills notes, 'the site of the body has been largely neglected in previous work on fan cultures' (2002: 158). Whilst the way in which fans might shape or fashion their bodies to articulate fan identity is part and parcel of many analyses of fan culture, the body as a specific site for the articulation of fandom has received less sustained analysis. In his book *Fan Cultures,* Hills (2002) redresses this imbalance with an explicit consideration of some of the techniques of the body employed in fan cultures.

In particular, Hills (2002) uses the term *performative consumption* to describe one formation of fan identity which uses the body. In using the term *performativity,* he considers the importance of enactment to fan identities. He uses the term *performative* (more often applied to a discussion of gender, as we will see in chapter 7) to describe both the origins of fan identity and the method by which this is made visible. He uses this term rather than the closely related *performance* to take into account the fact that when shaping the physical body in line with fan identities, fans are 'performing' this identity. At the same time, he argues, fans do not always exert 'agency' over the development of this fan identity. Fans, he thus argues, find it hard to identify a moment of 'becoming' but rather see fan identities as something 'realized'.

The notion that some social performances are so ingrained and internalized as normal behaviours that these iterations are unconscious forms the crux of definitions of performativity in relation to gender as posited by Judith Butler (1999; see chapter 7 for a more detailed discussion). Hills acknowledges the contradictions in his use of the word, arguing that 'fandom, perhaps unlike gender, possesses a moment of "emergence" rather than always

Figure 3   Elvis impersonator, Key West Club. © FloridaStock, 2010, used under license from shutterstock.com

already being citational, and this appearance cannot be readily placed within theoretical narratives of performativity, despite sharing their emphasis on the loss of individual agency' (2002: 160). Nonetheless, his use of the term *performative* aims to emphasize the passionate and irresistible drive that ardent fandom seems to provoke. Most importantly for this chapter, however, his work emphasizes the way in which fans seem to feel compelled to express this fan identity through their bodies.

Here, then, Hills focuses on the impersonation of star identity at the heart of much fan culture, often focusing on the professional Elvis impersonator (Figure 3) as the most spectacular example of this. He argues that such acts of iteration, copying and the adoption of star identity open an 'irresolvable space for playing, spectacularly and physically' (2002: 168). Whilst Hills's work aims to draw out the complexities of fan identities and critique previous approaches to understanding and organizing fan cultures which go far beyond the aims and remit of this book, his work offers us a model for thinking about the role of dress in fan cultures. This role is formed by the performative urge for iteration of fan identity through the body. Here, fashion and dress offer the tools to become, and fandom (and the star system which underpins it) creates the conditions and attachments that shape this becoming.

FASHION AND STAR/AUDIENCE IDENTIFICATION

In April 2010, British magazine *Glamour* announced pop star and *X Factor* judge Cheryl Cole to be the Best Dressed Woman of the year for the second year running, voted for by a reader's poll. More than her role as a member of Girls Aloud, it was arguably her position as judge on the reality show that brought Cole's style to the forefront. Magazines from *OK* and *New* to *Vogue* (see for example *Vogue* n.d.) featured issue after issue reviewing the female judge's look on each episode (often rather disappointingly and yet predictably placing her in opposition to the other female and somewhat older judge, Dannii Minogue). These accolades came despite criticisms of some of her outfits in the popular press throughout the duration of the series. In particular, a black and silver David Koma designed dress with curved, architectural black breastplates met with a great deal of condemnation in some publications (see Morales 2009; Jones 2009). The power of Cole as a promoter of zeitgeist fashion was clear, however, when by 6 November 2010, London stockists of Koma's collection, Browns Focus, sold out of the £1,900 dress (see Alexander 2009a).

Perhaps what makes Cole such a strong style icon is her own rise from reality TV star on the UK show *Popstars: The Rivals,* from which her band Girls Aloud were formed. Drawing on the work of earlier film studies theorists like

Dyer (1979), Gledhill (1991) and Stacey (1991, 1994), Ndalianis and Henry describe the kind of transformation from ordinary girl to icon undergone by Cole as 'the "rise to fame" mythos associated with film stardom' (2002: xiv). In their work, Ndalianis and Henry make the important point that the celebrity landscape can no longer be understood as finding its locus in Hollywood, and Cole's successful conversion from reality TV girl next door into fully fledged style star is illustrative of this. Still, it is perhaps her ordinariness—her strongly articulated identity as a working class 'geordie' girl from the north-east of England—that is part of Cole's appeal.

As Sandvoss (2005) has noted, classed identities play a part in consumer patterns and choices and consequently in cultures of fandom. Much coverage of Cole focuses on her multi-market appeal. Whilst on *X Factor,* she often wore expensive, high fashion, while most press coverage told consumers how to get the look at cheap, high street prices. The *Sun* newspaper celebrated Cole as 'groomed girl next door' (Jones 2008). In October 2009, British *Marie Claire* magazine recounted that in 'what can only be described as a natural progression for a nation's sweetheart who's constantly applauded for her sense of style, Cheryl has opened up about her desire to start her own fashion line.' Crucially, here Cole stated, 'It would probably be a high street collection. I would take inspiration from designer stuff, but turn it into high street' (*Marie Claire* 2009).

Thus, 'whilst it has become increasingly difficult to link specific fan texts, particularly those distributed through mass media of virtually universal reach, such as television, to specific positions in a multi-dimensional class model, this does not mean that they cease to function as signifiers of class, age or gender positions from the subjective position of the fan' (Sandvoss 2005: 37). Though Cole may have mass-market appeal that cannot be limited exclusively to a particular classed identity, it is certainly her broad, everyday appeal that is her value to the fashion media, and the continuing emphasis on accessibly priced fashion in much coverage of her style seems to attest to this. The strong and ever-apparent memory of her earlier ordinariness in her accent and her public persona forms her star identity. This is part and parcel of her 'charisma', defined by Richard Dyer as 'a certain quality of an individual personality by virtue of which he is set apart from ordinary men' (Dyer 1979, quoted in Gledhill 1991: 57)

It is Cheryl Cole's charisma, emerging from her ordinariness, that seems to define her appeal for both her fans and the fashion industry and media that have been fundamental in the creation of her style icon status. This is part and parcel of circumstances where, from the early part of the twentieth century, 'celebrity status became aligned with the potentialities of the wedding of consumer culture with democratic aspirations. The images of possibility provided by films, radio and popular music represented an accessible form of consumption. The discourse that surrounded these celebrities provided the evidence of access to stardom' (Marshall 1997: 9).

Charles Eckert has established the way in which mid-twentieth-century Hollywood recognized the value of star culture to money-making, where 'tens of millions of Americans provided the captive audience for the unique experiments in consumer manipulation that the showcasing of products in films and through star endorsements constituted' (cited in Gledhill 1991: 39). For Eckert, Hollywood here established a model of desire and consumption upon which both consumer culture and celebrity culture have grown. The star was presented as a commodity, but as P. David Marshall notes, one that 'possesses in its humanness and familiarity an affective link in consumer culture' (1997: 245). Here, goods offered the possibility for the consumer to 'declare his or her worth by spending money on items that will help them look like, play like, or in some other way, be like someone else' (Cashmore 1990: 409).

CELEBRITY FASHION RANGES

Fans, whatever their level of devotion, are, of course, good audiences for products offered by the object of their fandom, since these products offer a way of articulating the identification of the fan with the star. Practices of performative consumption identify the body as a locus for this identification. Because of the historical relationship between star and consumer culture, it is perhaps unsurprising, then, that so many music stars also market and, in some cases, design fashion ranges. (We have already explored the part that music stars play in promoting fashion labels which are not their own in chapter 1 and will look more specifically at the relationship between hip-hop music and stars as fashion entrepreneurs in chapter 6.)

Claire Beale, writing in the *Independent* newspaper, acknowledges that the real links between performers and the design of clothes themselves might be tenuous in some cases but also notes that the idea of a celebrity-designed range has more powerful promotional potential than ordinary advertising because 'getting your celebrity to infect your product, to become part of your product, your brand DNA, now that's a different game' (2007). As Sarah Harris (2007) writes in the same issue, the market on both sides of the Atlantic has been and continues to be flooded with celebrity fashion ranges. In 2004, Jennifer Lopez was at the height of her relatively short-lived musical success and developed a number of ranges in fashion and cosmetics. Others, like Britney Spears, Sean 'Puff Daddy' Combs, Jessica Simpson, Beyoncé Knowles and Gwen Stefani, to name but a few, have all launched themselves into fashion careers alongside music, as have, in the UK, Kylie Minogue, Madonna for H&M, Lily Allen and, more recently, Amy Winehouse for Fred Perry.

The press around the launch of these ranges always goes out of the way to emphasize the involvement of these stars in the production of designs for their ranges: to authenticate the role and thus the clothes. In the case of Winehouse at Fred Perry: 'We had three major design meetings where she was closely involved in product style selection and the application of fabric, colour and styling details' (*Guardian* 2010). Still, as Claire Beale notes, 'This is not about supplementary designer talent; this is about a shrewd, multi-layered marketing strategy that works seamlessly from initial product concept through to advertising, PR, and the bottom line' (2007).

There is a sense, then, that celebrity fashion ranges may exploit fan-consumers. Such manipulations of desire are endemic in consumer culture. This reveals the increasingly complex relationship of fan cultures to mainstream consumer culture and the often impossibility of separating the two. Fan cultures, which take the products of consumer culture and create sub-cultural meanings for them, become targeted and readopted into consumer culture as products are made directly for fan groups. Clearly, the relationship between fan and consumer cultures is cyclical and opportunistic. Here, 'the sense of autonomy and identity in consumption is placed constantly under threat' (Slater 1997: 31), and as soon as a countercultural space is carved out by fans, it becomes inspiration for another section of consumer culture.

PRODUCTIVE FANS, FASHION AND RESISTANCE

When fans adopt forms of dress to articulate their fandom, they undoubtedly participate in the wider power structures of consumer culture. This is because 'fan performances are in fact performances of symbols and images representing texts and commodities tied to the economic and symbolic power of the media industry' (Sandvoss 2005: 51). At the same time, Sandvoss argues that 'the consumption of popular culture in fandom thus forms part of the struggle of disempowered groups against the hegemonic culture of the powerful' (12)—a struggle which may, it appears, be never-ending.

Thus, fans participate in consumer culture as a means to articulate their fandom and, as such, are participating in the hegemonic culture—the dominant, mainstream, consumer culture which encourages them to consume and conform—of which Sandvoss speaks. Here, the objects of their fandom can be used by that consumer culture as powerful catalysts for consumption. But many writers have seen fans as making small resistances to this culture through their participation. This has been a central tenet of a great deal of debate on fan cultures: the desire to mark fans out as more productive individuals than mainstream consumers; to see consumption as leading to a meaningful act of creation. In particular, John Fiske focused on Madonna fans

in the early part of her career and found that an identity as a Madonna fan offered young women a useful model for working through their own social and
gendered identities. He argued, for example, that Madonna's star identity offered a model of femininity to these girls, one which allowed them to find their
own 'feminine sexuality' (1989: 100).

Fiske saw this fan identity as circulating an empowered version of femininity which provided a challenge to more limited notions of female roles. These
notions were put into action through the body and fashion. Here, the adoption of Madonna's style provided a 'site of semiotic struggle between forces
of patriarchal control & feminine resistance, of capitalism & the subordinate'
(1989: 97). Thus, Madonna's young female fans used fashion and style to
mark out an allegiance with a particular version of femininity, 'aligning themselves with a source of power' (101).

For Fiske, they also, in carving out an active and specific identity for themselves, were adopting increasingly productive modes of identity construction,
because 'the Madonna fans who, on MTV, claimed that dressing like Madonna
made people take more notice of them as they walked down the street were
not only constructing for themselves more empowered identities than those
normally available to adolescent girls, but were putting those meanings into
social circulation' (1992: 38). It is important also to mention that style plays
an equal part in the making of a community in this context. For Fiske, this
played a vital role in the female identification he also felt was important in
this context: both the identification of young female fans with Madonna herself and, by extension, the female-to-female friendships that formed around
this identification.

Sandvoss argues that resistances are made possible and come to fruition not because of the goods fans acquire but because of what they do with
them: 'It is ultimately of little significance to the culture industry what we do
with texts and commodities after the point of purchase. The way we wear our
jeans or engage with the symbolic resources of popular culture does, however,
have a profound impact on our social and cultural environment and interper-
sonal relationships' (2005: 15). It is when goods are put to work that ordinary
consumer products develop performative potential for fan identities.

In performative consumption, we see the central role of the body in the
experience of fandom. By extension, we also see the possibility that fan identities possess both creative and spectacular potential. This creativity might
be located in consumption patterns and the reappropriation of everyday objects into fan cultures. As such, Cornel Sandvoss argues that 'fans also become performers as others acknowledge their consumption' (2005: 45). But,
equally, we might see fans becoming more literally productive by putting into
action what Sandvoss calls 'textual productivity [which] refers to materials
and texts created by fans which are manifest concretely' (29).

On a Lady Gaga fan site (see Lady-Gaga.net n.d.), we see an example of this kind of creativity, which focuses on fashion. Fan 'St Louis (AJ)' posts images of his fan identity; one which we might argue is active, productive and performative. In a post of four images, two focus on a red leather or plastic jacket on a kitchen table. It is not entirely clear whether this garment is home-made or tailor-made, but it is certainly clear from this set of images that this sculptural garment is of great importance to this blogger's fan identity.

The two accompanying images show the jacket being worn at a meeting with Lady Gaga, cementing this garment's significance to the relationship between star and fan, providing a provenance for this object. This is an example of the 'cult body as written through a process of commemoration and impersonation' (Hills 2002: 161), not least because in its materiality this jacket evokes the red rubber dress worn by Gaga at the Royal Variety Performance in the UK in December 2009. Thus, this jacket is a demonstration of a commitment to a fan identity, via time and presumably also money, fandom is made visible through the body and through fashion. In such accounts, there is evidence of not only creativity in terms of identity construction but also in the very making of objects themselves. Here we see the potential for fan cultures to be productive and the possibility that a fan identity will feed into other experiences, other kinds of knowledge and the accrual of new skills and social networks.

In this example, then, we see not only the engagement of the body with fan identity, but also the re-presentation of this body and identity through the Internet and thus into a fan community. Hills sees online fan media as affirming for individuals, 'not only celebrat[ing] and validat[ing] the fan's knowledge, it also mirrors the fan's attachment back to him or her, validating the affective experience itself' (2002: 181). For Hills, the online fan community is a 'community of the imagination' which 'acts as a specific defence against the possible "otherness" or even "alien-ness" of the discursively inexplicable intensity and emotionality of fandom' (180). Online communities offer the means to create and access fan cultures, to validate the individual in his or her fandom and to provide an outlet for the products of that fandom.

TEEN FANS, TWEEN FANS, YOUTH MARKETS

Some of the most active fan sites, particularly for the discussion of style, centre on American teen stars. The fanforum.com site for American teen heartthrob Zac Efron, star of the extremely lucrative *High School Musical* film franchise, focuses not only on adoration for the actor, but also on his wardrobe and those of his female co-stars. Most importantly, it gives advice on how and where to access these looks (see fanforum.com n.d.). It is also a space of knowledge-sharing where users can post a picture and wait for a reply telling them how to recreate the look. Those answering provide links to other blogs for information as well as product sites detailing where some items can be found.

Efron's contemporary American teen star Miley Cyrus has a strong fan presence, much of which oscillates around her style both on screen—as Hannah Montana—and off. A seemingly ordinary girl with a secret identity as a rock star, the character of Hannah Montana resonates strongly with the requirements of both ordinariness and extraordinariness essential to the star system. As such, Cyrus embodies three possible identities with which her audience can identify: Montana; her offstage alter ego, also called Miley; and Cyrus herself.

Like many of the celebrities already discussed here, Cyrus has launched a fashion range in collaboration with US designer Max Azria which is sold in Walmart stores and retailed at very low prices for a pocket-moneyed youth market. With jeans priced at $20, this is a fashion range that understands its market: ordinary young girls. Thus, whilst Cyrus may be quoted as saying that she 'would pay $500 for the jeans that we make for $20. I'm really into high fashion' (see Glennon 2009), she recognizes that 'this is going to be good for, like, Middle America, and it will be great for kids that really want to be in fashion but don't have it available' (see Bitten and Bound 2009).

This youth market has been a target for companies since the end of the Second World War and the baby boom that came soon after. As Daniel Thomas Cook writes, 'From the outset, this demographic phenomenon—an increase in the birth of babies—was framed as a business opportunity. Children and babies, regardless of any specific tastes and preferences, represented prospective consumers whose effective demand for products would unfold in the near future' (2004: 123).

In particular, fashion and apparel 'was poised for the boom . . . Integrated into [its] infrastructure were age-graded merchandising, several concatenated age-style ranges, a consumerist conception of "the mother" and a construction of "the child" as an ever demanding and knowing customer. These elements, put together, provided the industry with the right tools at the appropriate time to accommodate and exploit the dimensions of the coming demographic explosion' (Cook 2004). As such, these youth markets are nothing new, but they have exploded into the world of the new media in recent years, and central to this explosion has been the music/acting star.

Like Zac Efron and many of these music/acting stars, the power behind Cyrus's career is, of course, the Disney network, a fact which clearly demarcates the intended audience for her music, TV shows, films and the associated merchandise, much of it fashion based. This carries with it certain ideas about youth and appropriate behaviour that are part and parcel of the marketing of stars like Cyrus. David Thomas Cook's work establishes not only the conditions that created both teen and 'tween' (or preteen) markets, but also the part that marketing to these groups played in managing a sense of age- and gender-appropriate behaviour for young girls. Here, 'markets are indispensable to the making of social persons in the ongoing consumer culture of childhood, and indeed, consumer culture at large' (Cook 2004: 144). In the case of fashion, 'sexuality . . . organizes the discourse around girls' dress' (128), or, perhaps more accurately, a certain discomfort around any tinge of sexuality in the dress of young girls informs reactions to this market.

In April 2010, the Irish newspaper the *Belfast Telegraph* reported that the high street chain Primark had halted the sale of padded bikinis for children after criticism from child welfare groups (*Belfast Telegraph* 2010). On 15 April 2010, British tabloid newspaper the *Sun* (see Hamilton 2010) reported that several high street stores retailed bras in size 28AA, which they estimated would fit the average seven-year-old, and on sale in Primark for the same age group were knickers with the slogan 'You've Scored'. All stores agreed to review their policies in relation to these items as a result of this coverage, with Primark pledging to donate all profits from these items to children's charities. That they were produced in the first place, however, illustrates the contradictions inherent in the marketing of fashion to young girls, when women's fashion has most often stood for 'sex' (see for example Craik 1994). As Daniel Thomas Cook (2004) demonstrates, there is a market imperative that requires these young girls to engage as increasingly sophisticated and mature consumers. However, there is alongside this a moral dualism that also demands they retain an innocence appropriate to their age.

Consequently, when Cyrus, aged fifteen, was photographed posing 'naked' for *Vanity Fair* magazine's June 2008 issue, Disney was quick to move, 'claiming the young singer and actress was "deliberately manipulated" into posing apparently topless with only a satin sheet draped around her' (Singh 2008). Photographer Annie Leibovitz defended her image, arguing that it was classic, natural and beautiful, but it clearly offended the representation of childhood, not only culturally and socially expected, but also marketed by Disney itself: what defines the child as 'a being distinguishable from adults [is] . . . its naturalness, its innocence, and the naturalness of its innocence' (Cook 2004: 22). Despite such criticisms, on the whole Miley Cyrus embodies a model of teen femininity, just edgy enough and polished enough (Figure 4), which Cook argues was established early on, projecting her as one who is 'fashion conscious, knows what she wants, and isn't shy of expressing her opinion' (131).

Cyrus's online communities follow a model of teen female engagement with fashion, also established at the very inception of the market, where 'stores institutionalized and appropriated the clique structure of white, middle-class

Figure 4 Miley Cyrus embodies teen femininity—polished and mature, but with chipped nail polish—Stadium of Fire, Utah, 4 July 2008. © Chris H. Galbraith, 2010, used under license from shutterstock.com

teen girl peer society into their merchandising strategy' (Cook 2004: 131). Many online communities do the same. The difference is, of course, that these communities are often self-created and self-governed. Here we see young girls behaving not just as consumers, but also as a productive community to which they can contribute through discussion and debate or through the creation of the site itself.

The Miley Cyrus fan site dresslikemiley.net advertised for members of the community to volunteer for jobs on the site (see Miley Fashion n.d.). As such, fandom becomes productive for young girls and a source of self-esteem and skills building. As a result, these fan communities could be argued to be an example of what John Fiske terms 'a shadow cultural economy' (1992: 30). The identification with Cyrus's familiar version of empowered girlhood, despite its problems and contradictions, becomes a potential source for more than a consumer experience for those participating in this community.

Thus, performative consumption is a method by which personal identities come to be shaped in homage to affective relationships to stars. It is made manifest by the shaping of the fashioned body along the lines offered by the star in a number of ways, be it through ranges created specifically for this purpose or the copying and borrowing of looks. Equally, the production of an object or objects by fans themselves might form the means by which a fan identity becomes performative. The possibilities of performative consumption as a bridging between musician and fan, via dress and fashion, become even more amplified when a fan has the opportunity to own or wear an item of clothing which has previously belonged to the object of their fandom.

FASHION, FANS AND COLLECTORSHIP

Elton John offers this opportunity via his Out of the Closet sales, the profits of which are given to his AIDS Foundation charity. Sales have been held in both London and New York and feature not only his own clothes, but also some of those belonging to his partner, David Furnish (see Harrison 2009). On the Elton John fan page The Fox (see The Fox n.d.), a fan previously involved in running fan clubs and communities displays items, mainly shirts and suits, bought from the Out of the Closet sales.

Key to the experience of making purchases from these sales is the possibility of authenticating items as actually belonging to and having been worn by Elton. The process of either identifying the same garment in existing pictures or finding 'on the inside it has a label which has Elton's name on it, which means in my opinion that it was custom made for him' (The Fox) seems to be the source of a great deal of interest. When reading through fan accounts which discuss making purchases from the sales, it becomes very clear that items are not necessarily bought to be worn: 'If I'd known then that I could actually fit/wear these suits, I would have bought black ones,' says 'The Fox', who ended up with something bright orange. Thus, the performative potential of such items is somewhat limited.

Here, then, we might argue that we see not only an opportunity for performative, fan consumption at its most personal and meaningful, but also an example of what Grant McCracken (1990) might also term 'curatorial consumption'. Here, personal relationships, a sense of identity and belonging are bound up in the possession of objects. Whilst McCracken did not initiate this term in order to understand the fan, writers such as Matt Hills (2002) and Tankel and Murphy (1998) have built on his ideas to develop an understanding of fan cultures. In McCracken's account, objects accrued and collected which have a significance to a sense of identity both past and present have 'special historical and memorial significance [which] constantly impresses it-self upon their curator' (1990: 45).

In such a context, the curator 'is in possession of objects that are charged with profound significance' (McCracken 1990: 46). In their work on memory and material culture, Hallam and Hockey demonstrate the role that clothing plays in the remembrance of the physical presence of individuals. Though much of their material focuses on the significance of clothing in mourning, it first establishes the important point that 'clothing . . . permits a desirable (physical) connection' (Hallam and Hockey 2001: 116). Just as clothing, for the bereaved, often becomes a locus for memories because of the 'material-ity of the body and its associated objects' (110), so the collection of stars' clothing by fans is valued because of the possibility that these clothes might have absorbed traces of the embodied self of the star, where 'personhood [might be] recognized as residing within the clothes' (115).

But beyond this personal connection, such forms of consumption seem to have at least equal value in the links they create to a community. This kind of consumption both rests on and also facilitates the development of personal knowledge. In accessing the objects at the sales, it is clear that existing fan knowledge has great currency: 'One woman rummaging among the shoes told her friend, "If they're size eight they're Elton's. David is an eight and a half"' (Harrison 2009).

This process, both off- and online, might be seen as a demonstration of what John Fiske has termed 'unofficial cultural capital' (see Lewis 1992: 33) or 'popular cultural capital' (Fiske 1989: 135). Here, fan cultures might be un-derstood as 'a sort of "moonlighting" in the cultural rather than the economic sphere' (Lewis 1992: 33). Whilst official cultural capital relates to the kinds of knowledge developed in official institutions like schools that can one day hopefully be exchanged for economic capital—for higher paid jobs, greater life choice and subsequently better self-esteem—unofficial cultural capital 'is a major source of self-esteem among the peer-group' (Lewis 1992).

CONCLUSION: FANDOM, FASHION AND NEW MEDIA

While Fiske argues that unlike official cultural capital, its unofficial form does not offer economic possibilities, the opening up of online communities may demand something of a rethink. As Dovey and colleagues note, 'Studies of fan culture have spearheaded the theoretical construction of [the] shift from "audience" to "user" in media studies' (2009: 222).

Not exclusively, but certainly more recently, the easy accessibility of new media has opened up prospects for fans to communicate much more widely and democratically. It has also been a space of opportunity, as we have seen in part already: a place where young fans can hone skills in new media production and communication. The recent success of fashion bloggers like Susie Lau—who started out as an everyday user of new media blogs but who is now courted by the fashion industry—attests to the potential of new media spaces to offer significant rewards. In the case of Lau: front-row seats at London Fashion Week, expensive freebies and a status alongside long-standing fashion journalists in the 'old media' (Wiseman 2009).

Undoubtedly, new media opens up marketing opportunities for companies at the same time. Further, fashion offers an opportunity for individual performers to expand their brand reach, and, here, new media plays a key role. As Jenkins states, 'Today the ideal consumer talks up the program and spreads word about the brand' (1992: 361). Fan sites provide an ideal discursive space for this kind of unofficial promotion because, in order to play out their fandom, individuals *must* consume and perform.

Fashion can thus be understood as a place where individuals might exert their fans identities and creativity through their bodies: a public declaration of their fan identity. New media dialogues open up new possibilities for how fashioned identities are created via the discourses of virtual fan communities; they offer spaces for the development of skills and self-esteem, but they may also eat away at the very notion of fan communities as something definable.

For Jenkins, the creativity of the fan comes under threat from new technologies: 'As fandom becomes part of the normal way that creative industries operate, then fandom may cease to function as a meaningful category of cultural analysis' (1992: 364). Jenkins argues that this is because by utilizing new technology, marketers have echoed the very structures of fan culture, in which new media encourages at least the idea of active participation on the part of the consumer. Thus, if fans of music are understood as productive individuals who create performative identities through fashion (and because of their fandom) within the parameters of consumer culture, then they become more difficult to locate in a sea of fashion-related new media that encourages all consumers to believe in their identity as producer as well as consumer.

–3–

Witchy Women: Fashioning the Womanly Body of the Female Singer-Songwriter

On the cover of her 1998 album *Ophelia,* the American singer-songwriter Natalie Merchant reclines on a sofa and gazes out at the viewer. She is wearing a silk dress of the darkest midnight-blue satin, trimmed with feathers. Her black hair flows onto her shoulders and melds with the sheen of her dress. This darkness of dress and hair is offset by her pale face, a white flower in her hair and white sandals. The look is suggestive of a 1930s female torch singer in a jazz club somewhere hot and humid—maybe New Orleans. She is a glamorous woman in a not-so-glamorous venue; the shell-shaped sofa on which she reclines looks worn, a slightly dirty-looking gold colour and shabbily fringed.

There is a dinginess to the background of the image and thus the room in which the narrative situates her. There is even a sense that she may be a woman of questionable morals. She is certainly exoticized and eroticized in this image. She wears too many beaded bangles—more than a good girl would wear in this period—and behind her is a vase filled with lilies, a flower with long-held connotations of the phallic, reminiscent of some of the iconic photographs of the artist Robert Mapplethorpe. The image is therefore tinged with sex, but the way in which this is represented is subtle: little flesh is exposed.

The title of the album in itself suggests a certain kind of woman: Shakespeare's tragic heroine Ophelia, used, abused and driven to madness by a man who loved her but who, unable to put her concerns before his own, could not demonstrate it. At the same time, the image is more reminiscent of Manet's Olympia, the affluent prostitute who reclines on a day bed; nude, she opens her body to be surveyed, inviting the look of a viewer whose stare she confidently returns. But though the comparisons between this painting and the cover of *Ophelia* are clear, there is an important difference. Merchant's body is not opened to the viewer. True, it is clothed, and this immediately changes the way in which her body and the image will be read and understood. But subtly, and most importantly, it is how she situates herself within the frame that changes its meaning. Her body is positioned to point towards the sofa, and her arm makes a barrier between viewer and body. Thus, she is turned away, and her body is closed to us.

THE REPRESENTATION OF FEMALE BODIES

Such subtleties can speak volumes. As John Berger (1972) has established, it is at the level of representation that the 'normal' position of women is established, controlled and managed, since seeing repeated images which show the same patterns of behaviour come to define our sense of how things 'should be'. Thus, such images or representations are the way in which we give meaning and order to the world (see Hall 1997). In an analysis which centres on the female nude in the historical trajectory of European painting through to more contemporary advertising, Berger demonstrates how the female body has often been portrayed in ways that 'make it available' to voyeuristic view. Thus, women are shown through representation to be a normally passive group. This has implications for all female bodies, naked or dressed, real or represented, because here the female body's function as a thing to be looked at is privileged through such imagery, over and above its main function: as something to be lived through.

In such representations women are therefore dehumanized—made an object and thus objectified. In such representations of nude, passive bodies, women become associated with contradictory qualities of both the submissive and the carnal. As such, these representations make the female body a visual stimulus, eroticized and formulated towards heterosexual desire, since this voyeuristic viewer is usually assumed, in the first instance, at least, to be male. Berger ably demonstrates, too, how such imagery becomes part of lived experience when it is, in turn, converted into a dominant discourse against which women are measured and measure themselves in all areas of life. This consequently defines a woman's value as something centred in her sexual desirability and, in association with this, her value as a visual object.

In the subtle act of repositioning her body, we might argue, then, that Merchant shows some suggestion of the kind of performer she is and the particular experience of being female that she presents through her music. Like many singer-songwriters, her work is often focused on her own subjective experience. As a *female* singer-songwriter, this is bound up with the experience of being a woman. Consequently, how she appears is of significant importance because, concerned as the female singer-songwriter's work is with female experience, their audience is made up of significant numbers of women who identify with their music.

As such, in connecting a female audience to a female musician, the female singer-songwriter's body must have more to say than just a passive avowal of heterosexual desirability. This means that, to some extent, the female singer-songwriter has to go against the grain of a music industry which has limited expectations of women's roles and value, but must do so in a way that does not threaten exclusion from success within this industry. This chapter looks at some of the ways in which the bodies of female performers—and later, more particularly, female singer-songwriters—can be understood to express such concerns. It establishes some of the looks which have become defining features of the genre and, thus, aims to suggest that these looks embody a sense of female experience rather than the more expected femininity, which fashion and dress usually write on the female body.

In discussing such looks, this chapter is in many ways concerned with anti-fashion. This is because, firstly, these styles of dress are more enduring forms of embodiment than the fast fashion trends favoured by female stars working in a more pop context who undergo almost seasonal changes of image, generally towing the fashion line. Secondly, these looks can be considered to go against fashion's usual emphasis on the female body as erotic object. James Laver's notion of the 'shifting erogenous zone' (1969) demonstrates the way in which the female body has been shaped by the position privileged to it as an erotic symbol. Here, the form of the fashionable silhouette—what is revealed and concealed, what is highlighted and reduced—follows the function of that body as a seductive source, managed, controlled and shaped towards the particular interests of men.

Whilst the chapter looks at a number of looks worn by female musicians that can be argued to challenge this eroticized and objectified female body, it finally focuses on a look, perhaps best described as witchy, adopted by many female artists with a personal and confessional style of music-making. Subsequently, this chapter will argue that this look, which creates a particular sense of space around the body and which uses fabrics and textures to create this space, hints at a deeper engagement with the world. This is amplified by references to religious and spiritual imagery. This look seems to endure as a device to powerfully embody female experience in the singer-songwriter genre. Thus, the chapter argues that this form of embodiment functions to emphasize the confessions of female experience on which the music focuses, formulating the performer's body for female identification rather than male desire.

WOMEN IN MUSIC

As Simon Frith and Angela McRobbie assert, 'Any analysis of the sexuality of rock must begin with the brute social fact that in terms of control and production, rock is a male form' (1990: 373). Writers like Longhurst (1995), Whiteley (1997, 2000) and Bayton (1990) have demonstrated that when women become part of the music industry, they must navigate its rather archaic ideas of female ability. Female roles in music are limited, and 'as musicians, women have traditionally been viewed as singers, positioned in front of a band, the focus of audience attention not simply for what they sing, but for how they looked' (Whiteley 2000: 53). Female instrumentalists are rare. Thus, this navigational process offers few choices to women as to how they might represent themselves or carve out a career in an industry which largely values female musicians as visual images rather than as producers of music. Such limitations have had an impact on the self-identities of women who make music; as Mavis Bayton notes, 'Most women starting out in groups do not define themselves as musicians' (1990: 253) in contrast to their male counterparts, who quickly identify themselves with such a professional identity. Therefore, the patterns of female behaviour that are sanctioned by the music industry echo the roles and behaviours stereotypically legitimated for women in Western society generally: a positioning of the male musician in the public, professional realm, valued for his technical abilities, alongside a certain domestication of the female musician in a private negation of professional identities, valued more often for the way she looks.

As John Fiske has noted, to analyse, understand and uncover the meanings of any cultural texts—musicians' bodies included—'recognizes that the distribution of power in society is paralleled by the distribution of meanings in texts' (1989: 97). Thus, how women operate within and are represented by the music industry and in the texts that it produces both reflect the expected role and behaviours of women in culture generally and play a part in perpetuating that role and those behaviours as the normal ones for women both within and outside that industry.

The power relations between men and women, in parallel with many aspects of cultural life, have been a focal point for a variety of discussions of both music and fashion. The music industry is posited as one which threatens to reject female music performers if the many long-established codes of appropriate role, position, behaviour and appearance are not followed. Sheila Whiteley (2000) argues that stereotypical representations of femininity have dominated many discourses of music since the 1960s. These were established not only by the dominant physical ideals of femininity of any given time, but also by the way that gender positions were reinforced and women were *discussed* in popular song.

In particular, Whiteley shows how popular music often depicted stories of what were *perceived* to be women's concerns, such as fey, romanticized and subordinate romantic love; how particular women characterized in songs fulfilled stereotypes by adopting nurturing, romanticized, passive and subordinate positions; and how such representations mirrored the fashioned styles of many female performers.

WOMEN PERFORMERS AND GENDERED IDENTITIES

In such ways, then, we might suggest that the popular music industry laid down its conventions early on. Along with other cultural representations, this played a part in establishing a set of normal behaviours and concerns for women against which all newcomers were judged and managed. Whiteley (1997, 2000) has analysed, in detail, the ways in which female performers have navigated their careers in such conditions. Of particular interest to many writers, including Whiteley, is Janis Joplin, who acts as a significant counterpoint for such discussions of women in popular music not least because she managed to both perceptibly contravene stereotypical codes of femininity whilst also enjoying professional success.

Joplin was possessed of a contradictory set of identity traits focused on her music, her behaviour and her body. Some writers suggest that Joplin's route to success in the male-oriented music industry was paved by her tendency to become 'one of the boys' (see Whiteley 2000): to be promiscuous, tough and hard drinking. Whilst this means that to see her as any kind of feminist icon might be difficult for some, she is a marker against which notions of the female singer-songwriter, and a corresponding set of traditions, have been established. There is a perceived resistance in Joplin's self-presentation, in her use of her body and her voice, which 'brought with it an opportunity to challenge the established conventions of beauty' (59)—and challenge them she did, whether she meant to or not (which always seems somewhat unclear). She is an important example because, as Whiteley's work suggests, her treatment by the press at the time reveals the boundaries of both acceptable female behaviour and physical appearance for the music industry which continue to persist. It also demonstrated the consequences for women who exist on or cross these boundaries.

Joplin's physical image has remained central to the way in which she was both discussed in her time and subsequently remembered because she failed to conform to conventions of female beauty. As a result, much press coverage converged on her lack of the traditional feminine attractiveness (which must be amplified, if not extraordinary, in the case of anyone in the public eye) required of female music performers and focused instead on her bad skin, frizzy hair and struggles with her weight. She was possessed of a stereotypically feminine love of clothing and dressing up, but her look was made up of thrift store items: scarves, patterned tunics, hats, feather boas, bangles and beads. This look spoke not of delicate femininity, but of an earthiness, and was just too 'plastic' to be acceptable (see Whiteley 2000). There seemed to be too obvious a juncture between her well-built frame and these feminine trappings; the very act of dressing up was all too obvious and revealed the artifice of her construction of herself as a woman. This played a part in isolating Joplin as something potentially dangerous because, to quote Mary Russo, 'to put on femininity with a vengeance suggests the power of taking it off' (1986: 224).

In the case of Joplin, then, we see the kind of inner struggle of being a woman, toiling for expression and acceptance, in a context where woman must 'survey everything she is and everything she does because how she ap- pears to men is of crucial importance for what is normally thought of as the success of her life' (Berger 1972: 46). Much of the criticism levelled towards Janis Joplin did not centre on her abilities as musician or performer, or her presence or lack of songwriting ability, but on the appearance of her body and the way she used it. This measure of attractiveness as value was not some- thing her male contemporaries were subject to. As such, we can see that music, like other aspects of the media, works within a tradition where 'women are constrained by representational codes which position them as passive vehicles of display and the object of the look' (Craik 1994: 45), where the physical image of the female music star has become an asset against which performers like Janis Joplin were and are judged. Joplin's female body was the main legitimated commodity for the female performer in a male-dominated music industry, and she was dealt with quite cruelly at times because she lacked enough of the obvious currency.

Whitley also discusses the way in which, in particular, Joplin's earthy sexu- ality construed her as something dangerous. Her performances were pos- sessed of an abundance of emotion and sexuality that spilled over, 'pos[ing] a challenge, and with the language of blues the solution is either to displace the problem on to a mythical other, to leave, or to situate the woman as doomed and unhappy' (Whiteley 2000: 57). Focusing on how Joplin looked was a way for the press to mark this out, and her inherent insecurity about her appear- ance acted as fodder. Still, whatever the tensions, Joplin's earthiness, her strength and the emotional honesty and pathos with which she imbued her performances was influential for many of the female musicians who feature later in this chapter. She 'offered women the possibility of identifying with rather than objectifying the star' (Ehrenreich, Hess and Jacobs 1992: 104). As a role model, she demonstrates the difficulties of being a woman in the music industry because she failed to fully traverse the numerous pitfalls that exist there. Moreover, her treatment reinforces the central role privileged to dress and the body in the success of female musicians.

FASHION, THE FEMALE BODY AND IDENTITY

The central role of the fashioned body to the identity of female musicians reflects the way in which fashion and dress have been seen to be heavily implicated in a system of social and cultural control of women and their bodies (see Craik 1994; Cranny-Francis et al. 2003; Entwistle 2000; Nead 1992). This positions women within a seemingly natural set of behaviours, establishing both a purported natural difference between men and women and the seemingly natural position of women as the 'second sex', to use Simone De Beauvoir's (1953) term. As Jennifer Craik asserts, 'clothed bodies are tools of self-management', and 'the ways in which bodies are fashioned through clothes, make-up and demeanour constitute identity, sexuality and social position' (1994: 45). A great part of this bodily management is invested in managing and controlling an appropriate gender identity—an appropriately masculine identity for men and an appropriately feminine one for women. These gender identities are constructed around sets of opposing, stereotypical and culturally formed but naturalized behaviours. This means that to be female might be biological fact, but to be feminine is a social strategy (see Craik 1994).

Fashion plays an important role here. Its historically perceived superficiality, artifice and inherently frivolous nature were seen to mirror these same attributes in the female sex (see Davis 1992). Fashion was established as primarily a feminine concern, and, as such, the successful adherence to the demands of fashionable dressing by women became a marker of female attainment. Thus, fashion has been regularly and negatively implicated in the management of power relationships between the sexes, both symbolically and, at times, physically pacifying women (in the case of the corset, for example, see Steele 2001; Summers 2001; Thesander 1997), comprising 'an effective and pervasive means through which women became objects of the gaze and of male sexual desire' (Craik 1994: 45; see also Berger 1972). As Frith and McRobbie (1990: 389) demonstrate, the dominant discourse of rock and pop is heterosexual desire—sometimes romanticized—within which 'oppressive images of women are built into the very foundations of the pop/rock edifice'. Here, as in fashion, where 'the emphasis on sexuality has been especially prominent in the consumer fashion system' (Craik 1994: 54), sex is the core commodity, but female sexuality is something which must be portrayed as still, passive and tentative. Fashion is a mode by which women's bodies are formulated towards and measured against the norms of heterosexual desire. This requires women to embody contradictory, stereotypical traits of femininity such as delicateness, passivity and innocence but also eroticized (though managed) display: the impossible Madonna–whore binary.

Sheila Whiteley's (2000) work has thus demonstrated that this is a shared ground for both music and fashion. Ironically, whilst fashion and music seem on the surface to be concerned with the *revelation* of sex, both have functioned, in a number of ways, to *manage* female sexuality. Reactions to Janis Joplin's mismanaged body and overt earthbound sexuality, which failed to be fully contained by either fashion or the music industry, demonstrate these boundaries.

FASHION, FEMININITY, EXPRESSION AND EMPOWERMENT

At the same time, although the history of fashion implicates it in the subjugated positions of women, like most forms of oppression, the key to symbolic emancipation may lie in the mechanisms of that oppression. Consequently, writers such as Elizabeth Wilson (1985), Pamela Church Gibson (2006) and Joanne Entwistle (2000) have seen fashion as a space in which women might find a creative voice and a symbolic language, finding expression within a structure ingrained in which is a design to pacify them. Whilst not focusing on fashion in her work per se, Sheila Whiteley (2000) identifies a number of female performers whose embodiment might be seen as a model for a symbolic resistance to the limitations placed on women by the music industry in a number of ways.

One of the most visually striking and confrontational examples discussed is Sinead O'Connor, who, in the 1980s, shaved her head and created a powerful and defining image for herself. This was a reaction to attempts on the part of her record company to coerce her into more feminine and sexualized ways of dressing (see Negus 1997). Importantly, there is no doubt that O'Connor's extraordinarily beautiful face was the sugar that made such a bitter pill easier to swallow, but she still managed to make her physical image a place to exert power, successfully marking herself out against other female performers. Through her body, then, she demonstrated her own set of concerns about her position as a woman in the music industry and continues to do so (Figure 5).

Whiteley also gives an impressive defence and feminist reading of the Spice Girls as purveyors of a variety of possibilities for female identity, presenting five different images that give 'an impression of independence within a group setting' (2000: 217). She argues that the Spice Girls, like Madonna, posited a model of potential liberation to young women from the constraints of demure femininity. This was symbolized through image and made available to fans through, in the case of Madonna, the Boy Toy fashion range—lace gloves, 'Boy Toy'—emblazoned belts, leggings, leather and miniskirts (Longhurst 1995)—and, in terms of the Spice Girls, in the instructional manual *The Spice Girls Style Guide* (Whiteley 2000).

Thus, fans were invited to shape their feminine identities in similar ways to their idols, and fashion and music came together as methods by which young women could negotiate their social identities and social lives. As John Fiske suggests, 'Madonna's appeal for her girl fans (wanna-bes) rests largely on her

Figure 5 Sinead O'Connor, May 2008. © Dariusz Majgier, 2010, used under license from shutter stock.com

control over her own image and her assertion of her right to an independent feminine sexuality' (1989: 131). Thus, these music stars are argued to have offered progressive models of femininity symbolized through fashion looks. When such styles are adopted by young women, then, we see the potential of both music and fashion to represent contemporary notions of femininity and to play a part in changing and adapting acceptable female behaviours more generally. Thus, these examples show how the emphasis on a fashioned image for female performers and the central role privileged to it in their careers makes it the place where limitations may be exerted but powerful points can also be made.

Whilst Whiteley notes the reticence on the part of artists such as the Spice Girls to articulate themselves as feminists, it is within the discourses of feminist concerns and practices that their fashioned bodies can be understood as having wider meaning. This is primarily because the female body has been the site of both tangible and symbolic struggle for feminist groups. Whiteley indicates that a more 'direct confrontation with the established codes of feminine representation became more explicit in the 1980s' (2000: 123). Punk had paved the way for more defiant forms of expression, she argues, and, in particular, Whiteley is interested in the gender ambiguity with which performers like Annie Lennox disrupted 'the traditional notions of sexuality and desire, playing with androgyny and wearing a man's suit to play down her femininity and, by inference, gain access to the male domain of artistic control' (123).

However, understanding androgynous dress as a method of symbolism suggestive of female emancipation is problematic because it might equally be argued that what we perhaps see is a reinforcement of the dominance of masculine power codes. This is because the word *androgyny,* when used as descriptor in both fashion and music, most often indicates a look dominated by masculine forms of dressing—particularly the suit, epitomized by performers like Chrissie Hynde (Figure 6). Further, androgyny indicates the *female* adoption of *male* forms of dressing rather than the true middle ground that a genderless androgyny would require. As Fred Davis notes, when masculine signifiers dominate androgyny, 'male power threatens to wipe out femininity

Figure 6 Chrissie Hynde epitomizes androgynous style, Ohio, August 2009. © 9507848116, 2010, used under license from shutterstock.com

entirely' (1992: 36). Thus, such looks may not be as disruptive as Whiteley suggests, and rather than expressing an alternative sense of female experience or redressing imbalances between the genders, androgynous dressing may, in fact, reinforce the gender divide and the dominance of masculine *culture* over feminine *nature*.

THE FEMALE BODY, MANAGED AND UNMANAGED

Many thinkers have identified a powerful equation between femininity and nature (see for example Russo 1994; Nead 1992). This connection is, in fact, so significant that a range of cultural practices, including the fashioning of the female body, have sought to manage this nature. This was fed by an understanding of the female body as inherently transgressive and potentially polluting, a notion provoked by its reproductive power and, thus, its hidden, mysterious and productive depths. As Lynda Nead has noted, aesthetics since Aristotle have established beauty as 'order and symmetry and definiteness' (6). By extension, the naturally bumpy and fluid female body has failed to conform to such a regulated ideal without much intervention. The female body has been seen to possess an atrocious potential: unmanaged, it is potentially abject and grotesque, 'lacking containment and issuing filth and pollution from its faltering outlines and broken surface' (6). Woman was broken, and a range of practices of representation, bodily management and regulation (of which clothing plays a significant part) aimed to fix her (Nead 1992).

Whilst Nead (1992) writes of the nude female body as represented in art, it is no leap of the imagination to understand that this has implications for the clothed, physical, material body. As Ann Hollander (1993) suggests, the very form of the painted nude is always etched with the outline of the idealized clothed body and fashionable silhouette contemporary to its production. Thus, in reality and representation, body and clothing seem to share an unassailable relationship. Therefore, to understand fully how fashion operates as a communication process, as a place of control and expression, it is important, also, to understand fashion as embodied practice: clothes as something that cannot be fully understood without also understanding the body with which they will work (see for example Entwistle 2000). Moreover, this suggests, then, that dress can be understood as a second, social skin, a covering for but also a representation and reflection of the naked body beneath.

Consequently, the clothed and naked body can be understood as 'not simply a text but also, more specifically, a *gendered* text. Elements of which may be obscured or repressed by various forms of cultural censorship' (Cavallaro 2006: 115). The control and censorship to which the female body is subject has focused largely on controlling female sexuality and, in particular, managing the at best ambivalent emotions felt in relation to the female role in reproduction. These are focused on concerns about the power this gives women.

This management adopted a particularly narrow and literal form with the onset of early-twentieth-century modernity, which demanded an industrialized, rationalized efficiency. Modernity caused 'the frame of the body [to be] sharpened, thus hardening the distinctions between inside and outside, between figure and ground, between subject and the space it is not' (Nead 1992: 19). In terms of fashionable dress, this shift manifest itself in a new attention to the management of the fashionable silhouette from within: through diet and exercise. This contrasted with earlier methods focusing on management of the body from the outside: via corsetry for example. Consequently, there is little room to hide under the demands of an increased visibility for the body and its boundaries with the concurrent expectations that women should not take up too much space.

Therefore, thanks to modernity's logical and functional approach to aesthetics, a tightening of clothing as the social frame of the female body opened it to closer scrutiny than ever before and transformed its ideal into something more defined, harder and arguably more phallic. This fulfilled the idealized 'hermetically sealed female body' (Nead 1992: 8): a cleaned up, rationalized and controlled body. This has little to do with the natural female form whose primary, fecund function is better signalled by a more fleshy imperfection in silhouette. In managing the female body in this way, the power of woman as re-producer is negated.

Thus, this management of the female body represents a battle between man/culture (male) and nature (female):

> The female is demoted to the role of passive nature and associated with the biological mechanisms of reproduction. Thus, in western metaphysics, form (the male) is preferred over matter (female); mind and spirit are privileged over body and substance and the only way to give meaning and order to the body in nature is through the imposition of techniques and style—to give a defining frame. (Nead 1992: 23)

Evidently, then, the female body has been viewed as possessed of an inherent and horrifying nature, rooted in the material and, to some extent, the animal. A resolution has been sought through a variety of cultural practices, including fashion and dress. At the same time, when clear and defined boundaries of right and wrong are established in this way, 'where vital distinctions are made between inside and outside, between proper and improper concerns' (Nead 1992: 6), then concurrently, there is a revelation of clear boundaries for transgression.

For Lynda Nead (1992), Julia Kristeva (see Kristeva and Moi 1986; see also Cavallaro 1994; Weedon 1997) and Mary Douglas (2002), the greatest transgressive potential is to be found in states of uncertainty: bodies and identities in a state of transition, indistinct, wavering on the borders between normal and abnormal, resisting control, difficult to define against dominant codes, rippling across established boundaries in a state of ambiguity. Thus, when considering the looks of the female singer-songwriters which follow, we must remember that not only is dress a legitimated, expressive space for women that subsequently provides the potential for transgression, but also that these transgressions, at their most powerful, might seem somewhat subtle and ambiguous. In each case, however, the power to transgress is rooted in the long-held associations between femininity, the body and the fashioning of it.

FABRIC, DRESS AND THE MUTABILITY
OF THE FEMALE BODY

In the video for 'Frozen', Madonna portrays an example of an identity that has become both synonymous with female singer-songwriters and which, it will be argued here, displays characteristics of ambiguity and malleability that might ultimately be understood to be transgressive. Like all her image changes, this was a temporary one, replaced first by a cowgirl for 'American Pie' and later by the infamous purple leotard for 'Hung Up'.

It is no accident that this was a look chosen for the album *Ray of Light* in 1998. This was arguably her most personal and emotive work, largely made up of self-penned songs written in the first years of her daughter Lourdes's life. This album seemed, in part, to work through feelings about a seismic shift in female identity from forthright single female towards motherhood (not that the two need necessarily be separate), alongside a rather melancholy response to other relationships.

The debt that the aesthetic of the video owes to Jane Campion's film *The Piano* (1993) is undeniable, but throughout the whole *Ray of Light* era, Madonna portrays an image that is an amalgam of symbols of the mystical, the folk inspired, the pseudo religious—in a way that differs to the kind of confrontational use of Christian imagery seen in the 'Like a Prayer' video (1989)—the witchy, and the earthy. Much of this symbolism seemed to act as a visual suggestion of the confessional content of the music it accompanied.

In 'Frozen', Madonna is a woman suffering: heartbroken, certainly disappointed by a relationship that has failed to come to fruition thanks to the emotional repression of some other person. In this relationship, she undoubtedly is made, then, the more powerful force through her emotional confidence—she is the person who is open, the active partner and the person to be given in to: her power, in comparison to the unknown other in the song, lies in her adaptability.

This adaptability is echoed in the way in which she is dressed in the video, as well as in the way she moves. There is, thus, a clear relationship between this body, its movement and the clothes that she wears. In a deep-black Victorian-inspired dress, her body is more covered than perhaps we have ever seen it before (or since). The colour of the dress matches her hair. It has full sleeves, a full skirt and layers that can be lifted or twirled; that can cover and uncover her face. As she moves, she moves the dress; there is a symbiosis between the cloth and her body that allows her form to shape and reshape itself.

This close connection becomes even clearer when body and clothing meld into animals: a running dog and flying birds. In using her body in this way, Madonna can be understood to be working within a framework which establishes women as 'more closely connected than men with the physical realm . . . capable of a greater and deeper involvement in body oriented textual activities' (Cavallaro 2006: 123). She is, as a female music performer, saying as much through her body as she is through her voice.

Femininity is represented here as multiple, decentred and fluid. In also talking about the realities of female experience, such as love, romance, heartbreak, sexuality, desire, addiction, ageing, motherhood, violence and abuse, the work of performers like Madonna—in the incarnation discussed here, at least—can be understood to be in parallel with the kinds of notions of female resistance posited by French feminist thinkers like Luce Irigaray (see Irigaray and Whitford 1991), Julia Kristeva (Kristeva and Moi 1986) and Helen Cixous (see Cixous and Sellers 1994).

For these thinkers, women have been silenced and controlled by culture in a number of ways. We have already considered, earlier in this chapter, the part that representation and fashion have played in managing the female body, but Cixous, Irigaray and Kristeva see the dominant position of masculine concerns and ways of being as embedded in the history of thought and in language itself. Practices such as representation and fashion are part of this. Here, logic and rationalism, attributed to be inherently masculine characteristics, become the most valued traits of humankind, upon which the very notion of society and culture is built. Consequently, issues of the mind (the male) are privileged over issues of the body (the female).

These writers consider that creativity—or what is often termed as '*écriture féminine*' (see Waugh 2006) is a process where women can find a voice by doing things their way. This can then redress some of the cultural imbalances weighted in the favour of the masculine, which 'subordinate[s] . . . the body to the mind' (Cavallaro 2006: 119). This would then represent a 'celebration of difference in both female language and the female body' (117). In one possible manifestation of such ideas, this might be achieved by acknowledging that rational, logical thought is not the only way of processing or presenting information and ideas.

With this emphasis on mythological symbols and transformation within performances of fashion and the female body of the kind seen in the video for 'Frozen', we might identify an effective disruption to such controlled modes of thought because 'reason fleetingly gives way to the imagination' (Cavallaro 2006: 120). Thus, in this context, it is dress which provides the form through which this imaginative power is connected to the body.

The body is also important here since 'patriarchy and Freudianism, in establishing male sexuality as the norm, have caused women to lose touch with their bodies. Asserting a female identity, therefore, means regaining contact with our physical selves' (Cavallaro 2006: 119). This might have the potential to reconnect us to the notion of woman as fluid and difficult to define, a reflection of a sexuality that is 'plural, for women's sexual organs are multiple and just about everywhere' (119).

Thus, there is a tacit understanding that femininity, in truth, equals complexity, a complexity which is negated by many cultural practices. Thus, female truth is best represented as something abstract, multiple and decentred. Consequently, for thinkers like Cixous, Irigarary, and Kristeva, woman is always in a heaving process of becoming and producing: this complexity means she can never just be. It follows, then, that creative practices which reassert the importance of the body and of nature to a complete understanding of womanhood are a method by which cultivated ideas of female identity might be challenged.

The style of dressing adopted by Madonna throughout the *Ray of Light* era is within a tradition that can be identified with a number of female performers. In particular, at this time Madonna described a certain admiration for the style of the American singer-songwriter Stevie Nicks. Nicks carved out this look for herself around the time of Fleetwood Mac's 'white album' in 1975; though it has had subtle modifications over time, it is a look she has kept throughout her almost forty-year career both with the band and as a solo artist. Her look is part Dickensian urchin, part fairytale princess, part ballerina, part gypsy, part earth mother and a significant part pagan high priestess. Such female figures emerge in her lyrics, too, alongside woman as ghost, as birds or as miasma.

The stories which make up her songs focus on mythological figures like the Welsh Witch (also the name of Nicks's publishing company) Rhiannon and make clear the connection between women and elements of nature, the moon and the cosmos. She thus characterizes, both through what she writes and how she appears, a certain multiplicity of female identity. On stage, she wears mostly black—occasionally white, cream or red—almost always dresses.

There is theatricality in the cut of the clothes: medieval- or kimono-inspired bell sleeves feature heavily, and skirts are ragged and full. There are scarves, hats, capes and coats.

However, it is the way the use of fabric creates space and volume around the body, alongside its potential to provide a sensuous surface for that body, that is of particular significance here. In a perhaps literal, but no less rigorous, analogy to the work of Gilles Deleuze—in particular *The Fold* (2006)—Claire Pajaczkowska understands fabric as something limitless, where 'in the fold there are surfaces and planes which are known to exist but which are inaccessible to view' (2005: 224) and where every entity, body, material, element and interpretation is constantly shifting and unstable. Thus, fabric might be understood as a mirror of the female body—a metaphor for it and a representation of it—because like the natural female body, fabric is always decentred, asymmetrical and difficult to define.

Deleuze's work has provided a seductive model for feminist analyses (though not without some concern that adopting a masculine model of theory might compromise such analysis; see for example Grosz 1994). His work has offered a model which questions restrictive and limiting ideas of cultural opposition and categorization. *The Fold* primarily aims to suggest that we should see the things we normally place in opposition to one another—man/woman, inside/outside, public/private, mind/body—as always interrelated.

Thus, in *The Fold,* nothing is rigid and fixed. The visible is always held firmly in place by its relationship to what is hidden, and the two must coexist. It has presented an abstract, but alternative, way to consider the aesthetic possibilities of culture and all that relates to the body within it. It suggests that we might see that if female power lies in abundance, the material, the emotional, the limitless, the process of transformation, the bodily that this does not mean such characteristics are necessarily separated from more spiritual and intellectual concerns.

This suggests a modality by which the subtlety of female, symbolic resistances might be made visible. This seems to resonate with the styles worn, not just by Nicks and Madonna, but also by many other female singer-songwriters: Canadian Tori Amos, Kate Bush as an exemplar of the form in the UK, alongside, in the US, Ella Bell and Sarah McLachlan. In both the construction of the clothes that make up this look and in their movement with and as part of the body, textiles act as a second skin. This formulates a sense of a body that is soft and fluid, creating space around it and blurring its boundaries. This softness does not reject femininity per se but reformulates it with symbols suggestive of the sensual and earthy, but also more spiritual. In these looks, texture is as important as shape, with fabrics like chiffon, jacquards and silks that give both structure and depth.

FABRIC, EMBODIMENT AND THE SUBLIME

Clare Pajaczkowska (2005) considers textiles to be sublime and finds parallel here with Linda Nead's (1992) ideas about the female body. For Nead, the notion of the sublime resides in the natural form of the human body and, in particular, its fleshiness. Thus, the sublime might be signified by limitlessness and excess of the kind suggested by the dripping layers of white chiffon and silks that coat Stevie Nicks's body on the cover of her 1981 album *Bella Donna*. Usually, the sublime potential of bodies must be managed because they have the potential to be obscene; in particular, the female body is conceived of as 'a mixture of pleasure, pain and terror' (Nead 1992: 26). Here, we see not a mismanaged body per se; Nicks is small, usually rather slight—certainly in her youth. She has a certain kind of all-American blonde prettiness. However, clothes act to give a suggestion or an etching of an alternative body around her smaller frame through dress which is fluid, voluminous and sensual.

Whilst, as Nead notes, the sublime has, in its conception, found fundamental links to the masculine, it 'is also where a certain deviant form of femininity is played out. It is where woman goes beyond her proper boundaries and gets out of place' (1992: 28–9). The sublime is defined by objects and experiences that create visceral responses. It is 'thus seen to be kinetic' (26) and is, therefore, located very much in the material, the bodily and consequently the female realm. For Pajaczkowska (2005), it is the materiality of textiles that first hints at their sublime nature. Their awe-inspiring potential exists within, not least because encounters with them demand a multiplicity of sensuous responses that cannot in all cases be located in language: their aesthetic is dual, operating at both physical and psychical levels.

Thus, the power of textiles lies in their ability to be excessively emotive. Claire Pajaczkowska argues that because of their ambiguity, textiles exist in liminal spaces between binaries of meaning: 'material and phallic, between distance and proximity, between sight and touch and between sacred and profane (2005: 224). Thus, her ideas are in concert with Deleuze's: textiles here are both opposing elements and the bridge between. Consequently, in Pajaczkowska's terms, they present the materials to create a bodily representation that is sublime. It is within their very boundlessness and ambiguity that this potential resides; used in abundance, they suggest hidden depths.

Consequently, if textiles are in themselves ambiguous, cavernous and sublime, then, as a covering for the body, they can become a representation of that body as something which is also ambiguous, cavernous and sublime. As a second skin, they come to be a suggestion of a different kind of body in the look of the female singer-songwriter. This is a body which demands a somatic and sensuous response: a return to bodily concerns. At the same time, this style of dressing also represents an internal sense of self appropriate to a music genre which is primarily concerned with female subjectivities. This is because such looks speak of both body, through sensuous styles of embodiment, and mind, through hints toward the spiritual and the sacred. Thus, we see not just that reclaiming the body and reuniting it to the mind is a way for women to articulate themselves, but we also see a tangible model for how this might look. In particular, it is in the *melding* of this fluid body with symbolism suggestive of the sacred, the spiritual and sometimes the openly religious that comes to provide a cohesive, embodied musical message for this genre.

EMBODYING THE SPIRITUAL

There are numerous images of performers who we have already discussed here who adopt imagery suggestive of some kind of spiritual life. Nicks is pagan high priestess—the archetype of the witch, in the most positive pre-Christian sense of the word; she is hooded, covered in sumptuous fabrics, flowers and lace. On the cover of her album *Exile in Guyville,* Liz Phair might be priestess or witch, too, but is made altogether more street by wearing thick chains. She screams out from beneath a dark hood that conceals part of her face. In the case of Sinead O'Connor, whose shaven head we discussed earlier, the religious symbolism is all the more direct: she is penitent monk draped in muted colours and sackcloth cloaks.

Kate McCarthy (2006) identifies religious symbolism of all kinds to be one of the signifiers often adopted by female musicians. She suggests that the employment of such imagery (for example Madonna's use of the crucifix) is a way to symbolically question the marginalization of women in relation to all kinds of spiritual and sacred experience. While she notes that this is not without potential flaws and ambiguities as a method, she sees this as a move towards a reinforcement of female voices previously marginalized. It provides an unofficial channel in which a woman can find a representation for herself as a spiritual individual with both a body *and* a mind.

McCarthy is particularly interested in how this might assist women in locating and accessing their spiritual lives in relation to religion very specifically. However, her work also facilitates more general links to both the articulation of female experience and its marginalization, alongside the representation of a woman's inner life. Thus, McCarthy positions a range of female music performers within a collection of articulations that use religious symbols and imagery to go beyond stereotypical representations of femininity in music and, in doing so, give authentic expression to womanhood: self, identity, body, intellect, sexuality. At the same time, identifying this theme also becomes a way of recognising that a shared identity exists between female singer-songwriters.

A chain of meaning is established for the genre passed from performer to performer.

In analysing the prevalence of religious symbolism, McCarthy (2006) considers examples from Christianity, Judaism, Hinduism and what she terms 'Neo-Pagan' communities, which all establish codes that can be drawn on and re-imagined in music performances. Thus, we might argue that to hint at the sacred through forms of dress which also represent the sensuous and the physical is to symbolically reunite body with mind to merge elements of the female that have been falsely separated by rational enlightenment thought—a separation maintained by all kinds of representation which mute female voices.

CONCLUSION

Thus, it is the part that dress can play in representing both the inside and the outside—of body and mind—that resonates with this particular kind of music performance. The enduring nature of this look also signals how many music genres come, in some way, to be identified with particular kinds of looks. This particular look might in some ways be considered anti-fashion, and yet, with each reemergence, it is modified to suit particular performers and contemporary tastes.

Most recently, Florence Welch (Florence + the Machine) has epitomized this style for the younger generation, wearing a silky white, thickly ruched garment that redefined the borders of her body away from a recognizably female form at a gig at the Brixton Academy in London (13 December 2009). Again, the female body and its relationship to space—both its own and that around it—is at issue. But most importantly for a book on fashion and music, a number of unifications are suggested through this recurring style. Here, we see not only body and mind fused in female music, but also the seamless blending of the visual and aural aspects of music performance. This signals the fundamental part that appearance can play in communicating and completing music performances, particularly for women, for whom fashion has been made an endemic part of their lives for hundreds of years.

–4–

White Suited Men: Style, Masculinity and the Boyband

When Gareth Gates became the odds-on favourite to win the first series of the British talent show *Pop Idol* in 2002, he expressed one of his greatest ambitions and was able to fulfil it in the video for his first single, 'Unchained Melody', released soon after he was—in one of reality TV's biggest upsets—trounced into second place by Will Young. It was not releasing a video, a single or an album, or accruing hoards of adoring female fans (young and old), money and trappings of fame and wealth, which symbolized pop success for the then 18-year-old. What Gates most aspired to was what best symbolized pop success to him: the opportunity to wear a white suit.

What he demonstrated, in many ways, was not so much why he was a favourite with the bookmakers, with the teenage girls and their mums and grandmothers who watched and voted for him, but, instead, why he was a favourite with Simon Cowell, the mogul who has so much to benefit from any of the young people who have won and will win shows like *Pop Idol, American Idol* and *X Factor*: Gates recognized his niche, he shaped his aspirations towards it and it was a lucrative one.

Gates had pure pop potential and thus, perhaps more accurately, pure market potential. His wants were focused on assuming a garment and a look that was synonymous with some of the most controlled and manufactured pop acts that had gone before him and, just as importantly, with the image of a nice boy. In directing his objectives towards this, Gates demonstrated himself to be malleable and compliant. He also showed that he had desires that did not seem to extend towards more troublesome creative control, which could result, ultimately, in lost opportunities in the marketplace for those who shaped and managed him, who had in mind only the immediacy of Gates's market potential as a nice boy. This market inevitably brings with it a very short shelf life and a brutal fall from grace when a young artist grows up, rebels and, in the case of Gates, alledgedly sleeps with the pregnant (with footballer Dwight Yorke's baby) glamour model Jordan. The transition from nice to nasty is not one that artists like Gates usually manage to make successfully, since niceness is the main commodity.

Thus, his career trajectory was written on his body at the moment he put on the white suit for the first time. In doing so, he established the kind of artist he was, whilst also projecting an idea of himself as a particular kind of young man; a projection which lacks the real complexities of the masculine condition and which, as such, can only ever be a fleeting moment in both his own, and pop culture's, histories. Yet as those behind such careers know—and with hindsight Gates now knows too, having carved out a new career in musical theatre—there is always someone else—more novel, younger, lacking in guile—to replace him.

It is the idea of clothing as symbolic of a particular kind of masculinity and, moreover, a particular kind of music phenomenon that is in focus in this chapter. This version of masculinity is considered as one constructed around the perceived wants and needs of a particular fan base: teenage girls. Considering this form of masculinity as a stereotype, specifically in relation to pop music, offers an opportunity to not only uncover the symbolism of this particular masculine identity and the core part that fashion plays in representing and embodying it, but also to view masculinity generally as a complex set of constructions, affirmations and denials upon which any representation of men is built.

In discussing masculinity, the aims of this chapter are twofold. First, it considers the enduring appeal of the suit—in particular, the white suit—to the musical category boyband in the late 1990s and into the early 2000s, aligning it with the accrual of meaning that makes such looks speak of a certain version of manhood. In doing so, it considers, too, the seemingly essential role of an often uniform and collective stylistic identity in the provision of a cohesive visual image upon which many such groups have been marketed.

Second, it considers the part the cultural and market conditions of postmodernity might play in making this an enduring marker of a particular kind of music experience and, even more importantly, in privileging and making persistent specific garments and ways of dressing. At the same time, in tracing the endurance of these forms of dress, we see, too, how the vagaries of fashion subtly shape not only the clothes worn by boybands, but also symbolize and reflect the shifting sands of gender politics and the construction of contemporaneous masculinities.

In chapter 3, we saw how the relationship between women and fashion is seen as strong and somewhat passionate, natural, even, but might also be understood to be complex, fraught and ambivalent. If the gender differences between men and women are often understood as a binary model (see Cranny-Francis et al. 2003; Hall 1997)—as sets of opposing characteristics—then we might be forgiven for thinking that the male relationship to fashion, dressing and dressing up must be altogether much more straightforward. Instead, fashion has been as much a contested ground for men as it has for women, but this tension rests on a disavowal of fashion rather than a compelling pressure to participate.

GENDER IDENTITIES

Women are traditionally seen to be subject to the power systems of men—passive, whilst men are active; private, while men are public; 'fashionable [when] men are not' (Craik 1994: 170). Clearly, then, both genders have been subjected to expected ways of being and modes of behaviour which are undoubtedly different, but equally limiting. The expectations of appropriate gender behaviour may change over time. Yet when such change happens, what is never eradicated is a sense of a clearly demarcated, if socially constructed, difference between men and women in behaviour, thought and appearance as the measure of normality. This runs alongside a sense of perceived natural masculinity and femininity as opposing concepts.

As Stuart Hall (1997) notes, any cultural understanding of personal and social identity and the very methods by which any society and its attendant cultural map is conceptualized relies on definitions which separate and make distinctions between groups. Thus, we understand people as much by what they are not as what they are. Gender is just one facet of identity that is managed in this way. Consequently, when any struggle for a redefinition or redistribution of power between the sexes happens, it takes place with the tacit knowledge that when they define and redefine themselves, they always do so in relation to one another. Fashion has been a way of writing such gender definitions and making any shifts in them, emphatic and visible, through the body.

FASHIONING MASCULINITY

Thus, in chapter 3, we saw how many writers have been concerned with fashion's potential to limit and confine women—both physically and symbolically—not least because fashion was seen to be a domain in which all women should and must be almost frenetically active in order to be naturally feminine. In contrast, for men, the limitations of fashion have been almost as stringent but for opposing reasons because the history of masculinity has sought to deny the employment of any artifice in the creation of masculine identities (see for example Breward 1999; Mort 1996; Nixon 1996).

Men are not free, but are instead subject to what Tim Edwards calls 'the anxieties and contradictions of masculine identity' (2006: 108). Thus, for some very specific historical reasons that will be explored in a moment, we may be given the impression that fashion has a stronger relationship to women than men. In fact, it is not a question of whether a connection exists between fashion and a gender group, or any inequalities of strength within these connections, but rather how this relationship manifests itself, that is the true marker of fashion's relationship to constructing gender difference.

It is the fear and loathing of apparent or possible abnormality that causes most people to adopt and maintain proscribed and stereotyped gendered behaviours of femininity for women and masculinity for men. This is because 'stereotyping doesn't just use visual clues welded . . . to cultural characteristics to distinguish one group from another; it also divides the normal from the abnormal, the acceptable from the unacceptable' (Cranny-Francis et al. 2003: 141). Thus, stereotypes are not just passive forms of organization and categorization but are instead active symbols which shape and control individuals, their cultural landscapes and the systems of power that surround them. Consequently, stereotyping sets up 'symbolic boundaries and then provides the mechanisms of cultural production for people to police those boundaries' (141). Fashion is one such mechanism.

Therefore, whilst women's relationship to fashion has been historically constructed as emphatic and natural, as Jennifer Craik notes, 'the rhetoric of men's fashion takes the form of a set of denials' (1994: 170). Such notions are traced by many writers to particular conditions within parts of nineteenth-century Europe and America: specifically, escalating industrialization and, alongside this, the rise of a business-oriented middle class with a value system that placed men at the forefront of a public world of work. As a consequence, a certain gentrification of labour came to be written through the male body.

J. C. Flügel terms this the Great Masculine Renunciation, where 'modern man's clothing abounds in features which symbolise his devotion to the principles of duty, of renunciation and of self-control' (1930: 113). This reassessment of masculinity was not just a matter of gender, important as this was, but was also an articulation of class values whose meanings lay in its difference to what had gone before—'the brighter, gayer, more elaborate, and more varied forms of ornamentation' (111). Such elaborate dress was rejected here because it harked back to a different set of class values: the kind of louche, spectacular forms of dress that signified aristocratic status, leisureliness and the prior dominance of the upper classes. The turn away from this kind of identity articulation was in part initiated by the French Revolution with a violent and outright rejection of such crude symbols of privilege and the establishment of the possibility of a different social order.

Political changes in Europe consequently created a seismic shift in the way in which masculinity was constructed and performed in industrialized countries. It meant that 'man abandoned his claim to be considered beautiful. He henceforth aimed at being only useful' (Flügel 1930: 111). The emphasis on utility was a change in the fashion of masculine behaviour, which was subsequently symbolized through a more utilitarian approach to the fashioning of the male body.

Therefore, in the nineteenth century, a new form of masculine embodiment was established alongside which many contemporary gender norms—though there have been further shifts—are to some extent still measured. The influence of this nineteenth-century period still seems to permeate much men's fashion, where 'men's clothing has generally been of darker colours, often monochromatic to symbolize the seriousness of their social position' (Finkelstein 1991: 131).

The maintenance of this appropriate façade is of fundamental importance because, as Rebecca Arnold notes, 'since masculinity is held up as a signal of the "norm" in western culture, any derivation from conventional male attire is viewed with great unease' (2001: 111). In particular, the man's suit—two or three piece—remains a staple of the male wardrobe, the only formal wear for men and an exemplar of masculine embodiment: for men, the suit is 'de rigueur', to quote Joanna Finkelstein (1991: 107).

This history means we might be fooled into thinking the suit has come to symbolize something of a masking of the male body, intended as it was to de-emphasize the spectacular potential of the male form. Its primary aim seemed to be to emphasize instead this body as a machine-like, functional entity and thus, implicitly, to de-eroticize the male body. This, then, seems to have little to do with a music world where one of the most prevalent concerns is sex and sexuality (see for example Frith and McRobbie 1990). However, this is not to say that any impression of masculine sexuality was removed. Instead, what was created was a 'sense of ambivalence towards the relation between male style and male sexual identity' (Craik 1994: 173). Here, there is not a blotting out of this sexual identity but, instead, an ambiguous and complex set of codes which both assert and deny facets of it: where 'as a fashion garment, the suit [comes to be] invested with sexual attributes of the new masculinity of the 1890s' (180). As male sexuality centres on notions of power, in emphasizing the strength and sturdiness of the male upper body, the suit symbolizes this power and thus an inferred male sexuality (see also Hollander, 1994).

Consequently, while music might be considered the place where transgression from the fixed codes and stereotypes of gendered dressing has often taken place, the men's suit—though sometimes diverting greatly from the stereotypical business suit—has featured heavily as mainstay attire for many male music performers. Whilst the design of the suit may be shaped by fashionable change and shifts in gender ideologies, it prevails as a key form of masculine dress in a number of contexts, including music.

MUSIC, MASCULINITY AND THE SUIT

For example, Joshua Sims (1999) considers the stage costumes worn by Elvis throughout his career as variations, however extreme, on the suit. This includes the kinds of rhinestone-embellished concoctions worn in the 1970s or the tight black leather revealed for his *Comeback Special* in 1968. His later ostentatiously bejewelled suits were rumoured to be modelled on Liberace's stage costumes, a music performer who, Jennifer Craik (2005) argues, established modes of dressing for performance that have been followed by many since.

In many ways, what Elvis and Liberace wore signalled few of the attributes of acceptable, mainstream masculinity: it was made feasible, in part, by their status as performers and because it was a look that might be best understood as symbolizing show business, more than anything (if we ignore Liberace's closeted homosexuality for the moment). It represented a certain kind of decadence and a notion of the excessive possibilities of fame. Sims attributes Elvis's increasingly outlandish forms of dress to a need to beat the competition and also to prevail over every other outfit he himself had worn before, which 'began with the gold lame suit . . . and culminated in the Bill Belew designed, camp, if not feminized jewelled white leather jump suits, pearls and furs' (1999: 12–13). But as much as show business legitimated this ostentatious dress, what is perhaps most interesting is that it is around the suit as a core concept of male dressing that these staged identities oscillate and meanings are produced—sometimes subtly, here less so. Consequently, we see both the endurance of the man's suit as symbol of masculine embodiment alongside a clear assertion of the part that variations on the suit play in demonstrating and articulating the complexities of masculinity itself alongside its relationship to other facets of a fashioned social identity.

Transgressive as Elvis was in his stage clothes, he never went as far as David Bowie and wore a dress (though he dabbled in eyeliner, see Sims 1999). Any assertion on Bowie's part that he was wearing man's dress for the cover of his album *The Man Who Sold the World* failed to convince anyone, but it did achieve his artistic intentions to reveal the artifice of gendered dressing and the way in which particular garments come to be gendered. The shock that Bowie prompted, demonstrated that 'traditionally, men who blurred definitions of masculinity by expressing an overt interest in fashion were viewed suspiciously within Western culture' (Arnold 2001: 111).

But not so for Elvis. The suit provided both a frame on which all his stage costumes were built and a frame of core masculine embodiment. This was arguably a significant contributing factor towards enabling him to successfully tread the difficult and ambivalent path of both being a man and dressing up, becoming, as he did so, the personification of 'masculine sexuality' (Sims 1999: 12).

The suit is thus imbued with gendered meaning and has acted as the crux against which many male musicians have formulated an image for themselves, whilst also articulating a sense of their particular masculinity. It has also provided the stable ground from which transgressions grow. This acknowledges and enacts the complexities of being a man, revealing 'masculinity [to be] composed of many masculinities' (Benyon 2002: 1; see also Edwards 2006). Popular music has been home to diverse masculinities; in their modes of dressing, male musicians have been able to get away with more than ordinary men.

MASCULINITIES IN MUSIC

In their essay 'Rock and Sexuality', Simon Frith and Angela McRobbie (1990) examine in some depth two contrasting forms of masculinity which contribute to music's constellation of identifiable masculinities. What Frith and McRobbie demonstrate is the way in which types of music have attendant to them stereotypical attitudes, where gender is often at the forefront. As such, they show implicitly how stereotypical gender stances are articulated through embodiment.

Thus, we can surmise that the fashioning of the body is centre stage. We can see this most clearly when they examine what they term the 'cock rock' performer—'aggressive, dominating and boastful'—an image which dominated the 1970s rock music that forms the focus of their work. They argue that cock rock performers' 'stance is obvious in live shows; male bodies on display, plunging shirts and tight trousers, a visual emphasis on chest hair and genitals' (Frith and McRobbie 1990: 374). If a suit is worn here, then there is rarely a shirt underneath. Instead, the chest is exposed in an aggressively masculine stance; a posture designed to dominate and intimidate.

In viewing this kind of male embodiment as threatening, Frith and McRobbie also make useful connections between particular forms of embodiment, stereotypical gender articulations and audiences. They argue that these aggressive poses and presentations of the body are formulated for a male teen audience, who identify with such stances and construct their own masculinity and sexual identity in relation to them, since 'rock constitutes sexuality for its listeners' (1990: 389). This is something they suggest a young female audience would find intimidating. In making this analysis, they contrast this male-to-male identification with the other form of masculinity they analyse in their essay, one they argue is specifically produced for this female audience: the 'teeny-bop' idol.

Unlike the cock rocker, the teeny-bop idol's fan base is stereotypically fe-male and teenaged. He produces pop music, instead of rock. There is, then, a tacit understanding here that the music is likely to be formulaic, manufac-tured, market led, unchallenging artistically and also somewhat fey. Where 'cock rock allows for direct physical and psychological expression of sexuality; pop in contrast is about romance, about female crushes and emotional affairs' (Frith and McRobbie 1990: 380). The teeny-bop idol is 'consumed almost ex-clusively by girls . . . [with an] image based on self-pity, vulnerability and need. The image is young boy next door: sad, thoughtful, pretty and puppylike' (375). This was the perceived niche for Gareth Gates, and the wearing of a white suit was his embodiment of it. It is in the articulation of masculinity for a teen audience that the suit as a symbol of masculinity really comes into its own.

THE BEATLES, BOYBANDS AND UNIFORMITY

The Beatles are the archetype of a group of young male musicians whose image was stage-managed to appeal appropriately to this demographic. Whilst the band are also symbolic of the 1960s concerns with the future, free-dom, youth and 'social, class mobility through their accents' (Marshall 2000: 164), they are in many ways—despite their undoubted musical talent and the fact that they formed themselves into a band—one of the first groups to be contrived and manufactured into a music phenomenon by an entrepreneurial manager: Brian Epstein (Marshall 2000).

Much of this engineering focused on how the band looked, and thus, while their 'musical style may have relied on a "leather and rockers" image' in their early days, 'they traded their leather jackets to present something less threat-ening' (Marshall 2000: 170; see also Sims 1999), and a suit was the gar-ment chosen for this purpose. By wearing a suit, The Beatles portrayed some sense of respectable masculinity, since woven within it are all the nineteenth-century symbols of rational, decent manhood. Their suits were monochrome, dark and, as such, fulfilled many of these stereotypes. At the same time, they were extremely fashionable suits, not the business suits that middle-class city gents wore to work with bowler hats, but 'Beatle suits (based closely on a design by Pierre Cardin), a fairly tight-fitting jacket fastening to the neck with no collar, usually in black (though grey with black trim was also a key look)' (Sims 1999: 24) (Figure 7).

Thus, the transgressive potential and rock credentials of these suits are embodied in the finer points of cut, style and finish: their collarlessness, for example. This seems to be a symbolic rewriting of the rulebook where the devil is in the details. This kind of subtle modification is within the tradition of men's dressing and, indeed, contemporary menswear design, where 'the line

Figure 7   The Beatles wearing grey Beatles suits, Republica de
Guinea Equatorial stamp, 1960s © akva, 2010, used under license from shutterstock.com

between acceptance and rejection of the norm was and remains thin' (Arnold
2001: 114). We might understand this as in a tradition of 'exaggerated sobri-
ety' (114; see for example also Craik 1994; Finkelstein 1991; and Breward
1999) that formulated the body of the Regency dandy, foregrounding issues
of masculinity, taste and sexuality in a relatively restrained way.

The restraint of the Regency dandy's approach to dressing did not remove
spectacular potential, but instead reattributed the spectacular aspects of
male dressing to features of cut, quality, detail and types of fabric. We might,
in fact, understand many male musicians who are widely acknowledged to
have in some way rewritten the rulebook of dressing—Mick Jagger, David
Bowie, Bryan Ferry, Elvis, Little Richard, Prince (Figure 8) and Lou Reed—to
have been contemporary dandies. They have arguably worn suits more than
any other garment, but always suits that deviated in form, fabric, pattern and
cut from the sober business suit.

Figure 8   Prince wears an unconventional suit: turquoise, flared, with an orange shirt and his hair tied in a scarf © Anthony Correira, 2010, used under license from shutterstock.com

Thus, through subtle and contemporaneous modifications to stereotypical styles of male dressing, The Beatles embodied just enough transgression for their audience. Through these garments, they posited a notion of themselves as nice boys, true or not, but also boys of the 1960s. There was also an essential hint of eroticization in the closeness of the cut, a way of dressing reminiscent of the suits worn by mods (see Hebdige 1979). The mods could equally be considered to be contemporary dandies whose 'obsession with detail smack[ed] of vanity and a lack of concern for the things that are deemed to matter' (Arnold 2001: 114).

In the image of The Beatles, we see something of a melding of the interests of manager and band, where 'although their hairstyles came from their Hamburg days and the influence of artist friends, the suits of the early years (at the insistence of Epstein) were a sign of moulding their personalities into a successful and industrial act' (Marshall 2000:169–70). In many ways, then,

The Beatles represent the reference point for most of the male pop acts, both groups and individual, who have come after them. They appealed to the same demographic audience. Since the suit was so synonymous with this point in their careers when they made it an 'essential part of the rock wardrobe' (Sims 1999: 24), we can begin to see the suit as symbolic of the industrialization of not just pop music itself, but also of the bodies of the young male musicians who populate it.

Arguably, every male pop band since The Beatles has been understood, in many ways, as a product of them. A uniformity of dressing which centred on the suit was certainly something they established as a specifically pop articulation (though it clearly drew on forms of dressing which evolved from Motown acts of the same period). The idea of dressing a band in a uniform way to either completely standardize its identity or to provide veiled hints of individual identity within a whole through subtle variations in detail pervades as a method of constructing many pop band images, both male and female. Jennifer Craik (2005) briefly discusses both the wearing of standardized dress in bands as a kind of quasi-uniform and vintage uniform as a common trope in music. The adoption of military uniform, in particular, has, for her, the potential for social and political comment. In the case of protest singers of the 1970s, this may be true in part, but such uniforms were adopted by many groups as much for stylistic reasons as for social or political ones.

Certainly it is interesting to note, as an aside, that military uniform and tailoring in its most literal sense has been a regularly occurring look for pop bands from a range of eras: The Rolling Stones, Duran Duran, Spandau Ballet and My Chemical Romance. At the Grammys in 2009, Coldplay wore a look created for their album *Viva la Vida or Death and All His Friends* with ragged uniforms reminiscent of revolutionary France (Figure 9). Lead singer Chris Martin acknowledged the irony of having Paul McCartney in the audience, joking that they had stolen the 'Sergeant Pepper' look.

In more unofficial terms, though, uniformity of dress traces its history back to the traditions of black music of the mid-twentieth century, where, as Jennifer Craik notes, 'the culture of popular music has been long linked to the adoption of uniforms and uniform style. In the 1940s, zoot suits—synonymous with gangsters—were popularized as the look of black music and radical nightclub sounds' (2005: 212). In the case of girl bands, Motown set the tone with groups like The Supremes and The Ronettes. For Jacqueline Warwick (2007), uniformity of dress for girl bands in the 1960s represented, on the one hand, a method of creating a striking visual look and, on the other, a kind of armour. In the case of The Ronettes, she notes the following:

Dressing them outrageously meant (in this case at least) also dressing them identically, and their uniforms . . . provocative though they may seem to have

Figure 9 Coldplay's Chris Martin wears military uniform, Melbourne, 2009 © Rovenko Design, 2010, used under license from shutterstock.com

been, also marked them powerfully and instantly as belonging together and may have made it difficult for any adult to prey on them individually. (Warwick 2007: 186)

Thus, Warwick establishes the potential of fashion to symbolize and to be part of the kinds of controlling mechanisms to which any body is subject in any context into which it enters—here, the music performer in the music industry. As Jennifer Craik notes, 'uniforms are a major technology for not only controlling the body but also producing the particular attributes of the self that are deemed desirable' (2005: 54). In many ways, this may be a method of constructing the kind of docile body that Craik argues school uniforms produce, where acceptable codes of behaviour and the values of an institution are embodied in a uniform that has a controlling effect on the wearer, making individual human identity incidental. When a uniformity of dress becomes an archetype, then, and when such a look is imposed on one group (musical performers) by another (record companies, moguls and managers), it removes at best any notions of individual creativity and at worst the value and worth of any individual person inhabiting it.

Uniform is thus seen to make people more vulnerable and compliant to systems of control. The Beatles and many of their contemporaries elided such consequences because, as the first to produce such a look, they were still pioneering. Thus, despite being subject to management and control in their early years, they developed a status that attributes to them a significant role in their careers and successes, receiving critical acclaim for being, at the end of it all, real musicians. But in working within a system which made style and appearance important, alongside establishing uniformity as significant, they established a model of a possible boyband image.

As well as docile bodies, uniformity in dress can also signal more than an adopted collective identity, especially in the case of groups whose members are related. In the case of Motown's girl groups, Jacqueline Warwick (2007) argues that such uniformity domesticated female music performance of this kind into a private sphere with an image that was suggestive of familial relationships (indeed, in several cases members of such girl bands were, in fact, related). Dressing the same might, on the one hand, seem reminiscent of gangs and aggression. In pop, it might suggest something different: the clean-cut safety of the bosom of the family, the house and the home.

THE WHITE SUIT

On such terms, by the 1970s, the suit worn by the Osmond brothers, from Little Jimmy right up to Wayne, was white and as squeaky clean as their image. The Osmonds were unabashedly family entertainment formulated to appeal to young fans but without any hint at transgressions that would alienate their parents. Thus, they appealed, wholeheartedly, to a family market, not least because of the TV show that placed them at the heart of light entertainment on both sides of the Atlantic.

They could sing, play and write their own music (though they performed plenty of covers and voraciously ran the gamut of music styles from country to an attempt at hard rock with 'Crazy Horses'), but it was this clean-cut image that made them really marketable. In their stage outfits, there is a convergence of the different images of masculinity in music that surrounded or preceded them; their look was an amalgam of everything from Elvis's white rhinestone jumpsuits to The Beatles' uniformity. Their stage outfits were, therefore, an example of 'cultural life . . . viewed as a series of texts intersecting with other texts, producing more texts' (Harvey 1990: 49).

Thus, as a respectable Mormon family making music, The Osmonds' adoption of a suit that was, in particular, *white*, is an example of some sense of 'value systems [that were] inevitably embodied in dress', to quote Elizabeth Wilson (1992: 14). The colour white has meanings relating to purity, innocence and cleanliness, all attributes the band embodied. Where the *suit* became the uniform of the boyband, thanks in great part to The Beatles, so The Osmonds made the *white suit* synonymous with the 'nice boy' band.

Both between The Beatles and The Osmonds and after came many boybands sharing similar characteristics: mainstream, manufactured for a teen market with a voracious appetite for this kind of entertainment. In order to fulfil the needs of this market—which is always in constant renewal—focus has been placed as much on the appearance of the young men in the bands as their music. Thus, gradually, how a band looked arguably became as important as how they sounded. In order to maintain this lucrative market, a formulaic look became synonymous with such groups. This focus on rather conservative measures to maintain market appeal suggests that, as a result, we might argue that embodied here, too, were a set of wider cultural values relating to postmodernity.

THE BOYBAND AND POSTMODERNITY

One of the most well-known statements relating to postmodernism, and one that begins to demonstrate the conditions that create postmodern culture, was made by Frederick Jameson when he argued that 'postmodernism is nothing more than the cultural logic of late capitalism' (Harvey 1990: 63; see also Jameson 1991). The very notion of postmodernism is complex, its characteristics much contested. It is best understood as a cultural mood that was identified by designers, critics and commentators somewhere around the 1960s (though this is one of the most contested factors of all).

This represented something of a shift, or 'cultural transformation' (Harvey 1990: 39), from the values of modernity. Most important, here, is the notion that 'postmodern culture . . . celebrates consumerism, hedonism and style' (Strinati 1995: 236), which in part resulted in 'the commercialization of history and cultural forms' (Harvey 1990: 62). Here, 'in an advanced capitalist society . . . the need for people to consume has become as important, if not strategically more important, than the need for people to produce' (Strinati 1995: 236).

In terms of fashion, for example, one of the most significant effects of these postmodern conditions has been an increasingly fast-paced and diverse fashion industry, where there is no longer one proscribed, correct, fashionable skirt length or trouser cut, but instead a myriad of possibilities. Consumers are encouraged to purchase far beyond their need. Fashionable change happens at more regular intervals with interim, mid-season and cruise collections.

On the high street, pile it high, sell it cheap, buy it now or lose it dominates as the rhetoric of consumer fashion; these kinds of market behaviours are related to postmodernity (See Kratz and Reimer 1998; Wilson 1992).

Thus, we see, on the one hand, that postmodernism has some possible negative aspects: that it encourages consumers to understand consumption as a meaningful and necessary experience when in fact it might be a rather negative and transient one that benefits multinational companies significantly more; that postmodernism is wasteful; that the consumer culture that is part and parcel of postmodernity is exploitative, but also that it has a feverish sense of excitement and possibility to experiment, to create through consumption and to indulge in the joy of playfulness. Elizabeth Wilson argues that postmodernism as a cultural mood 'expresses at one level a horror at the destructive excess of western consumerist society, yet, in aestheticising this horror, we somehow convert it into a pleasurable object of consumption' (1992: 4). Postmodernism and our relationship to it is thus best understood as something hard to define, elusive and consequently—most of all—ambivalent (Wilson 1992).

One of the greatest criticisms of postmodernism, then, is that it might present empty experiences as meaningful ones, primarily because this may, therefore, provide greater fiscal rewards for a capitalist economy which includes those who create such experiences for a marketplace. This is closely linked to 'the rise of forms of mass communication' (Strinati 1995: 236). As 'the associated proliferation of popular media culture . . . becomes central to the explanatory framework of postmodern theory' (236), and because 'there are no dependable alternatives, popular culture and the mass media come to serve as the only frames of reference available for the construction of collective and personal identities' (221). As such, individuals are encouraged to conceptualize themselves through such references. Consequently, the central position of the music industry to both contemporary popular culture and the mass media places it at centre stage as an example of how such a culture manifests itself in artefacts and events.

There is, therefore, the implication that postmodern experiences have little concern with a sense of real values, histories and meanings and that they are instead caught up in a system that values surfaces and images, where life becomes more and more a mass media experience. Harvey defines this emphasis on the visual as being endemic of 'postmodernism's preoccupation with the signifier' (the image/visual at only a descriptive surface level) 'rather than the signified' (any deep, cultural meaning of the image/visual) 'with participation, performance and happening rather than roots' (1990: 53). As such, postmodernity contrasts with the ideals of modernism that had gone before, which had focused on real political possibilities, hope for the future and a better world. In polar contrast, postmodernism is concerned only with the here and now, 'the reduction of experience to a series of pure and unrelated presents' (53) where there is 'little overt attempt to sustain continuity of values, beliefs or even disbeliefs' (56).

Despite a perceived lack of continuity from past to present and future, what postmodernity does hold dear are images and appearances of the past. It enjoys a love affair with visual display because it 'can judge the spectacle only in terms of how spectacular it is' (Harvey 1990: 56–7). Thus, there is an onus on the most powerful visual forms. This may explain the enduring appeal of uniform styles of dress for pop bands and, in particular, the white suit as an enduring trope for the boyband, particularly in the 1990s, since such forms of dressing create a striking visual impact. This recurrence of particular types of image and, indeed, the commercial boyband itself is an example of how, in postmodernism, 'the fiction of the creating subject gives way to frank confiscation, quotation, excerption, accumulation and repetition of already existing images' (55), showing 'an incredible ability to plunder history and absorb whatever it finds there as some aspect of the present' (54).

As postmodernism has both its pleasures and its problems, so the relationship between the particular image of white-suited masculinity in music has both its lighter and darker sides. One of postmodernism's greatest pleasures lies in its playful ability to create humorous references to history. Whilst there is a danger of trivializing deeper, past, embedded meanings, there is also a joyous abandonment in enjoying its images.

THE WHITE SUIT, POP AND POSTMODERN PASTICHE

The band 50 Kaitzen is one of the many Japanese bands that revels in references to an idea of past pop. Like other popular Japanese bands such as Shonen Knife, influences of British and American pop in particular, and certainly that of the 1960s, make up a significant amount of what currently influences the sound and visuals of contemporary Japanese pop. Dressed like the love children of Austin Powers and Ringo Starr, both 50 Kaitzen's music and their appearance are pure pop pastiche. Core to this are the mop haircuts of Merseybeat and slim-cut modish white suits. A postmodern and ironic appearance here is a greater part of the musical point of 50 Kaitzen: dress is almost everything. This is parody at its height, a recycled past image and a nod to humour. This is not a realignment of an earlier look that demonstrates any passage of time or any modifications to the vagaries of fashion. Instead, we see simply how a whole history of a particular type of pop is absorbed into surface style, made all the more ironic because of a merging not just of a variety of time-spaces, images and histories, but also of cultures. These Japanese men dress like British men of fifty years ago.

Here, then, we see postmodernism's global reach, thanks to fast-moving mass media, increasing globalization and the two-way street that is either cross-cultural cannibalism or cosmopolitanism—depending on how positive one feels about the phenomenon that does not just have West plundering East. Thus, a look which began as something peculiar to a particular cultural moment has spread, thanks to postmodern mass media and communication, to be an enduring, global image. Ultimately, however, this is postmodernism's fun side—images for images' sake, produced by performers for ironic and pleasurable effect. In the case of boybands of the 1990s emerging from Britain and America in particular, the effects of postmodernism can be seen to be in play in a much darker sense. Here, the image of the white-suited nice boy is deeply implicated.

EMPTY VESSELS: THE SUIT AND SIMULATION

In the 1990s, a glut of mainstream boybands portrayed a very similar form of masculinity, which, despite some subtle differences between bands and band members, was, broadly speaking, largely unthreatening. This emerged, in particular, from Britain, the United States and Australia. More than in any other period, it was here that the white suit became an exemplar of the boyband image. Just as the suits of bands of the 1960s and 1970s gave a nod to the contemporary fashionable styles of the time, so these suits reflected, to some extent, the masculine ideals of dressing of the time, whilst keeping, at the core, the good repute of the boy next door.

For example, in the US and UK, respectively, the Backstreet Boys and Boyzone both sported versions of a white suit that demonstrated a development of particular kinds of 1990s masculinity. Despite the fact that in each band there was at least one member who was grungier, earthier or tattooed—for the girls who liked dangerous boys—there was also a certain yielding of the hard, broad male silhouette that suits traditionally emphasize. This look replaced the white blazer of the two- or three-piece suit with a softer, longer, flowing coat. This can be read as symbolic of certain shifts in mainstream masculinity that had, by the 1990s, become accepted.

Masculinity in this period had become a little less hard edged thanks to the gender shifts of the 1980s, which were finally bearing fruit in the conventional context of manufactured pop. The members of these bands are, to some extent, the children of the 'new man' (see Mort 1996; Nixon 1996). They are masculine, but in touch with their softer side—'a rejuvenated peacock, a man who is aware of his body not just as a machine but as an object of sexual attraction enhanced by his choice of clothes and ways of wearing them' (Craik 1994: 192). This represented 'the transition of the male from primitive state to cultural commodification' (Triggs 1992: 27). The white suit *suited* both this softer man and his commodification through cultural practices such as fashion.

Importantly, this white suit is somewhat symbolic of uniformity not just within bands, but also across them. For example, when Irish band Boyzone were coming to the end of their shelf life (though by 2009 they had been able to reunite as a man-band for nostalgia's sake), their manager, Louis Walsh, and band member Ronan Keating put together and managed Westlife. When Boyzone begat Westlife, the change was fairly imperceptible to the idle viewer because the formula was the same: young Irish boys, some better looking than others but all fairly conventionally attractive, dressed in similar ways, producing cover versions of popular songs. There was little attempt to make anything new, but instead, a desperate attempt to keep a good thing going.

Thus, a way of dressing and an image became a perennial form in music thanks to its appeal to a lucrative market. This image was linked to a particular teen market, had textures of the kind of teeny-bop idol written about by Frith and McRobbie in the 1970s (see Frith and McRobbie 1990) and was reminiscent of the kind of standardized identity of early boybands like The Beatles, but music was far from the main reason for the existence of these bands. Instead they are pure marketing images, and their images are commodities to be bought into: music is an incidental part of this commodification. With a reliance on cover versions of earlier boybands and Barry Manilow songs—or of new songs, not original as such, but more derivative—the boyband was less a music experience than a marketing one. The ability to recreate the formula was wholly facilitated by a particular way of dressing which acted as an empty vessel that had an immediate market appeal.

Jacqueline Warwick notes that when Cindy Birdsong replaced Florence Ballard in The Supremes in the late 1960s, what mattered most was that Birdsong fitted into Ballard's clothes. The reasons behind the choice of Birdsong were, then, primarily fiscal because 'Motown had made significant financial investment in the clothing of its star female group and considered the wardrobe to be more valuable than the sound of The Supremes' (Warwick 2007: 78). We see here a sad dehumanization where 'individual members of girls groups—and male vocal groups to be sure—were considered by many record producers to be replaceable as long as the look of the group was maintained more or less intact . . . In this regard, wardrobe was key' (78). This is an early example of something that has become much more commonplace. In the case of manufactured pop bands, young music performers are often treated as nothing more than cannon fodder for a music industry bent on making money. They are made easily replaceable because of the overwhelming significance of the clothes they wear.

We might understand the uniformity of the white-suited boyband to be, in part, then, concerned with portraying a certain sort of masculinity: something safe, pure, domesticated. We might even suggest that such an image finds reference not just in popular music with the dress of The Beatles of the 1960s or zoot suit–wearing jazz musicians. We could, for example, draw comparison to the presentation of band members as respectable, innocent choirboys, particularly when we see how Westlife were shown in a photograph by Karl Grant against a heavenly sky (see EW.com n.d.). Ecclesiastical dress is, after all, 'a dress of innocence' where 'colours . . . acquired religious significance after papal regulations were introduced in 1570: White or silver symbolized joy, purity and innocence . . . these associations carried over into civil life' (Craik 2005: 205) and perhaps then, too, into this musical image.

But we might also understand this look to be an example of what Jean Baudrillard (1994) termed a simulacrum. This is defined as a copy of something that was once a reality, but which has become a meaningless image where repetition and reproduction, of the kind common in postmodernity, gradually empty out any essence of real, profound meaning, leaving only the image itself. Here, the boyband uniform makes incidental the reality of the individual identities of both bands and those populating them and presents a popular and tested image as the marketable commodity. The white suit can be understood to be a simulation in this context because it privileges production and money over individuality and any profound reality or purpose. This is one of the negative but inevitable consequences of a postmodern culture that recycles and plunders ideas with an eye that is often firmly on market success.

It is also the consequence of market success because 'for Baudrillard, it is the success of capital/value/production/the real that leads to its demise through saturation' (Hegarty 2004: 54). When a phenomenon is lucrative, when a market still exists for a cultural artefact or experience, then, in postmodernity, methods are found to continue this phenomenon—by remaking it, by copying it, by making versions of it that are indistinguishable from each other. Thus, the 'death' of any boyband 'becomes total in simulation because it is hidden away' (80), replaced by another version of the same thing where nothing new is really being produced at all: the white-suited boyband is pure simulation, and it is the white suit that provides the means for it.

CONCLUSION

Fashion studies has made familiar the concept that fashion has the ability to express individual identity; that it has the potential to be a site of personal creativity; that it brings pleasure and pain; that it acts as a language and thus speaks of a variety of possible facets of our identities, our genders, our class origins, our tastes, our similarity to some and our difference to others, our sexuality and our ethnicity. Dressing the self is thus constructing the self for public consumption, and much of the work that forms fashion studies is interested in how individuals create meaning through this process. The ways in which some styles of dressing might be understood to be transgressive are framed by such notions.

In examining masculinity in music, we come to see how, whilst music is assumed to be one of the most gender-transgressive contexts where boundaries of normal and acceptable are established and sometimes broken, the suit features heavily as a core form of masculine dressing around which the different masculinities of music happen. Equally, the suit forms a background from which masculine transgressions emerge and are managed, made palatable and understood.

In focusing on how the clothing worn by boybands and the image created might relate to shifting notions of masculinity or reveal the relationships between certain kinds of masculinity and certain audiences, what speaks loudest is the potential for some forms of dress to, over time, become an archetype. This can, in turn, become a much-copied simulation which has, not the potential to describe and communicate individual identity, but, like uniform, the ability to obliterate it, creating docile bodies malleable to the whims of the music industry and its desire for monetary reward.

It is not that the form of this image does not subtly shift over time: indeed, thanks to the New Lad of the 1990s (see Edwards 2006) and the dominance of indie music to the American and European markets, the boyband archetype is undergoing something of a sea change in terms of how it is fashioned. What does not change is the uniformity that crosses the genre: that crosses bands; that crosses oceans. In postmodernity, a concept which is itself framed by a capitalist economy and which consequently focuses on the constant growth of markets and a consumer ethic, the boyband image has appeal for a market that, so long as it exists, has its needs met by a repetitious image: emptied of meaning, uniform, hinting at individuality but containing little. This, in turn, contravenes many of the long-held ideas about authenticity in music and performance because here bodies are given over to the control of an industry and fashioned towards the perceived desires of a lucrative market.

–5–

Dressing Your Age: Fashion, the Body and the Ageing Music Star

On 6 August 2009, Hollywood actress Sharon Stone appeared on the cover of the French magazine *Paris Match*. It is, of course, far from unusual to see an image of a high-profile celebrity like Stone on such a magazine's cover, but this particular image caused something of a tumult amongst printed and online media. What made this picture such a talking point was not just that Stone was aged over fifty and, as such, fell into a category of women who fail to enjoy the kind of cultural visibility of younger members of their gender and, indeed, men of similar age: actresses in this age group seem to have to fight to maintain their careers and their profiles. The real focal point for the press attention the image enjoyed was that, at her age, Sharon Stone posed topless in bondage rubber and high heels.

For the cover image, Stone strikes a pose with attitude, revealing pert, gravity-defying breasts. Of course, it goes unmentioned in the accompanying article that on a woman of fifty, such a chest could only, surely, be thanks to surgical intervention. Still, when coupled with the firm legs and flawless skin also on display, the image is an arresting representation of the *possibilities* offered to the fifty-year-old female body by a consumer culture that provides a variety of methods to potentially hold back the ravages of time. All kinds of bodily maintenance—managed diets, personal trainers, treatments, cosmetics and creams, alternative therapies and cosmetic surgery—are made available and offer the possibility of resolution for this age-old problem to those who can afford it in terms of both time and money.

It must be acknowledged, too, that this image of an astonishingly youthful fifty-year-old body might well owe some debt to image manipulation and airbrushing. In 2008, another actress celebrated turning fifty with a topless image of herself, although markedly less provocative, showing only head and shoulders on the cover of a somewhat less glamorous publication. For the May/June 2008 issue of *AARP Magazine,* Jamie Lee Curtis celebrated natural ageing, arguing that 'older women . . . can remain beautiful if they take care of themselves'. Her response to ageing into her fifties was to 'let my hair go gray. I wear only black and white. Every year I buy 3 or 4 black dresses that I just keep in rotation' (see World Entertainment News Network 2008).

Curtis had set herself up early on as a champion for the ageing woman. In 2002, she had appeared in the US magazine *More* at the age of 43—un-airbrushed, with a body that showed imperfections rarely seen in celebrity photo spreads—in an attempt to reveal the artificial nature of many published images of those in the public eye, particularly women. Still, it cannot be taken for granted that Curtis offers women a possible model for ageing where Stone does not. In *More* magazine, she admitted to having had a 'nip and tuck' in the past (see Wallace 2002). Whilst she promotes real beauty, it has to be remembered that hers remains an unattainable image for millions of women worldwide without the time and/or money to direct towards their appearance.

Whilst there is a great deal of celebration in the way in which these women present themselves, there is also often plenty of criticism, too. Perez Hilton, one of America's biggest powerbrokers of celebrity gossip, posted on his Web site that 'we've got to admit she looks damn good for 51, despite the work done by her surgeon and Mariah's retoucher!!!'(see perezhilton.com n.d.), giving a backhander to both Stone and the much-younger Mariah Carey. While many bloggers contributing to the site acknowledge that Stone looks good, with the proviso 'for her age', many also recognize that this is thanks to plastic surgery. On other parts of the Web, the measure of public opinion shows something altogether more venomous, with charges such as 'you are so embarrassing, Grandma!' (see dailyfix.com n.d.). Generally, though, Stone seems to get at least a 'good for her', if not quite a thumbs up (she is criticized for lack of fashion taste, the tackiness of this particular pose, a perceived lack of acting ability and too much of a tendency to strip off), as the general public opinion.

British newspaper *Metro* was on the side of Stone, admiring the way in which she 'has peeled off to hand Madonna a beginner's guide of how to work the sex factor at age 51' in these images (see Harmsworth 2009). Comparing the similarly aged women's bodies, Madonna is criticized for the 'gristle and veins usually dished up . . . in her leotards' (Harmsworth 2009). The focus on the very texture of her body, which is treated more as meat and matter than human form, seems to reveal that her particular type of honed physique may be at issue here as much as her age. Thus, there may be something about how Madonna has aged, how she chooses to present herself and the type of body she has created through exercise (which may just not be stereotypically feminine enough) that encourages such vocal criticism—something which will receive further discussion later in this chapter. But such reactions also raise important questions. Could it be that being a music star poses particular challenges when it comes to ageing that may be greater than those that exist even for actresses like Sharon Stone and Jamie Lee Curtis?

Firstly, this chapter considers how engagement with many forms of popular music has come to be established as an age-specific activity. It pinpoints some specific historical moments that have cemented music and youth in a seemingly natural coexistence in the popular consciousness. In doing so, it also considers how this relationship has been played out through practices of embodiment and representation. In particular, subcultural groups, for whom both fashion and music were key ways in which group- and age-specific identities and behaviours were defined, form the background to discussions here.

The chapter then moves on to consider some of the specific problems this presents to those who produce and consume popular music when they age. Here, in particular, the focal position of the body and fashion as places where physical ageing might and must be managed is central to the analysis. Thus, this chapter examines some of the ways in which individuals and groups have attempted to resolve the problems of ageing in relation to music performance and the part that the fashioning of the body plays in such resolutions. Finally, and inevitably, embedded throughout this discussion is a consideration of the way in which ageing might pose different challenges for male and female musicians.

OUT WITH THE OLD: MUSIC, FASHION AND YOUTH

Whilst, as Patrizia Calefato would argue, the past is always present in music and fashion, with 'citations, experiences, influences and suggestions from the past' (2004: 121), it is not a place in which either industry likes to be seen to dwell. As Calefato establishes, music, like fashion, relies on progress—the next big thing—not necessarily entirely new, but with at least an impression of constant movement and development. In music, she argues, 'each successive generation [is] consciously living anew the state of perpetual and sensory doubt and displacement of the previous generation' (118). For Calefato, this is music's most dominant ideal: it is seen to work most powerfully in harmony with a sense of transition, particularly in relation to life stages, and, even more specifically, it is viewed as being in concert with the concerns of the younger generation.

Undoubtedly, many writers have seen popular music as having a particularly powerful resonance with the young (see for example Bennett 2000; Frith 1996; Frith and McRobbie 1990; Longhurst 1995; Fiske 1989), most often for two reasons. First, a great deal of popular music is concerned with the discovery of love and sex. As such, it seems to say more about an unresolved, developmental life stage than the settled one which is the expectation of middle age. As Frith and McRobbie note, 'Of all the mass media, rock is the most explicitly concerned with sexual expression' (1990: 371), and popular culture would have us believe that sexual expression is the preserve of those under forty-five, so invisible is the sexuality of older people (see for example

Sontag 1972). Thus, for Frith and McRobbie, the mosh pit at a rock concert is a place where the aggression of developing male sexuality is played out whilst the teeny-bop, pop idol is a convenient locus for pubescent female romantic love, tinged with the danger of sex, an experience often to be held at arm's length—somewhere in the future—and viewed with a mixture of fear and expectation.

The second place in which music and youth have a strongly established link is in the notion that a rebellious nature is keenly important to both making and experiencing music to its fullest. As David Buxton argues, 'Rock Music [has become] synonymous with radicalism *tout court*' (1990: 435). Youth, music and rebellion are inextricably linked, cemented together by particular historical conditions relating to popular culture in America and Europe during the 1950s, 1960s and through to the 1970s. In this period, music and fashion are part and parcel of not only the way in which youthful transgressions were formed and expressed, but they also offered ways in which social ideals about morality, sexuality, gender, the body, social class and politics could be questioned. With 'the arrival of rock 'n' roll . . . not only did the stylistic direction of popular music radically alter but it also acquired a distinctly youth-oriented and oppositional stance' (Bennett 2000: 34). On both sides of the Atlantic, one of the first and most influential music performers for youth culture in this period was Elvis Presley.

The alarm and astonishment, fear and fascination caused by Presley's clothes in tandem with his bodily movements, which focused on a thrusting pelvis (never until that time seen in the living rooms of polite homes), are well documented and known to many. The powerful influence of rock 'n' roll on the younger generation was evidenced by the speed with which the shockwaves caused by performances on TV rippled onto the street, where 'Presley's image . . . was quickly emulated by many white male teenagers, and his stage performances . . . injected a source of spectacle into rock 'n' roll that was, up until this time, unknown to white audiences' (Bennett 2001: 14).

YOUTH CULTURE, SUBCULTURES

The development of a specific youth culture in this period was thanks in great part to what was also a period of demographic change. This shift meant that youth itself came to be established in particular ways, defined by cultural spaces like music and fashion, which were accessed as symbols of youthful experience. In the long run, such experiences have become fundamental to the cultural understanding of youth and the very definition of the state of being youthful. In his seminal work on youth subcultures, Stanley Cohen (2002: 150) notes the following:

In the years between 1945 and 1950 the grounds for change were laid by a constellation of economic and demographic variables. There was a large unmarried teenage generation (between 15 and 21) whose average real wage had increased at twice the rate of the adults. This relative economic emancipation created a group with few social ties or responsibilities and whose stage of development could not really be coped with by the nuclear working-class family.

This life stage, furnished by greater economic wealth than the generation before, offered the young an opportunity to explore the cultural spaces offered by fashion and music and, in doing so, to aim to 'negotiate a meaningful intermediate space somewhere between the parent culture and the dominant ideology: a space where an alternative identity could be discovered and expressed' (Hebdige 1979: 88).

The perspectives of both Cohen and Dick Hebdige, quoted earlier, are part of a broad body of work examining youth or sub*cultures* (see also for example Bennett 2000; Muggleton 2000; Thornton 2005). Rather than being explicitly concerned with fashion or music per se, many such texts sought to understand the ways in which young people were organizing and expressing themselves in this fast-changing period. Fashion and music came to be themes extrapolated from this work because of their significance to the way in which these subcultures marked themselves out. The visual and physical resonance of fashion and style made them a powerful tool for the young. As Cohen argues, 'Whether the objects for decoding are Teddy Boys, Mods, Rockers, Skinheads or punks, two dominant themes are suggested: first that style—whatever else it is—is essentially a type of *resistance* to subordination; secondly, that the form taken by this resistance is somehow *symbolic* or *magical*, in the sense of not being an actual, successful solution to whatever is the problem' (2002: liv).

The problems these groups of young people were attempting to symbolically resolve centred on both the state of being young and of being working class. Much of this early work on subculture focused specifically on Britain and on groups of young working-class men. These groups were argued to be attempting to find ways to express and resist the limited future mapped out for them by their classed existence. For many young working-class men in this period, there was little hope of an education that extended beyond the age of about fifteen (unless they were exceptionally gifted), and, as such, their hope of freedom of choice and mobility in the future was limited.

Whilst being teenaged was not exclusively the right of the working classes, much fear centred on the idea of the young male delinquent, and, as Stanley Cohen argues, 'working class yobs are the most enduring of suitable enemies' (2002: viii). Almost as soon as the teenager was identified as a nomenclature for this life stage, it also became a problem which—in the media and on the news, at least—focused on subcultural groups' 'emerging styles, [which] became associated with deviant or publicly disapproved values' (151).

Youth was presented as a generation in limbo, and many within the older generation and the establishment (the media and the government, for example) feared that this represented some kind of breakdown of society. The way in which the young used activities like fashion and music to symbolically mark themselves out as different from their parents and the parent culture which governed them created 'violations of the authorized codes through which the social world is organized and experienced [having] considerable power to provoke and disturb' (Hebdige 1979: 91).

Like Elvis, one of the most powerful and public ways for these groups to provoke and disturb was through the presentation of the body. Often described as 'spectacular subcultures' because of the privileged status of the visual spectacle of the body in subcultural identity, groups like the Teddy Boys in the 1950s, the mods and rockers in the 1960s, and punks in the 1970s expressed a resistance to the limitations of class through that body. In the case of the Teddy Boys, 'their style was adapted from a different social group—the Edwardian Dandy—and its exaggeration and ritualization were mirrored in the groups activities: a certain brutality, callousness, indifference and almost stoicism' (Cohen 2002: 154).

Hebdige named this use and reuse of clothing styles 'bricolage', defined as an activity where 'prominent forms of discourse (particularly fashion) are radically adapted, subverted and extended by the subcultural bricoleur' (1979: 104). In a text which focuses specifically on subcultural style, Hebdige argues that 'in this way the Teddy Boys theft and transformation of the Edwardian style revived in the early 1950s by Saville Row for the wealthy young men about town can be construed as an act of *bricolage*. Similarly the Mods could be said to be functioning as *bricoleurs* when they appropriated another range of commodities by placing them in a symbolic ensemble which served to erase or subvert their original straight meanings' (104).

In subculture there was clearly an acknowledgement, then, that clothes could have a symbolic function. While Cohen would argue that it is impossible to unpick and attribute individual meaning to every minute detail of any individual subcultural style in bricolage, 'the objects chosen were, whether intrinsically or in their adapted forms, homologous with the focal concerns, activities, group structure and collective self image of the subculture' (2002: 114). These objects and styles became what Celia Lury (1996) would describe as 'totems', items which, when adopted by a particular group, come to symbolize ideas and ideals, taking on almost magical properties in their changed, subcultural meanings.

While Cohen's text focuses on the notion of youth and delinquency generally, noting that not all forms of juvenile deviance are articulated through clothing, Hebdige (1979: 93) argues that it was the way in which subcultural groups in the 1950s, 1960s and 1970s dressed that was the catalyst for the kinds of moral and media panic that ensued:

> In most cases, it is the subculture's stylistic innovations which first attract the media's attention. Subsequently deviant or 'anti-social' acts—vandalism, swearing, fighting, animal behaviour—are 'discovered' by the police, the judiciary, the press and these acts are used to explain the subculture's original transgression of sartorial codes.

Embedded in this desire to explain the problem of subcultural youth there was doubtless, too, some long-held puritanism at work that was suspicious of the emphasis on leisurely consumption that defined many subcultural groups as 'cultures of conspicuous consumption' (Hebdige 1979: 103). Consumption practices were core to many subcultural identities, whether in a keen adoption of shopping habits or in a perceived refusal of mainstream consumer habits (as in the case of punks and skinheads; see Hebdige 1979). In particular, the participation of young men in practices that made the body a focus of display was often viewed with great suspicion. Thus, subcultural identity created a sense of fearful fascination for mainstream culture, tinged as it was with a frisson of danger, transgression and rebellion. But such identities have also played a significant role in establishing ideas about how generations work to define and understand themselves and, in particular, the relationship between the youthful life stage, music and style.

Still, despite the extensive enquiry that has taken place into the notion of subculture (though the nature of these subcultures has shifted over time), as Gary Clarke (2005) argues, there has been little detailed exploration of how subcultural groups, and those populating them, adapt or modify themselves and their bodies as time progresses. As he describes, 'There is an uncomfortable absence in the literature of any discussion as to how and with what consequences the pure subcultures are sustained, transformed, appropriated, disfigured or destroyed' (Clarke 2005: 170).

Many writers (see for example Hebdige 1979; Polhemus 1994) attribute the gradual degradation of subcultural identity to the adoption of similar styles by the mainstream. Few consider, however, what happens to those who had established a subcultural identity for themselves—probably held very dear—when they cease to be young. Is the expectation that they are to give this up at an appropriate but fairly arbitrary and difficult-to-recognize moment within a society that perceives them to be too old to continue? Thus, while Andy Bennett (2000) notes that punk music and style has seemed to endure in Germany, for example, he is interested only in what this says about the part that locale plays in music culture. He does not tell us whether the audience for this punk music was there from the start and has endured or has been replaced by a younger generation of fans.

MOD STYLE AND 'MIDDLE-YOUTH' CULTURE

In British newspaper the *Independent* (see Walsh 2008), the musician Paul Weller and the designer Paul Smith discuss fashion, music and bespoke suits and give a hint to the continuing significance of one subcultural style, at least to older men. The article features alongside the launch of a book, *A Thousand Things,* which celebrated Weller's career as music icon and was to be sold at £250 a copy in Paul Smith's stores. Described by Weller as a scrapbook, *A Thousand Things* was largely a pictorial record that harmonized with the slim-cut aesthetic of the Paul Smith suit (always reminiscent of the 1960s) and target cufflinks being sold alongside it.

A love of good tailoring and the kind of attitudes to dressing adopted by the mod subculture in the 1960s is a shared ground on which much of the discussion hinges, though, at age fifty, Weller was part of the 1980s mod revival rather than the original subculture. The conversation focuses on memories of looks past and present—Tonik suits, ox blood shoes, Fred Perry shirts—and the origins of their sartorial tastes, which lie, in both cases, with subculture and music. Whilst there is a clear awareness that both men have been in the public eye for a long time and are getting older, there is never a sense that anything about the way the two dressed ever needed to be modified. The way in which the preamble to the interview identifies Paul Smith's approach to tailoring might suggest a reason why—'classic but funky' suggests a timeless and ageless appeal.

As Dom Phillips argued in a further article in the *Independent* newspaper, mods will always be with us. He recounts a project by one of his friends whom he describes as a 1970s 'suedehead'. Part of the 1980s mod revival himself, he photographs ageing mods in an attempt to see how this subcultural style has shaped their sartorial codes as they have grown older. As Phillips describes, 'Mod is about well-styled, working-class aspiration with an obsessive attention to detail: the right shoes, records, shirts, everything . . . A wink of mod style works well for men in their thirties and forties' (Phillips n.d.).

Stanley Cohen has clearly established how mod style was one of the most commercially appealing subcultural looks in the 1960s, and it came to dominate both the subcultural landscape and subsequently mainstream dressing. Here, 'the rockers were left out of the race: they were unfashionable and unglamorous just because they appeared to be more class bound . . . the Mods on the other hand made all the running and although the idiom they emerged from was real enough, it was commercial exploitation which made them completely dominant. This was the Mod era' (Cohen 2002: 156).

The commercial appeal of mod style was part of what Dick Hebdige identifies as a process by which 'each subculture moves through a cycle of resistance and diffusion . . . Subcultural deviance is simultaneously rendered "explicable" and meaningless in the classrooms, courts and media at the same time as the "secret" objects of subcultural style are put on display in every high street record shop and chain store boutique. Stripped of its unwholesome connotations, the style becomes fit for public consumption' (1979: 130). As such, what was once outlawed becomes mainstream through its assimilation into consumer culture. Through this process, confrontational symbols begin to lose their potency.

This move of subcultural style to mainstream fashion is part of what Ted Polhemus (1994) terms 'bubble up', an explanation for the cyclical nature of fashion change. While this was read as the sad but inevitable fate of subcultural style—the emptying of politicized meaning from the looks and a watering down of its spectacular potential—the move of mod style to the mainstream has clearly offered a model for the successful, stylish fashioning of the ageing male body. The Web site modculture.com dubs those who return to subcultural style later in life 'third-age mods'. For many of those who populated the pure subculture, style was the main remaining vestige of their participation, as Chris Hardy (age fifty-nine) says on the site: 'I'm a bit too old to be called a Mod now but I still like to dress nicely' (see Parker n.d.)

Thus, what was once a youth style actually offers a model for the successful, stylish fashioning of the ageing male body for many men: both for those who were part of the original subculture and equally for those who were not. The look works for these older men because, at its core, it centres not only on many of the traditional staples of the menswear wardrobe, but also on ways of fashioning the male body that hark back to the traditions of the dandy, which we explored in chapter 4. This is because the spectacular potential of mod style lies in its focus on quality, attention to detail and a certain nontraditional styling of traditional menswear garments: shirts, slim-cut trousers and sharp-cut suits.

THE AGEING ROCK STAR

Whilst for some baby boomers, then, subcultural style has come to offer a form of dress seen to be appropriate for older men, most significantly for this chapter, subcultural groups and the historical conditions within which they emerge set out a landscape where popular music was core to the youth explosion of the 1950s and 1960s. This, in turn, established a link between style, the body, music and youth. The consequences of this have been far reaching. On the one hand, as Andy Bennett argues, 'the continuing centrality of popular music in youth culture since the 1950s has underlain much of the theoretical debate about how to approach the study of popular music and the various stylistic sensibilities to which it has given rise' (2000: 35). On the other, it led the forty-six-year-old George Michael to announce his (semi) retirement from the music industry when he stated that 'the pop scene . . . was about youth culture and "shouldn't be an endurance test"' (see virginmedia.com n.d.). It is a contradiction that Sheila Whiteley acknowledges in her postscript to her book *Too Much Too Young* (2005).

Indeed, the notion that music is for the young surrounds many of the discourses of popular culture and seems to shape the reactions of audiences, the media and, indeed, artists themselves to older music stars. When Michael Jackson died of a heart attack just before his fiftieth birthday in June 2009, the possibility that the pressure of performing fifty dates at the London O2 arena might have contributed to his death tinged much of the press coverage, at least in the early stages. In March 2009, rapper 50 Cent suggested that his colleague Jay Z was close to being 'past it'. He argued that as Jay Z approached the relatively young age of forty, the deal Jay Z signed with Live Nation to control his tour schedules, recording and marketing was a way of slowing down towards his dotage (see insider.com n.d.). What such examples demonstrate is that while music—and along with it, style—are firmly imprinted as part of youth culture, older people continue to participate.

However, they equally reveal the kind of close monitoring of what constitutes age-inappropriate behaviour to which the media contributes significantly. The ageing rock star is, like any individual in middle age and beyond, subject to 'the vocabulary of aging, or its discourse, [which] provides the aged with limited potential for the expression of their subjective, personal feelings, separate from prevailing stereotypes' (Faircloth 2003: 17). But, importantly for this chapter, it might be argued that this subjection is amplified around popular music when youth is such an emphatic part of its identity as culture and industry.

THE BODY AND THE AGEING PROCESS

The body clearly plays a significant role in the ageing process. This is not to say that ageing is merely the gradual physical decline of the body. Instead, becoming older can be understood as a vital part of the life course, where 'adult life . . . is process' (Featherstone and Hepworth 1991: 375). At the same time, it is a process with which individuals are expected to engage in an active dialogue, not something to be passively accepted. Thus, it is argued that there is a 'contemporary global understanding that the ageing process cannot be adequately explained solely in biological and medical terms, but is an interactive process involving social and cultural factors' (Featherstone and Hepworth 2005: 355).

The dilemma for the ageing music performer originates in their status as part of 'the baby boomer generation which explored counter cultural lifestyles in the 1960s and who are now entering what used to be called "middle-age". As they do so they are taking with them many of the values and cultural tastes of youth' (Featherstone and Hepworth 1991: 375), and these ideals are shaping the way in which they move through the life course and the ageing process.

Mike Featherstone and Mike Hepworth (1991, 2005) have undertaken some of the most sustained work on ageing and its cultural meanings. Much of their work focuses on the ageing body in the context of post-war consumer culture. As Bill Bytheway notes, 'While older people have always been active consumers in a variety of traditional marketplaces, they have increasingly been targeted as a group who, through their participation in new markets, are being persuaded that there are alternative lifestyles that they too might enjoy' (2003: 39). This has meant that traditional notions of the elderly as infirm and passive have broken down. Hence, 'chronological age continues to be discredited as an indicator of inevitable age norms and lifestyles and a new breed of body maintenance experts optimistically prescribe health foods, vitamins, dieting, fitness techniques and other regimens to control *biological* age, which, it is argued, is the true index of how a person should feel' (Featherstone and Hepworth 1991: 374).

For Featherstone and Hepworth, the notion that a real self—one which is constant and youthful (though adult)—lies just beneath the maturing surfaces of the body prevails as a defining idea about ageing in Western culture. While they acknowledge that to 'adopt a view of the life course in which culture is granted the overarching power to mould nature in any form it chooses' (1991: 375) is a mistake, many areas of consumer culture offer the possibility of holding off ageing; of extending what they define as 'middle-age', which has come to refer 'to a very loosely defined age stage covering the wide chronological range 35 to 60, if not beyond' (373).

Thus, there is a perception that internally, individuals change little, but they are let down by the external realities of the ageing body which place both physical and cultural limitations on their lives. In contemporary consumer culture, in particular, this has created a pressure to maintain an external self that matches this perceived, real, internal character. This, in turn, places bodily practices, including fashion, to the fore, and 'for those of the middle-classes with the prospect of generous pension incomes and who have planned for their retirement, old age holds out the prospect of a prolongation of the plateau like phase of adult life, with continued relatively high consumption of consumer culture lifestyles, body maintenance and styles of self-presentation' (Featherstone and Hepworth 1991: 374).

Whilst this might suggest that, in the contemporary period, ageing has new possibilities and freedoms unavailable to earlier generations, there are consequences. Christopher Faircloth argues, for example, that ageing provided 'women . . . more leeway in their bodily presentation . . . a . . . resource for defining their bodies in a more laissez-faire manner. Unlike younger women, older women used the very constructions that society imposed on them due to their age as a way of invoking a kind of freedom in bodily construction and presentation' (2003: 8). Instead of such freedoms, however, pressures grow, and 'we act on or work to maintain the body because of the images of the perfect body presented to us by the media, advertising and so forth' (10).

In the pursuit of idealized old age, there is 'a contrast between ideal perfection and failures [on the part of] the individual' (Faircloth 2003: 18). Like many other images of consumer culture, an almost unattainable ideal remains always just beyond the consumer's grasp, driving the consumption process ever forward in a contradictory progression which both demands the retention of youthfulness but also the creation of an age-appropriate identity for those past middle age.

Thus, ageing is a discursive process where the individual is in dialogue with the boundaries of contemporary ageing and its expectations. This process is made difficult by the fluidity of these boundaries. In 2000, Pamela Church Gibson noted the way in which older women, thanks to both the possibilities presented by new definitions of ageing and the constant threat of getting the process wrong, remained somewhat alienated by the fashion industry despite the fact that the new concept of old age suggested they should continue to participate actively in such areas of consumer culture. The individuals who contributed testimony to Church Gibson's study felt that the inevitability of wearing safe, sensible fabrics, body-covering garments and beige blousons from the British brand Country Casuals lay somewhere just ahead for women in mid-life. There was a sense of growing confusion about how any individual in any age group should look and an increasing uncertainty about how to navigate the fashioning of an ageing body.

What Church Gibson's (2000) work clearly identifies is that fashion is a place of expectations and possibilities for managing and moving through the ageing process. Here, consumer culture—and, in relation to it, fashion—plays a central role. A fashioned identity that acknowledges that ageing has happened whilst diametrically resisting giving in to old age has become a difficult to attain ideal. To cling wholeheartedly to symbols of youth risks being labelled tragic or 'mutton dressed as lamb'. Instead, the aim is for a youth*ful*ness that conveys a sense of the irrelevance of physical age to social life.

THE AGEING FEMALE BODY: MADONNA

Clearly, achieving such a fashioned identity is not easy. Achieving it as a star figure, open to the scrutiny of the media, can only add to the challenge. At the same time, the ageing of those in the public eye reveals the central part the scrutiny of others—media, audiences and peers—plays in making such identities. As Madonna approached the age of fifty, the press awaited her milestone birthday with baited breath. Coverage seemed to focus more and more on the problems that lay just over the brow of a hill, as though, at fifty, things would be very different for Madonna than at forty-nine. Thus, while Featherstone and Hepworth argue that 'adult life . . . need not involve a predetermined series of stages of growth' (1991: 375), the old idea that numbers matter seems to persist. Whilst Madonna is not the only ageing female star to suffer at the hands of the press, her ageing process has arguably received more ferocious attention than any other and demonstrates some of the specific problems for women in relation to ageing.

In Britain, the tabloid press has shown a particular interest in Madonna's ageing process. In January 2009, the *Mirror* newspaper focused on what it clearly saw as the tragic inappropriateness of sexualized images of women her age in an article entitled 'Put It Away, Granny Madonna—You're Too Old to Be Flashing Your Crotch'. These headlines came about in response to images created for the Louis Vuitton accessories campaign of the same year. Here, with her yoga-toned body, Madonna demonstrated the ability to strike a number of contorted poses for which any fifty-year-old should normally be congratulated. Instead, the *Daily Mail* asked on 28 July 2008, 'Have age and stress launched a shocking attack on Madonna's face?' (Wilkes 2008), and declared on 4 May 2006 that 'Madonna can't hold back the hands of time' (Simpson 2006); in the *Telegraph,* Jan Moir (2008) proclaimed that 'Madonna sups deep at the fountain of youth', entering the 'anti-ageing battle with the zeal of a warrior looking into the whites of the enemy's eyes'.

Whilst the work of Featherstone and Hepworth (1991, 2005) suggests that resisting traditional notions of ageing through consumer culture has become an acceptable process through which individuals work through their life course, Madonna, as an archetypal example of someone inside this process, reveals its boundaries: she seems to be too desperate to remain young for the taste of many.

Thus, where as Faircloth argues that old age was historically understood to be biological, it has, thanks to 'the visual representations of aging [which] in our culture [made] for a constant self-monitoring of bodily transformation' (2003: 8), increasingly come to be understood as a social process against which the individual is measured to have been successful or unsuccessful due to a number of different factors and contexts: gender, race and occupation being just some of these. Thus, the rules of ageing and the monitoring to which it is subject—both internally from the individual who makes decisions for his body and externally from a society which establishes rules which govern normal and appropriate behaviour—follow the kinds of power structures within society identified by the French philosopher Michel Foucault.

Whilst Jason Powell notes that Foucault himself never looked explicitly at age and ageing, focusing instead on issues such as madness, illness, criminality and sexuality, his methods of analysis have been adopted by a few writers whom Powell terms 'Foucauldian gerontologists' who have 'recently recognised the validity and importance of his theories, methodologies and concepts in relation to "old age"' (Powell 2004; see also Katz 1996). In particular, his ideas have been used to consider how the institutions of old age, like medicine and elderly care, institutionalize the ageing process in order to organize and manage it.

Much of Foucault's work (see Foucault 1990, 2003; Rabinow 1991) examined the way in which societies organize themselves through processes of categorization and surveillance, and, as such, it is equally prescient for considerations of the ageing body in society and popular culture. In particular, his work often revealed the internal power systems within these societies that constructed what we might understand as a disciplinary framework, focusing in particular on a sense of the normal and abnormal behaviours to which those constituting a society were subject. This means that a number of public entities—the media, systems of government and education and the images such institutions produce—set out the boundaries of acceptable behaviour against which individuals shape and measure themselves and each other.

Similarly, such methods of categorization and surveillance can apply to the representation of ageing bodies in popular culture: the ageing music performer, positioned in the context of music, with all its youthful associations, is one such body. For ageing music stars, the problems of ageing are clearly amplified. Star bodies are both expected to provide the kind of image to which others aspire, but are also subject to all the cultural constraints around ageing. In particular, the ageing star provides a very visible ageing body open to scrutiny by and via the media—subjected to what Foucault termed 'the gaze' (Foucault 2003; Rabinow 1991).

For Foucault, 'the gaze'—the process of looking at ourselves and one another—is an active rather than passive pursuit. It is not only a process of social engagement and perhaps pleasure, but also a means by which the body enters into what he terms discourse. Here, the body becomes part of social life, a tool of communication and a representation of power. In turn, it becomes something to be worked with and on to move through social life and navigate its power systems. As such, this body has to be shaped, managed, presented and disciplined in accordance with these social norms. Here, the body becomes part of the power systems and social ideals against which it is regulated. This regulation does not necessarily happen by overt or violent means, but instead is an insidious process where individuals risk being singled out as different—rejected, even—because of any failures to adhere to accepted behaviours within their social context: they may thus be deemed abnormal and in need of rectification (see Rabinow 1991).

These ideas also acknowledge that the adherence to and achievement of these social norms is also a route to power. Thus, as the physical locus of social identity, the body is core to the process of adherence to social norms of various kinds: gender identity, cleanliness, body shape, body language and maintenance, body size and, most importantly for this chapter, age-appropriate behaviour and appearance.

Thus, media and public scrutiny are central to the management of appropriate age-specific identities, and the treatment of the older musician reveals this process in action. After all, the very term 'ageing rock star' is rarely intended to be complementary and carries with it some often negative connotations, as evidenced in the almost gleeful reporting of the physical vulnerability of older stars. When Steven Tyler, the sixty-one-year-old frontman of Aerosmith, fell from the stage into the crowd while dancing at a gig in August 2009, it seemed to some like divine retribution for a perceived vanity: the denial of age. For older musicians, then, contemporary notions of ageing suggest that continuing to be active, to work and to live a full life *should* be possible. Yet at the same time, echoes of past attitudes and the possibility that being old and being a rock star does not constitute age-appropriate behaviour past a certain age endure. Thus, navigating ageing asks individuals to follow a narrow path where pitfalls are lurking on either side: neither letting oneself go into old age with abandon, nor clinging onto youth in desperation, are acceptable responses to growing older.

As a performer attempting to work through the ageing process in an industry obsessed with youth, Madonna, it may be argued, suffers particularly because she is a woman. Writing in 1972, Susan Sontag argued that 'getting older is less profoundly wounding for a man, for in addition to the propaganda for youth that puts both men and women on the defensive as they age, there is a double standard about aging that denounces women with special severity' (1972).

One element of the discipline and adherence of the body to socially acceptable ideas of age-appropriate presentation is how the ageing body is concealed. As Rabinow argues, in these 'normalising' processes, 'it is always the body that is at issue' (1991: 172). This is particularly prescient for women since, in youth, the revelation of flesh is a key part of fashion, femininity and sexuality. Pamela Church Gibson identifies a 'particular trend for older self exposure' which she argued began 'in the pages of *Playboy* when Ursula

Andress celebrated her sixtieth birthday by recreating her famous emergence from the Caribbean, bikini clad in the very first Bond film' (2000: 80). Madonna represents the current incarnation of this trend in the music industry, and negative reactions to images and clothing which reveal her body both on and off stage (Figure 10) have become part of a tradition in the press that places older women, particularly, under a critical spotlight. Here, women like Madonna are judged for attempting to maintain a sexual identity for themselves as they age in an industry where women understand early on that their value is managed against their sexual allure. Thus, newspaper articles which ridicule Madonna for attempting to remain youthful, sexual and relevant demonstrate that, as Sontag argues, 'for most women aging means a humiliating process of gradual sexual disqualification' (1972). Thus, whilst all ageing musicians suffer similar problems in an industry and creative practice that defines itself against notions of youthful expression and rebellion, it may be that women suffer more.

As a woman in the public eye and in the music industry, Madonna illustrates debates around ageing in a number of ways. She is, first and foremost, part of an industry obsessed with youth, with a history that imprints youth

Figure 10 Madonna shows off an age-defying, youthful body, Sticky and Sweet tour, Munich, August 2009 © photoproject.eu, 2010, used under license from shutterstock.com

as an essential element of successful music-making and authentic musical engagement. Second, she is open to media scrutiny and must navigate the difficult ageing process in the public eye—opening her up to regular criticism by media producers and audiences alike. But thirdly, Madonna is part of 'our contemporary cultural imagery of ageing [which] is enlivened by heroes and heroines who vigorously deny the relevance of age-graded statuses' (Featherstone and Hepworth 1991: 373). Madonna acts as a model for how the contemporary aging process could look for women.

For the journalist Jan Moir (2008), this adds new pressures on women over fifty, where, 'with dear Madge still on the scene, complete with her apple-sized rear and biceps like bulldozers, there is no chance of any of us going gently into that dark pair of elasticated trousers with the nice, forgiving seams'. For writers like Moir, then, Madonna plays a part in maintaining fashion's stranglehold on women's bodies. For Susan Sontag, attempting to rid themselves of the signs of ageing is not, for women, the route to freedom from its tyrannies. As she argues, 'the model corruption in a woman's life is denying her age. She symbolically accedes to all those myths that furnish women with their imprisoning insecurities and privileges that create their genuine oppression, that inspire their real discontent' (Sontag 1972). In denying the ageing process, all consumers, women in particular, 'let the direct awareness they have of their needs, of what really gives them pleasure, be overruled by commercialized images of happiness and personal well-being; and, in this imagery designed to stimulate ever more avid levels of consumption, the most popular metaphor for happiness is youth' (Sontag 1972).

CONCLUSION

Thus, it is difficult to separate any discussion of ageing from one about gender, since gender difference frames many social and cultural attitudes to human bodies. In many ways, music is something of a leveller in relation to ageing since it is a space within which any individual, male or female, might feel its tyrannies. This is identifiable in the kinds of finger-wagging that older performers are subject to, particularly through the media, both old and new. Most importantly, attitudes and ideas about ageing are formed largely by appearances: the body becomes the locus for judgements about good and bad ageing and for the very evidence that the process is happening.

Fashion, as part of consumer culture, has offered a means through which this ageing process can be negotiated. However, this is far from straightforward, and older consumers can feel alienated by the products that seem to be offered to them and confused by regularly shifting boundaries of appropriate behaviour. All these issues are made visible through analysis of many older music performers, but still, the iniquities in the treatment of men and women also become clear.

Ultimately, older music performers demonstrate some important points about our cultural attitudes to both popular music and fashion. First, both are largely conceived of as youth industries. Popular music is understood to articulate particular aspects of what are falsely understood to be the preserve of the young: rebellion, resistance and an abundant sexuality. Equally, fashion is a youth-obsessed industry, and, whilst many products are now marketed towards older consumers, this can require a seismic shift in self-identity and an ability to self-monitor and adapt in rapid response to the ageing process.

Second, an engagement with both music and all its attendant rebellion has become a cultural requirement of youth. This only serves to reinforce a disjuncture between older people and music. In a similar vein, there is an expectation that the 'new' so desired by the fashion industry will be found amongst the young. Consequently, there is an equal expectation that young people be fashionable. Thus, the life course holds tyrannous expectations to conform to age-appropriate behaviour at both ends of the spectrum. Such expectations can be understood as tyrannical whether they are recognized or not and whether they are pleasurable or not. Fashion and music are implicated in making these attitudes to the life course material and visible because, as facets of identity-making, there is a requirement that we make careful choices in relation to them . . . if we wish to conform.

–6–

Clothes and Cultural Identities: Music, Ethnicity and Nation

In the ways in which they have been discussed and understood, both fashion and music are seen to have a strong relationship to the spoken word. In the work of writers such as Alison Lurie (1981) and Roland Barthes (1990), fashion has been examined alongside linguistic models and is broadly understood as having potential as a nonverbal language; a language that is in greater part an expression of social position. Consequently, when fashion articulates this social position, it also therefore expresses facets of identity such as taste, gender, social class, ethnicity and national identity because it is through such means that patterns of social position are first established and then negotiated.

By extension, fashion is seen to be as much about belonging as it is about being individual. As such, ways of dressing are methods of allying oneself to a group of people with whom one identifies. One of the functions of style has been to express belonging to a particular group or membership in a particular community, but it may equally be a means of creating distance from other possible groups and communities.

Musical taste and methods of production are seen to have the potential to speak of similar issues. Simon Frith has examined the way in which both the lyrical structure and the content of music find a linkage to the traditions and ideas of the people producing and consuming it and play a part in forming communities. He focuses, for example, on country music, which, 'like blues, is a vocal music concerned with the realistic presentation and appraisal of the problems of the common people, of the workers and the oppressed' (Frith 1978: 182). In such examples, music was a way of publicly speaking in one's own voice long before other forms of media became conscious of an imperative to represent people from a variety of communities. Thus, fashion and music share the potential for expressions of the self and the community from which one originates.

When thinking about community, we are considering fashion and music's relationship to space and place. In this way, we think not only about the part that physical space might play in shaping identities expressed through fashion and music—where one comes from—but also about a cultural space through which identities can be articulated in a variety of ways. Separately, both fashion and music have offered the means for such identity expressions. The overarching concern of this chapter, then, is how people's engagement with fashion and music might relate to their sense of who they understand themselves to be and where they are from. In particular, it considers how fashion and music, together, might be understood as expressions of ethnic and national identity.

The aim of this chapter, then, is to examine the ways in which such facets of identity have come to be spoken through types of music and, alongside this, embodied through dress. Here, we consider the potential of both fashion and music as cultural spaces with an occasionally unofficial status as cultures of the street. It argues that, unguarded, they have acted as spaces where the realities of lived existences could be represented. Through such means, marginalized groups could represent themselves rather than be represented by others. This allowed a voice for the complexities of ethnic and national identities and the maintenance of traditions. As an alternative to more traditional and closed media routes, music offered a space to gain access to such channels, making what were once marginal, muted voices more dominant.

This chapter thus argues that it is the melding of fashion with music—the embodiment of politicized, lived existences and personal and collective histories; ethnic, national and, by extension, often classed—that has created a language powerful enough to allow previously marginalized and thus subdued voices to speak more loudly, gaining access to spaces and places previously denied them.

DEFINING IDENTITIES

Martin Stokes contends that music has provided a means by which individuals and communities come to understand themselves in relation to other groups with whom they contrast themselves, thus establishing the 'difference between'. Therefore, he argues that 'music is socially meaningful not entirely, but largely because it provides means by which people recognise identities and places and the boundaries which separate them' (Stokes 1994: 5).

Music operates to assist in the formation of identities and also in the recognition that these are something constructed rather than fixed or factual since it is the concept of boundaries and differences that creates demarcations rather than any tangible, physical separations. Consequently, music has long had a social function to assist in the negotiation of identities within communities where 'music has been tied to social rites and unified by them' (Foucault and Boulez 2000: 164). It has also been a means by which the complexities of such negotiations of identity become clear. As Paul Gilroy argues, 'Music and its rituals can be used to create a model whereby identity can be understood neither as a fixed essence nor as a vague and utterly contingent construction to be reinvented by the will and whim of aesthetes, symbolists and language gamers' (1993: 102).

Thus, the 'places constructed through music involve notions of difference and social boundary' (Stokes 1994: 3) but are not concerned with differences and boundaries that are grounded in fact so much as constructed in order to develop identity and community. For the purposes of this chapter, then, identity is best understood as lying somewhere between our sense of what we are and what we might become; is established by the boundaries between what we understand ourselves to be and how we understand ourselves to be different from others and is expressed through a range of cultural practices, including music and fashion.

The method by which identity operates on a structure of 'similarity and difference' (Hall 1997: 17) correlates with the ways in which societies organize themselves, how power systems are structured within them and how meaning is produced to, in part, manage the power systems within a society. This is not least because we shape our identities against the kinds of categorizations that organize the society from which we come. In chapters 3 and 4, we examined gender and saw how stereotypes act as organizing principles that maintain men and women in largely opposing gender roles. In such situations, power relations tend to be weighted towards one group. With regard to cultural identity—be it ethnic, national or regional—stereotypes operate in similar vein 'as part of the maintenance of social and symbolic order' (258). These stereotypes are communicated most clearly through the ways in which groups of people are represented. Stuart Hall (19) asserts the following:

> At the heart of the meaning process in culture then, are two related 'systems of representation' the first enables us to give meaning to the world by constructing a set of correspondences or a chain of equivalences between things—people, objects, events, abstract ideas etc.—and our system of concepts, our conceptual maps. The second depends on constructing a set of correspondences between our conceptual map and a set of signs, arranged or organized into various languages which stand for or represent those concepts.

Thus, if we apply the principles of representation to an understanding of how a particular group of people are constructed, then it is through the ways in which they are talked about, written about, visualized through images of all kinds and discussed that we come to a cultural understanding of what that group is *understood* to be like. This is the heart of the process of representation, which Hall defines as being the 'production of meaning through language' (1997: 17). One of the problems with representations is that they reduce a group of people, made up of any number of individuals with diverse characters and characteristics, to a few 'essences' that are *seen* to identify all. A further significant problem lies in the fact that within any given culture, a dominant group usually wields much of the representative power and thus has an invested interest in maintaining groups which differ from them in marginal positions.

If we begin to unpick such notions of representation by examining ethnicity, for example, then we can begin to see how issues of similarity and difference, of power and marginalization, shape such representations. The very language which we use to discuss such issues is accompanied by associations with the history of race relations. To mark groups out by their ethnicity is in itself to use the power-riddled control systems of culture, and 'there is a difficulty both with creating and using categories, that is, in deciding how many categories there should be and determining who fits where, and with being sure what is being measured' (Fenton 1999: 2). This is not least because personal ethnic ancestries can be extremely complex. There is always the danger that judgements are often primarily decided upon by the colour of a person's skin.

Equally, the language choices used to discuss such issues carry some difficult connotations. The term *race*, for example, is often deemed to be problematic because it has negative associations with past, disproved scientific theories that suggested that different racial groups could be distinguished as different species through the identification of biological and physical differences (Fenton 1999). 'By contrast, the term "ethnic group" is used primarily in contexts of cultural difference, associated above all with an actual or perceived shared ancestry, with language markers, and with national or regional origin' (4).

It is important to note here that cultural difference in itself is not problematic. It is, as Steven Fenton notes, 'a central facet of life-as-lived on both a global and local scale' (1999: 6). It is when cultural difference is stereotyped, based on physical characteristics rather than individual identity constructs, and when it is used as a justification for subordinating a particular group to shut them out from aspects of life as lived and its possible privileges that cultural difference becomes a problem.

Thus, the categorization of culture that relies on the demarcation of difference is a concern because 'one pole of the binary is always the dominant one' (Hall 1997: 235). In looking specifically at black ethnicities, Hall (243) notes these distinctions:

Racialized discourse is structured by a set of binary oppositions. There is the powerful opposition between 'civilization' (white) and 'savagery' (black). There is the opposition between the biological or bodily characteristics of the 'black' and the 'white' 'races', polarized into their extreme opposites—each the signifiers of an absolute difference between human 'types' or species. There are the rich distinctions which cluster around the supposed link between the white 'races' and intellectual development, refinement, learning and knowledge, a belief in reason, the presence of developed institutions, formal government and law, and a 'civilized restraint' in their emotional, sexual and civil life, all of which are associated with 'culture'; and on the other hand, the link between the black 'races' and whatever is instinctual.

Thus, there has been what Hall terms a culture-white/nature-black distinction between white and black 'races' (note Hall's tendency to place the word race in inverted commas to somewhat neutralize its negative connotations), with a privileging of culture and civilization over nature as a marker of human over animal. Thus, there has been, historically at least, a tendency to dehumanize some aspects of black culture in relation to white and, certainly, a subordination of it (Hall 1997).

BLACK MUSIC, COMMUNITIES AND CULTURAL HISTORIES

Music has long been a legitimated space within which marginalized black cultures could find expression; as David Hatch and Stephen Millward note, 'those designated as black have made the major contributions to the development of pop music from its earliest origins' (2000: 88). This contribution builds on a whole tradition of music as a key part of black culture and expression as well as a lack of recognition of the power of music historically so that, as Paul Gilroy would have it, music was a 'grudging gift' (1993: 76) to slave communities. Indeed, Gilroy notes that music was a way of symbolically drawing the boundaries of what was and was not, what is and is not, authentically black and, in particular, notes that this traces itself back to 'slave music [which] signalled its special position of privileged signifier of black authenticity' (91).

This was also a method of drawing together collectively; of carving out and maintaining a community, and, though Gilroy (1993) would argue that this is a somewhat false construct in the much more fragmented contemporary period, for Patricia Maultby, 'the conceptualization of music making as a participatory group activity is evident in the processes by which black Americans prepare for a performance . . . Since the 1950s for example, black music promoters have advertised concerts as social gatherings where active audience involvement is expected' (2000: 92). Thus, music has been an opportunity for black culture to be expressed, alongside the assertion of a sense of community. Through such means, black culture defines its boundaries and maintains its history and traditions.

Equally, this sense of culture has been expressed through dress, where 'in African-American culture, the element of dress in musical performance is as important as the musical sound itself' (Maultby 2000: 93). This emphasis can be seen strongly in hip-hop and rap music, which we will come to later in this chapter, but is also identifiable in other traditionally black musics like gospel and soul. Here, Maultby argues that 'performers establish an image, communicate a philosophy, and create an atmosphere of "aliveness" through the colourful and flamboyant costumes they wear' (93). The focus on the embodiment of music can be seen in the way that 'black people consciously use their entire bodies in musical expression, and music and movement are conceived as a single unit' (94). Embodied expression of this kind remains a way for 'African idiomatic style [to] maintain cultural continuities through the black fashion imagination' (Chandler and Chandler-Smith 2005: 234). Thus, music and dress have become synonymous as methods by which black communities and performers express their own cultural histories, ideas and ideals and mark out communities and cultural spaces.

One such convergence of fashion and music as cultural expression has been identified in jazz music in the early part of the twentieth century, primarily in America. The male jazz performer became synonymous in this period with a particular type of elaborate suit—the zoot suit, cut very squarely, with broad shoulders. This suit became, in its later adoption by young black and Mexican gang members, a powerful 'emblem of ethnicity and a way of negotiating identity' (Cosgrove 1988: 4; see also Craik 2005).

Cosgrove argues that 'the zoot suit was a refusal: a subcultural gesture that refused to concede to the manners of subservience' (1988: 4). It was a method of marking oneself out from a more dominant white culture that evolved as a method by which antiwar attitudes could be embodied since 'wearing a zoot suit was a deliberate and public way of flouting the regulations of rationing' (9). This transgressed the pared down silhouette of the time, informed by the limited use of fabric during and after the Second World War. At the same time, it symbolized 'the enigmas of black culture' (20)—perhaps, more accurately, cultures other than white since, in America especially, the relationship between Mexican and Latino youths and such resistances through music and dress often parallel those of Afro-Caribbean and African American youth. Thus, wearing a zoot suit came to signify a symbolic, subcultural resistance, not of a classed existence per se, which, as we saw in chapter 5, was the locus for much subcultural expression in 1950s, 1960s and 1970s Britain, but an ethnic, lived existence for young men in mid-twentieth-century America.

EMBODYING CULTURAL IDENTITIES: MUSIC AND STYLE

Clearly, 'the zoot suit is more than an exaggerated costume, more than a sartorial statement: it is the bearer of a complex and contradictory history' (Cosgrove 1988: 3). Whilst Jennifer Craik (2005) notes that this suit gradually became part of the repertoire of popular music styles and thus almost a uniform for music, Joshua Sims (1999: 21) establishes the power this particular cut of suit had in the early stages of popular music:

> In order to play white clubs, Little Richard was also suited, but he wore a deviation of the zoot suit; baggy trousered, pocket-chained and long jacketed . . . As for Richard it was a race thing. Fats Domino wore the innocuous uniform of all subservient black performers, the dinner suit when he pumped out his hits like 'Blueberry Hill' and 'Aint that a shame' . . . but Little Richard went for threat, the danger, immediately.

As a result, the power of fashion to symbolically resist the limitations placed upon a particular group, and to be in and of itself confrontational, was established early on in music. Equally, the role that fashion and clothing could play in maintaining and articulating a cultural identity was also in place. It should be no surprise, then, that in writing on both music and fashion, black music has been identified as a place where these two forms of expression powerfully intersect. Much of this discussion has emphasized the significance of the music of the Black Atlantic in this regard.

It is the influential reach of black music and fashion across both industries that make it of significant interest to many writers (see Arnold 2001; Chandler and Chandler-Smith 2005). To others, it is the part that music and fashion have played in creating a space for the articulation of cultural identities and histories that is of greater import (Tulloch 1992; Gilroy 1993). In all cases, the ultimate aim is to examine the way in which black music—in particular, hip hop and rap—articulates itself through lyrics, music and embodiment. This is a way for black identity and cultural expressions to maintain themselves against a historical threat of oppression and possible erasure. This threat was made manifest as much by symbolic as real violence. In societies where whiteness was established as the dominant culture through stereotyping, cultural imperialism and ethnocentricism, much expression sought to apply the ideals of white culture onto other groups and to suggest a sense of whiteness and white culture as 'naturally' superior (see for example Hall 1997; Brown 1965).

This tension becomes particularly important in the Black Diaspora: the movement of black communities from Africa and the West Indies to countries like America. Such moves have a tendency to create more complex cultural identities in subsequent generations with intricate and conflicting national and ethnic allegiances. Thus, diaspora shapes and reshapes the boundaries of identity. Paul Gilroy (1993) would argue this creates what he calls a double consciousness: a sense of being both inside and outside the culture and society within which one lives. This would particularly apply to the second generation—for example, those who have an African heritage but were born in America and whose identities (and the negotiation of them) subsequently exist in a tension between their ancestry as African and their nationality as American.

Paul Gilroy argues that the history of black music as rooted in systems of oppression and subordination is still perceptible in contemporary music, thanks, in part, to double consciousness. This equates to an inner struggle that must be externalized in some way. For him, 'the irrepressible rhythms of the once forbidden drum are often still audible' in hip-hop and rap music, and 'its characteristic syncopations still animate the basic desires—to be free and to be oneself—that are revealed in this counterculture's unique conjunction of body and music' (1993: 76). Indeed, so important did music become to expressing the cultural position of black communities that black music, for Gilroy, became 'the central sign of black cultural value, integrity and autonomy (90).

Gilroy locates the emergence of hip-hop and rap music within the convergence of a number of different areas of culture. In part, burgeoning technologies such as cutting, mixing and sampling gave music an accessible, do-it-yourself aspect, while 'hip hop culture grew out of the cross-fertilisation of African American vernacular cultures with their Caribbean equivalents' (Gilroy 1993: 103). Thus, the forms of hip-hop and rap sounds owe much to black cultural linguistic histories. As a consequence, we see the central role that particular forms of language and accent play in forming cultural expressions of this kind.

Chandler and Chandler-Smith argue that 'if dressing is a language, then black dressing is a dialectical language' (2005: 245). In particular, they acknowledge that this is shaped by a contradictory sense of both belonging and alienation for many African Americans. Early hip-hop and rap music used this dialect to reflect both the exclusions exercised against black communities and some of the transgressive and symbolic ways that such exclusions could be made visible through dress, style and language. In later gangsta rap, this symbolism was amplified and aggressive; growing 'out of the burgeoning Black Music scene in California [gangsta rappers] represented a hardening of attitudes amongst young Black people who, unwilling to wait any longer for a change in their situation through passive political routes, sought to assert their strength through music and visual style' (Arnold 2001: 40). This form of rap was knowingly confrontational in both music and fashion and 'flaunted references to shootings, drug dealing and sexual domination as a mark of power rather than degradation' (Arnold 2001). Here, being an outsider was embraced as a means of exploiting the fear and fascination that surrounded the politics of race in America in the late 1990s.

This confrontational stance was expressed through fashion; 'while early rappers like Public Enemy had used an aggressive stance and military inspired dress to speak of black awareness and the message of Malcolm X, gangstas used hard black leather and Palladium boots to assert their own harsh lifestyle as it already existed rather than seeking change' (Arnold 2001: 41). The history of rap and hip-hop fashion was built on a base of sportswear, where 'artists like Run DMC and LL Cool J had celebrated the swagger given by the obvious wealth of real jewellery, coupled with the laid back kudos of sportswear brands like Adidas and Nike' (11–12). Gangsta rappers developed this language, adding 'work-wear to the sartorial mix, as well as references to prison dress in light denim shirts and baggy jeans worn low slung to reveal the top of boxer shorts' (40).

Other than these very political and belligerent symbolisms, the most important facet of hip-hop and rap fashion is its emphasis on 'conspicuous consumption' (Arnold 2001: 42). In this context, the ostentatious purchase of goods becomes a marker of status within a group. This is not a bourgeois conspicuous consumption of the kind described by Thorstein Veblen (1994) in the nineteenth century, but instead an adoption of such patterns of consumption as a symbolic way of constructing an affluent identity for those not expected to enjoy such a position—historically, at least. This results in something of a visual and lyrical glorification of the limited (and often illegal) avenues available to attain such affluence, revealing concurrently the way more legitimate avenues are closed off.

Affluent consumption is a somewhat natural way for such symbolism to emerge because, as Chandler and Chandler-Smith note, 'why would hip-hop aspire to any other dreams when to be American is to *bling bling*' (2005: 241). Thus, bling is in fitting with notions of the American Dream—the mythological possibility of achievement through hard work that is supposedly open to all. It also simultaneously demonstrates some of the inconsistencies of the social networks (and their attendant myths) within which the appropriation of such a dream can happen—that it may be harder to achieve if one is not white. Thus, the notion of bling has become synonymous with black music as a symbolic way of demonstrating access, of a kind, to a status system from which one would once have been excluded.

Of course, in particular, *bling* describes the kinds of flamboyant jewellery favoured by hip-hop and rap artists: gold pendants and medallions, large 'truck jewellery', diamond watches and earrings and teeth embedded with precious stones or capped with twenty-four-carat gold. This phenomenon is argued to have begun in New York, specifically growing from the opening of the jeweller's Manny's, whose main clientele was understood to be made up of Hell's Angels and 'notorious drug dealers such as Leroy "Nicky" Barnes' (Atolliver and Ossé 2006: 16). Thus, as befits a street style, its origins lay firmly in underground culture.

Atolliver and Ossé define bling as 'anything and everything today in pop culture that expresses wealth to the highest degree', formed by 'the lesson that the hip-hop generation took . . . that in order to be accepted in this society, one had to be successful . . . and mega paid' (2006: 7). Consequently, to have the ability to consume conspicuously was to demonstrate wealth and status, and bling was the method by which this success was made material. Indeed, so central was conspicuous bling to a hip-hop lifestyle that Atolliver and Ossé add to their overview of bling's jewellers and wearers a small postscript which shows readers that 'if you can't afford to buy any diamonds, make your own' using charcoal briquettes and a microwave (2006: 167).

In looking at the operation of hip-hop fashion in the contemporary period, Chandler and Chandler-Smith (2005) highlight the emphasis on 'keeping it real' and the import given to special kinds of 'in' knowledge. Forman notes the following:

> Claiming one's place within Hip Hop culture involves more than simply exhibiting particular consumption patterns, sartorial tastes, or other surface gestures; it also encompasses the demonstration of deeply invested affinities or attitudinal allegiances that shape one's modes of expression and inform the core of both self and group identity simultaneously. (2002: 102)

In relation to this, the necessity to recognize that the subtle details and idio-syncrasies within hip-hop fashions speak volumes is an essential part of op-erating within hip-hop culture. Equally, the sense of do-it-yourself reflects the music style's origins, and making one's own mark is an essential part of hip-hop success (see Arnold, 2001; Chandler and Chandler-Smith, 2005).

As Paul Gilroy argues, hip hop 'routed and re-rooted Caribbean culture [and] set in train a process that was to transform black America's sense of itself and a large portion of the music industry as well' (1993: 33; see also Chan-dler and Chandler-Smith 2005). Hip hop is significant because of its early links to the street and its status as counterculture, where 'fashion becomes a tool of assimilation and nationalism, affluence and materialism and finally cultural transference' (Chandler and Chandler-Smith 2005: 243). Its influence has spread beyond America, becoming what Chandler and Chandler-Smith argue is a 'global dress code' 'that transcends the politics of race' (232). Thus, 'the hip hop movement, . . . reverberates with the reinvention of style which has deeply influenced youth cultures around the world, thereby trans-mitting broader American culture and ideological referents to remote corners of the globe to maximum effect' (234).

INTO THE MAINSTREAM: HIP-HOP MUSIC AND STYLE

Hence, the influence of hip-hop and rap music and the fashions that embody it now reach far beyond its origins in street style and countercultures. It is

in itself a multimillion-dollar global industry. In many ways, this could represent what David Hatch and Stephen Millward see as 'the promotion of the
concept of black music which has been motivated largely by non-musical factors [that] might be described as the marketing of a heritage' (2000: 88–91).
However, the danger of a straightforward cynical adoption and exploitation of
black street credentials by the fashion industry as a signifier of coolness has
been diverted by the active part played by many hip-hop and rap artists and
performers.

The concern has always been that 'comparisons between the earnings and
acclaim achieved by, on the one hand Elvis Presley, and on the other, Chuck
Berry . . . demonstrates the continuing discrepancy in financial reward and
popular acceptance' (Hatch and Millward 2000: 89) between white artists
and black artists. This emerged from a history in which 'in the pop business,
until very recently, it has always been the white musicians and entrepreneurs
who have clearly profited' (Hatch and Millward 2000). The relationship between hip-hop and rap music and the fashion industry has presented a unique
opportunity to redress this imbalance.

In 2005, US rapper Pharrell Williams launched his fashion brands Billionaire Boys Club and Ice Cream, in conjunction with his manager, Robert Walker,
and the Japanese designer Nigo. Billionaire Boys Club produces limited quan-
tities of men's and women's streetwear-cum-preppy cool: jeans and cardigans,
US high school cardigans, check and striped shirts, sneakers and bow ties.
Inevitably, the limited-edition approach gives the brand an inbuilt exclusivity so
essential to the hip-hop sensibility (see Chandler and Chandler-Smith 2005).

Williams himself is a fashion icon. He has also been invited, by Louis Vuitton, to design a jewellery range for the brand. He is apparently on friendly
terms with editor of US *Vogue* and one-woman fashion powerhouse Anna Wintour. He features regularly in magazines like *InStyle, GQ,* international editions
of *Vogue* and the fashion pages of the major international newspapers. How
Williams dresses and his personal fashion taste seem to be almost more important than the music he produces with his band, N.E.R.D.

Williams's style represents a recent shift in hip-hop and rap style. Like all
rappers, sportswear forms the basis of his wardrobe and influences the designs of his label. As he says, 'Sportswear and hip-hop have always been
linked. As a kid, I wore bad T-shirts and plaid pants. I admire Rakim. He was
the best rapper and stylistically, he was about classic sneakers and customized Dapper Dan threads' (Arlidge 2008). But melding with this old-school look
is what the *Guardian* newspaper describes as 'preppy golf chic' (Arlidge 2008),
for which *Giant* magazine coined the phrase 'Return of the Prepster' (Wilbekin
2008). Williams is at the forefront of this look. In both Williams's Billionaire
Boys Club range and also that of his contemporary, André Benjamin (alias
André 3000, one-half of the band OutKast), a more tweedy, upper-middle-class

and polite notion of sportswear is integrated with traditional hip-hop style, re-writing the rules of hip-hop fashion in the twenty-first century.

For Williams, this look is American nerd chic. He has always admitted his nerd credentials, and, of course, they are written into the name of his band. They are also written through many of his fashion choices, such as geeky shirts and chunky sweaters (Figure 11). They are even more clearly reinforced by his role as not only creative driving force, but also model, for Billionaire Boys Club, where, wearing tan chinos, a coral knitted sweater just like mother used to make and a bow tie, Pharrell gives Dr Spock's Vulcan hand gesture.

Like Williams, André Benjamin is, to use the *Guardian's* term, a 'rapper-turned-fashion mogul'; his label Benjamin Bixby is comprised of '1930s-influenced American football clobber' (Mills 2008). At the same time, Benjamin has expressed a fetish for all things British aristocracy, citing Beau Brummel and the Duke of Windsor as some of his style icons. His range is available in the UK, exclusively at Harrods—the retail bolthole of upper-class exclusivity. When in London, he shops at Hackett, the spiritual fashion home of the hunting-and-shooting country set. The *Guardian* describes him as '80% Brideshead' (Mills 2008), referencing Evelyn Waugh's epic story of the fag ends of the British aristocracy in the interwar period.

There is clearly something of a fascination with forms of dress that are deeply rooted in social systems that would initially seem at odds with the

Figure 11 Pharrell Williams in chunky knitwear epitomizing N.E.R.D. chic, March 2009 © arvdix, 2010, used under license from shutterstock.com

values of hip-hop culture. Reappropriating forms of dress so synonymous with very particular classed existences is, of course, within the traditions of sub-cultural style. This is the kind of reappropriation entered into by the Teddy Boys in the 1950s, where the Edwardian suit, a particular embodiment of upper-class nobility, was parodied by young working-class men who wore this look for leisure (see Cohen 2002; Hebdige 1979). In effect, an object whose traditional class values would have rendered it unavailable to some becomes the means by which issues of separation, oppression and subordination can be symbolically played out. Thus, the wearing of what one should not wear becomes a sort of rebellion, a method of accessing privileged experiences intended for someone else.

We might understand this as an example of what Chandler and Chandler-Smith describe as 'a reach for a kind of nobility' (2005: 241). It might be a more literal reach for nobility—particularly in the case of Benjamin—than Chandler and Chandler-Smith describe. But, just as with the hip-hop artists and fans whom they consider as in 'pursuit of recognition and upward mobil-ity through wearing the "in" fashion' (2005: 241), this way of dressing is a method of both accessing and displaying a look synonymous with class cul-tures historically at odds with black hip-hop style. It equally suggests an ability to access the tastes and knowledge of other classed groups.

As such, we might argue that fashion—for both performers and fans of hip hop—seems to be related to cultural capital. 'Cultural capital' is the term used by Pierre Bourdieu (1984) to describe the kinds of knowledge that act as a currency with which we negotiate our lives. In greater part, what Bourdieu describes is the kind of value an individual is likely to have in the society in which they live, which is largely determined by the individual's level of educa-tion. The more education one has, the more possibilities for work and leisure one has access to, in part because this should also equate to greater afflu-ence and a more privileged existence, which gains greater social respect.

Thus, 'cultural capital' can translate into economic capital. What Chandler and Chandler-Smith (2005) describe is what John Fiske might term 'popular cultural capital' (1989: 135): knowledge of the kind not provided by the formal education system, but knowledge that has value in particular social groups. For performers and fans of hip hop, knowing what to buy and where to get it, how to wear it and in some cases how to customize it displays this popular cultural capital and is a way of gaining status within the culture of hip-hop music.

Celebrity fashion ranges are not exclusive to musicians working in music of black origin, as we saw in chapter 2. However, there does seem to be a particu-lar attitude amongst artists like Williams and Benjamin for whom gaining new access to the fashion industry via a career in music also seems to be a way to accrue more formal cultural capital. There is no sense in the media coverage of such brands that these artists are merely fronting the range. Instead, they take pride in articulating particularly active roles which require them to develop skills that have nothing to do with performing hip-hop music per se.

For Benjamin Bixby, André 3000 'makes factory visits, has the help of collectors and fashion archivists, and employs a technical director and a vice-president of design' (Mills 2008). He takes his part here very seriously, telling the *Guardian* that 'I would like to go to fashion school to learn the correct terminology and the correct technique'. He argues that 'this is not a celebrity brand. I am not a fan of celebrity brands to be honest' (Mills 2008), and, in so doing, Benjamin aims to mark himself out not as part of the glut of celebrity ranges, but as someone who just happens to be active in both the music and fashion industries. In similar vein, Pharrell Williams, when asked to design his jewellery range for Louis Vuitton, attended trade shows in Europe and spent time in the offices and factories where his designs would be produced and refined (see freshnessmag.com 2008).

In business, then, 'keeping it real' might have a different meaning, but it is just as important for these hip-hop artists' professional identities as it is for their subcultural ones. Thus, music has long been a legitimate space for black individuals to gain success and wealth, but it also represents a means by which other cultural areas come to be accessed, subsequently facilitating the accrual of new knowledge. Consequently, it is in the connection between black forms of music and fashion that opportunities for self-development exist: the development of technical knowledge, professional knowledge and historical knowledge and, alongside these, a particular pride in doing these things right.

In discussing the origins of his particular patterns of taste in dress, André Benjamin hints at the key part that familial relationships—or, in his case, a lack of them—plays in their formation; 'Benjamin became fascinated by the understated Anglophilia and Gatsbyish exotica of Ralph Lauren adverts, which peddled dress codes that appeared to have been handed down from father to son like family heirlooms' (Mills 2008). Benjamin himself argues that 'I think a lot of African-American kids don't have fathers to teach them how to dress, so you end up being taught by pictures in magazines and movies. You see cowboys, Indians, old Hollywood films, Cary Grant. It has an effect on you' (Mills 2008). As such, dressing seems to be a way of reaching back and creating an ancestral trajectory from which one's own style, masculinity and, therefore, identity can be understood to have grown. Here, 'clothing choices signify cultural points of identification and self-identity' (Forman 2002: 124).

BEYONCÉ, FASHION AND THE FAMILY BUSINESS

Whilst a sense of familial ancestry is important in its absence in the case of André Benjamin's personal approach to both dressing and design, it is the ready presence of a familial ancestry that shapes Beyoncé Knowles's relationship to fashion and style. With the band Destiny's Child, she long fulfilled a tradition identified by Jacqueline Warwick (2007) of embedding female black music in family relationships: her father as manager, her mother Tina Knowles as stylist and her cousin Kelly Rowland as band member. Destiny's Child also marketed a very specific notion of sisterhood with songs like 'Independent Women' drew on 'the notion of sisterhood in 1970s feminist thought [that] may have been partly inspired by the relationships among girl group singers' (Warwick 2007: 18). In the case of both the girl bands of the 1970s and Destiny's Child, the notion of a family business that extends beyond sisterhood is of significant importance to the way in which the bands are formed.

This concept of family converges in the fashion range, House of Dereon, established by Tina Knowles. The name itself is a family one—the maiden name of Beyoncé's maternal grandmother. The range was originally launched in 2006 as a streetwear brand for younger women and was later relaunched as something with more upmarket elements: evening wear, 1940s-inspired suits with fur collars and the tagline 'Couture, Kick, Soul'.

Whilst this, like many celebrity brands, offers an opportunity for the consumer to buy into Beyoncé's style, it also places her mother centre stage. Tina Knowles has long designed Beyoncé's stage outfits during her solo outings and also acted as stylist for Destiny's Child. In the advertising for this brand, there is a particularly strong emphasis on this idea of a female lineage. Beyoncé models for the brand's advertising campaigns. Her sister Solange sometimes features. Significantly, in most of the images, three generations of Knowles women are present: Beyoncé as the face of the brand; Tina Knowles as its creative force shown dressing and styling her daughter in many images; Grandmother Dereon's picture in the background establishes its ancestral inspiration.

This sense of family might be embedded both in personal familial ties but also in more general notions of black cultural identities in the Black Atlantic. As Paul Gilroy has argued, 'the idea of racial community as a family has been invoked and appealed to as a means to signify connectedness and experiential continuity that is everywhere denied by the profane realities of black life amidst the debris of de-industrialisation' (1993: 99). Thus, in consumer culture, this notion of interconnectedness as a much cited—though, as Gilroy (1993) argues, somewhat essentializing—notion of black identity has the potential to be a powerful symbol arguably brought into play as a layer of reference in the marketing for House of Dereon. This, we might propose, is an extension of a tendency to use 'the discourse of authenticity [which] has been a notable presence in the mass marketing of successive black folk cultural forms to white audiences' (99).

Equally, as Jacqueline Warwick (2007) has established, family relation-ships formed the foundation of many female groups, from black and Latino backgrounds in particular, in the 1960s. Taking, for example, The Ronettes, she argues that 'the fact [they] were related was an important component of their success. For one thing, the girls had a distinctive appearance and looked very much alike so that they were a visually striking trio. Under the guidance of their mother and aunts they cultivated a unique look, with teased up hair, dramatic make-up and matching clothes' (185).

For Warwick, this emphasis on the family had two effects. First, it gave a context to female music-making, placing it in the traditional realm of the femi-nine, often termed the 'domestic' sphere. In relation to this, it secondly had a protective effect: it provided greater safety from possible exploitations of all kinds, both physically and emotionally, for young women. In closing ranks in both their engagement with the music and the fashion industries, then, the Knowleses not only provide opportunities for one another, but also form a co-hesive and protective unit in which the idea of family unity—and, in particular, female unity—is of central importance.

Equally, female performers like Beyoncé offer something of an alternative to the more negative representation of femininity in some hip-hop and rap music. Much writing on this form of music has seen it as riddled with the mi-sogynistic treatment of female bodies. This is evidenced in many videos by male hip-hop performers, where women play peripheral roles, such as danc-ers dressed like hookers, valued only for their bodies (see Caracino and Scott 2008). Beyoncé is an example of a female hip-hop performer 'whose fashion choices are focused on "real" women-centred concepts of fashion' (Chandler and Chandler-Smith 2005: 244). These relate to her own construction of her-self as an African American woman with an African American woman's body, which she dresses to emphasis its curvaceousness (Figure 12).

The range Apple Bottoms by male hip-hop star Nelly makes an even clearer declaration of its celebration of this 'real' female body. The company profile is marketed as 'a clothing line that caters to trendsetting women of all shapes and sizes. Celebrating and liberating the natural curves of a woman's body is Apple Bottom's supreme mission' (see Apple Bottoms shop n.d.): this de-spite the fact that a UK size 16 equates to XXL.

When the real body and curves are evoked by this brand, then, the focus is clearly placed on one particular part of the body. The booty as a marker of non-white womanhood has been important to the public profile of not just this brand, but also to non-white female hip-hop artists including Beyoncé, Rhianna and Latin American Jennifer Lopez. This fascination finds its locus in what Janell Hobson has argued is 'a history of enslavement, colonial con-quest and ethnographic exhibition [which] variously labelled the black female body "grotesque", "strange", "unfeminine", "lascivious" and "obscene". This

Figure 12   Beyoncé dresses to amplify her curves, a woman-centred approach to fashioning the body, September 2009 © arvdix, 2010, used under license from shutterstock.com

negative attitude to the black female body targets one aspect of the body in particular: the buttocks' (2003: 87).

CULTURAL IDENTITY AND THE BLACK FEMALE BODY

The historical interest in the black female body of which Hobson talks traces its history to what we now understand as racist scientific methodologies which focused on attempts to understand racial difference as a hierarchy. These approaches aimed ultimately to prove an a priori attitude—that whiteness equated to a 'natural', racial elite (see Hall 1997). Such enquiries were at their most virulent in the late eighteenth and early nineteenth centuries. These scientific methods focused a great amount of attention on bodily characteristics fed by a fascination with bodily difference. These interests subsequently carried over into questionable popular entertainments of the time. As Stephen J. Gould notes, in this period, 'when anthropological theory assessed as subhuman both malformed Caucasians and the normal representatives of other races, the exhibition of unusual humans became a profitable business both in upper-class salons and in street-side stalls' (1985: 292). 'Supposed savages were a mainstay of these exhibitions' (293).

One of the most important and recounted stories (Gould 1985) of such shows centres on a woman named Saartjie Baartman who was encouraged to go to Europe by the brother of her 'slave-owner' in the belief that participating in these shows could bring her wealth and freedom. Here, she was called the 'Hottentot Venus'. For Stephen Gould, this name makes the relationship between Baartman and those both exhibiting and looking at her very clear. The focus is placed keenly on notions of her perceived fecundity and exotic, lascivious sexuality—all seen to be embodied in a particular female form very different from the white female ideal. This sense of difference was located in a fascination with two areas of her body which were conceptualized as being in anatomical contrast to the white female body: her genitalia and her buttocks.

After her death in 1815, Baartman's body was dissected by the anatomist Georges Cuvier, who focused much of his 'scientific' fascination on these two parts of the body. From his investigations of a few individuals from various parts of Africa, Cuvier attempted to understand and construct a hierarchy of racial identity embedded in bodily difference; 'Cuvier regarded Hottentots as the most bestial of people', partly because, as Stephen Gould also notes, 'he fell into an interesting error, arising from the same false association that had inspired public fascination with Saartjie—sexuality with animality' (1985: 299). As Gould writes, 'Cuvier focused on an unsolved mystery surrounding each of her unusual features. Europeans had long wondered whether the large buttocks were fatty, muscular, or perhaps even supported by a previously unknown bone' (297).

In view of his questionable findings, Cuvier attempted to construct links between bodily characteristics—primarily skin colour, alongside other 'distinguishing' bodily characteristics—and degrees of animal nature (as opposed to Western, white civilization). In the contemporary period, writers like Martin Stokes encourage us to recognize that 'ethnicities are to be understood in terms of the construction, maintenance and negotiation of boundaries' (1994: 6); in the case of the Hottentot Venus and the scientific methodologies that aimed to study race in the late eighteenth, nineteenth and early twentieth centuries, we see it reduced to 'the putative social "essences"' (6).

If, as Stokes also argues, 'performance is a vital tool in the hands of performers themselves in socially acknowledged games of prestige and power' (1994: 97), then, in connecting fashion and music together, we might understand performers like Beyoncé as reclaiming cultural and economic power. Here, they might be seen to take power not only with regard to their own part in the music industry and thus conceptually over both cultural spaces—establishing some autonomy for themselves—and cultural identities: through music, lyrics and the presentation of cultural histories and identities. This can equally apply to their

attitudes to bodies shaped by a celebration of physical attributes that had previously been open to ridicule.

Thus, the conflation of contemporary black music with a host of cultural expressions—'fashion, style and language and personal history' (Ogbar 2007:
68)—has presented, in many senses, opportunities for black musicians both
male and female to enter into a variety of areas of cultural life. This might be
viewed as having both positive and negative traits because, as Jeffrey Ogbar
argues, 'unlike the hyperexploited black musicians of earlier generations; hip-
hop entrepreneurs, for better or worse, have embraced capitalist principles
with zeal, boldness and business savvy' (177). This seemingly quite uncriti-
cal involvement in a capitalist consumer culture is viewed with suspicion by
some (see Ogbar 2007) but is somewhat forgiven in a group of individuals for
whom participation of this kind was difficult for so long. Thus, the involvement
of black music stars in the fashion industry is part of an 'incredible expan-
sion of commercial opportunity for members of the hip-hop generation beyond
rapping' (176).

NATIONAL IDENTITIES

The notion of cultural community can be identified strongly in the cultures
of black music, made more emphatic through its relationship to fashion and
style. But such a sense of cultural community does not, of course, work exclusively in relation to ethnic identities. Such notions apply as strongly, in music,
to national identities. We have seen already how cultural identities can be
complex—difficult to define and contradictory—in diasporic communities; it
would be a mistake to see national identity as more straightforward.

As Keith Cameron writes, it is 'difficult . . . to define a nation . . . the concept of the nation varies according to the historical moment, geographical situation, linguistic affiliations, political climate etc' (1999: 1). Nations are fluid,
their populations constantly in flux. However, Benedict Anderson (1991), Lynn
Williams (1999) and Susan Hayward (1999) all demonstrate how the very
concept of *nation* has been something not necessarily tangible or easily defined, but certainly imagined, constructed and reconstructed. Here, 'the bond-
ing and, where necessary, assimilatory functions of language are thus crucial
to nationalist ideology' (Williams 1999: 8). Such a sense of community 'plays
a vital role in maintaining social order' (Hayward 1999: 93). Consequently,
as part of the social discourse that surrounds everyday life, and despite its
imagined status, a national identity became part of the context within which
individuals constructed their sense of self.

Since it is primarily an imagined concept, Fiona Clampin argues that 'defining the national in art has always been a contentious issue, particularly

in music which is believed to be free from political, social and cultural associations because of its "abstract" nature' (1999: 64). Nonetheless, as part of cultural life and as a method by which identities are established and played out, concerns around nation and the articulation of it have found a locus in music. For example, Clampin describes how 'at the beginning of the 20th Century composers in Britain were particularly anxious to create a sense of national identity in music' (64). Whilst she notes that such articulations of nation are not without their problems, her work establishes the part that national identity can play in creative pursuits, including the production of music.

AMERICANA

A notion of an American national identity has been important to a diverse range of performers whose presentation and style might come to be defined under the broad term *Americana*. According to the Web site of the Americana Music Association, 'Americana is music that honors and is derived from the traditions of American roots music. It is music inspired by American culture traditions which is not only represented in classic man made/roots based sounds but also through new and contemporary artists whose music is clearly inspired by these great traditions' (see Americana Music Association n.d.). That the site and the association exist at all demonstrates the central role privileged to the American in a great deal of American music. As a genre, it is vast. As Barry Mazor writes in *No Depression,* a magazine devoted to American 'roots' music, 'Robert Plant, Joan Baez, Glen Campbell and Charlie Louvin, despite their very different career starting places, are all being presented as Americana acts. Darius Rucker and Jewel are country. Taylor Swift and Alison Krauss are topping the pop album charts' (2009).

BRUCE SPRINGSTEEN: DRESSING THE AMERICAN WORKING-CLASS HERO

On the cover of his album *Born in the USA,* released in 1984, Bruce Springsteen gives a visual articulation of his position as 'the voice of blue-collar America' (Wazir 2002). On a background of the red and white stripes of the US flag, Springsteen posits the archetype of a stereotypical, American, working-class identity. Photographed by Annie Leibovitz, the image focuses on Springsteen's rear. Wearing blue jeans and a white T-shirt, his muscular body hints at an active working life; the red rag in his pocket suggests a particular kind of working life.

As Tim Edensor writes, 'Clothing is, of course, highly symbolic as an expression of national identity. In ceremonies, folk dancing, tourist displays and official engagements, clothing becomes an important marker of national identity' (2002: 108). He notes that, in more contemporary terms, 'traditional elements are fused with modern designs. Here national identity is expressed as *style*' (108). Springsteen presents the stylization of American working-class identity on this album cover and, in doing so, emphasizes the 'everyman aspect of [his] music [which] best describes his ongoing appeal to his audience' (Wazir 2002). As Jim Cullen notes, Springsteen wrote 'about situations he knew first-hand. For much of his career this meant charting the psychic or external landscapes of the white working class to which he belonged. He was able to describe, and embody, a familiar American Dream of such people because he shared it' (2005: 67).

Thus, Springsteen embodied ideals in relation to American identity and, more specifically, American working-class identity in a number of ways: through his performances, movements, gestures and musical references and also through his body and style. Aaron A. Fox sees country music as the 'roots' of much of what would be termed Americana, 'a class specific cultural response to changes in the regional, national and global economy in which American blue-collar manual workers have experienced a loss of both cultural identity and economic security' (2004: 21). In the early days of country, such identities were embodied by 'the cowboy persona' which 'envelop[ed] country music. Cowboy hats and boots became standard uniforms for country music performers' (Harkins 2004: 95). This offered 'romantic possibilities' (Harkins 2004). Equally, such constructions make clear the central part that clothing plays in the embodiment of national identities no matter how romanticized or imagined these may be.

In Springsteen, we see a convergence of concerns about national and classed identity embodied through music and dress. Whilst Cullen (2005) rightly notes that in focusing on such concerns, Springsteen ignored questions about ethnic identity in relation to American-ness, nonetheless, articulations of national identity through music and dress demonstrate similar symbolic resistances to those of race. These all circulate around the remembrance of cultural identities whether consciously adopted or not.

CONCLUSION

Thus, the origins of these types of music and embodied styles begin with roots music but diverge in different ways. At the core of these styles is the urge to mark out cultural histories. These styles have at their heart a sense of an authentic identity which, whilst it may, in truth, be nothing other than an imaginary construct, is nonetheless an important marker of a cultural identity for many. Of course, what constitutes an authentic American identity, then, is always in question.

Equally, what constitutes authenticity itself is fluid, too. In the case of hip hop and other types of contemporary black music, what we understand to be authenticity is a response to past denials of access to success, money and the trappings these can provide. Gaining access here is integral to how hip-hop music comes to symbolize.

Americana, as the music of the American working class, shares similar concerns about the limitations that may result from the possession of a particular kind of identity. But the authentic articulation of this identity through fashion rests on maintaining a sense of a stable style—a romanticized look that is *seen* to be rooted in traditions—rather than an increasing participation in areas of consumer culture. Thus, just as we saw in chapter 3, a congruence between an attitude to fashion and an adornment which communicates an identity, which matches the themes of the music, is integral to the power of music genres which self-consciously maintain a sense of roots. This seems to demonstrate the potential of music and fashion, when welded together, to signal not just an individual, but also a political engagement with ideas of personal and collective identity, providing a means by which such identities can be made visible and material.

–7–

Spectacle and Sexuality: Music, Clothes and Queer Bodies

In 2006, a trail of twenty dark-caped figures stalked around Hammersmith in West London, followed by gangs of music fans. This ominous parade of grim reapers—faces hidden by dark hoods—announced a one-off show by the American band My Chemical Romance to be held in August that year at Hammersmith Palais as a precursor to a new album entitled *The Black Parade*. The album aimed to tell the story of a character called only 'the Patient'. This character's death at the start of the album heralds a journey through the afterlife represented through the narrative device of the street parade.

For the tour which both preceded and then accompanied the global release of this album, the band renamed themselves after the album title and costumed themselves in eighteenth-century, military-inspired black uniforms—evocative partly of toy soldiers and partly of Halloween skeleton suits thanks to white-piped details on breastplates and epaulettes (Figure 13). These uniforms were revealed only after the lead singer, Gerard Way—who was wheeled onto stage on a hospital trolley—removed his surgical gown. The revelation of his and his bandmates' uniformed bodies was intended to represent the move into the afterlife that was a focal point for most of the theatrics of the show.

MORAL PANICS: EMO FASHION

In a band which might be understood to have a close relation to the emo subculture, whether technically part of it or not a creative focus on notions of death and deathliness would seem wholly appropriate. Growing partly out of the American punk scene of the 1990s and partly also a substrata of goth, emo shares similar 'primary values . . . expressed through visually perceptible aspects of personal style: dress, coiffure, jewelry and tattoos and other bodily modifications. Goths are determined to face down death, as it were, and they achieve this almost entirely through the eroticization or even the simple valorization of appearances and objects associated with morbidity and decay' (Siegel 2005: 19).

Figure 13 Frank Iero of My Chemical Romance in his *Black Parade* uniform. © Adam Gasson, 2010, used under license from shutterstock.com

Thanks to the theatrics which formed both the promotional campaign for the tour and the tour itself, in August 2006, emo seemed to take centre stage in much media debate, with My Chemical Romance as its poster boys. On 16 August 2006, in the UK, the *Daily Mail* newspaper issued a stark warning to its readers, embedded in which was the clear indication that this readership must be largely made up of the middle-class parents of teenage children.

In an article entitled 'EMO Cult Warning for Parents', concerns are predictably focused on the content of emo music—its morbidity and a notion (generally unproved but regularly re-emerging) that such music culture might feed into depression and melancholia for young music fans (Sands 2006). In this article, there is a clear inference that emo glamorizes somatic and psychological symptoms like self-harming. However, whatever the validity of such concerns about content, even more attention in this article is directed towards the 'look' of emo and, even more particularly, the stranglehold this look was seen as having on youth fashion generally: 'Flicking through the autumn glossy fashion magazines, I noticed that some of the models did not look very well. A few of them appeared to be dead. This is because one of the key looks, especially at the younger end of the fashion spectrum is Goth' (Sands 2006).

As we saw in chapter 5, moral panics around youth culture looks are noth-ing new: each new subcultural style seems to herald—to the mass media, at least—the possibility of a new degradation of middle-class social norms and a younger generation more troubled than those before. But we also see the powerful part that fashion and dress plays in symbolizing both youth itself, with all its dark uncertainties, and the perceived (rightly or wrongly) power of the fashion and music industries to shape the tastes and behaviours of a whole generation, to hold a cultish power over young minds. These moral pan-ics around any individual subculture become all the more clear when a news-paper argues that 'it is irresponsible for the fashion and music cultures to encourage it' (Sands 2006).

Of course, as we saw in chapter 5, parental concern, be it family, media or state, does little to dissuade young people from their interests, obsessions and subcultural identities. Equally, such negative media coverage gives a very one-sided view, failing to see how subcultural membership might demonstrate a more critical engagement with the world. Carol Siegel sees goth culture as a 'stylistic departure from rationalism' (2005: 18). This creates 'new bodily plea-sures . . . ultimately to enact a resistance to the dominant powers of our so-ciety which function to structure our lives in ways beneficial to the state' (16).

STYLE OVER SUBSTANCE? PROGRESSIVE ROCK

The Black Parade was primarily a concept album because, in and of itself, it aimed to create a self-contained narrative augmented by the theatrical presen-tation both in terms of staging and promotion. As such, much about this pack-age seemed to borrow from some of the most important musical moments of thirty years earlier. Both the creation of a cohesive musical narrative through the album and an emphasis on the power of theatrical imagery—much of this focused on the body—seemed to hark back to the values and strategies of the progressive rock, or 'prog rock', of the 1970s.

Kevin Holm Hudson (2002) argues that prog rock was a subgenre of rock music which in its very inception demonstrated the difficulties of defining and organizing rock music. In prog rock, the emphasis tended to be placed on music which 'aimed at incorporating some degree of cultivated musical influ-ence' (Holm Hudson 2002: 2). This aimed to create high-end mass or popular culture through the inclusion of elements from, very often, classical music. This has meant that whilst some define prog rock from a musicology perspec-tive, seeing it as 'a style of self-consciously complex rock often associated with prominent keyboards, complex metric shifts, fantastic (often mythological or metaphysical) lyrics, and an emphasis on flashy virtuosity' (Holm Hudson 2002), for many, prog rock has become associated just as strongly with the visual elements of performance.

During the 1975 tour for the album *A Lamb Lies Down on Broadway*, lead singer Peter Gabriel unveiled one of the most outlandish costumes ever to be seen in a rock music performance. Gabriel is well known for many surreal and eerily theatrical costumed performances during his tenure with the band Genesis. These included the donning of a fox mask and red dress for the finale of 'The Musical Box' in 1972–73, a flower with petals worn around his head and his body covered in a cat suit—somewhat resonant of a child's school production costume—and a cloak with a winged headpiece for 'Watcher of the Skies' in 1974 (Figure 14).

Eight-millimetre footage of the shows in Bern, Germany, in 1975 show Gabriel's presentation of a strange amorphous, nebulous and lumpy figure and what seems like a rather bewildered reaction from the audience of fans. Gabriel is indiscernible in this costume. The only human characteristics of this figure are the arms and the legs, and, as he unfolds himself from a crouching position, a very ordinary red party balloon inflates, extraordinarily, between his legs.

Strictly speaking, this emphasis on visual theatrics does not in itself define prog rock, but writers like Holm Hudson (2002) and Katherine Charlton (1998)

Figure 14   Peter Gabriel in his costume for 'Watcher of the Skies', 1974. © Peter Albrektsen, 2010, used under license from shutterstock.com

agree that a convergence between prog rock artists and what might be better termed as art rock bands like Roxy Music, Velvet Underground and Talking Heads emphasized the visual aspects. Here, many bands 'appropriate[d] an image in a cool, ironic way reminiscent of 1960s pop artists' (Holm Hudson 2002: 2). Prog rock thus represented something of a convergence of music and art culture, but for many this was either a betrayal of the core values of music or ridiculous theatrics that had a self-indulgent disregard for real life. One blogger wrote the following:

> The worst thing about prog has always been its image, in fact it doesn't have much of a image at all and if it does, it's a totally random and ridiculous one . . . Progs 'image' is one of the main reasons it is so unpopular with the media . . . Comparing it to pop punk is ridiculous. Pop punk bands (and punk bands in general) have the entire 'we're rebels, we're misfits' image going for them, and kids everywhere eat it up . . . What does prog have? . . . A bunch of ugly old farts in halloween costumes? . . . How is that a marketable image? (Booboo, 2006)

Whilst this music fan argues that prog rock lacked marketability—perhaps a peculiarly twenty-first-century attitude to the values and purpose of popular music—prog rock was unpopular with many music critics, and its emphasis on style over substance was clearly a significant part of the reason (Sheinbaum 2002). In such critiques, 'authenticity was characteristically the key weapon: the farther a progressive rock album was from rock's natural rhythm-and-blues roots, from the ideals of "natural" unstudied simplicity, the more seditious and treasonous the result' (21). Thus, as Sheinbaum also notes, 'when considering progressive rock within a more general history of rock music, the style and its chief progenitors [are seen] as little more than a blip on the radar screen' (22).

ART ROCK, AUTHENTICITY AND THE AVANT-GARDE

These negative attitudes towards prog rock can be traced, to some extent, to a suspicion of a music form that seemed to betray rock music's history, embedded in countercultural styles—the cultural roots of black music and working-class resistances. There was clearly a fear that 'progressive rock, which supposedly eschews those roots in favour of "artistic" complexities, results in a "hollow emptiness", in a degeneration of rock's former glory' (Sheinbaum 2002: 23). Most of these negative evaluations are made on the basis of how rock music should be positioned and understood as part of culture; where it is placed in the dialogue between high and low culture and what its very purpose should be.

Much of this tension focused implicitly on the visual and the role of the body in music performance. To a great extent, such attitudes seem to oscillate around long-held ideas about how types of music have defined themselves in terms of a perceived authenticity. Such concerns would seem to find congruence with some of the points discussed in the introduction to this book. Here, I argued, in support of ideas already presented by Noel McLoughlin (2000), that the lack of discussion of the relationship between music and fashion in either music journalism or the academy may well be the result of a general negation of artifice in music performance; the enjoyment and expression found in physical image can only threaten the integrity of a music style whose values are bound up in notions of authentic purity, however questionable these might be.

Nonetheless, the visual elements of performance are undoubtedly important, which must suggest that physical image has always seemed to be more of a problem for those writing about music than making it. Indeed, those who aspired to art rock postures were no doubt aiming towards a position as the avant-garde, which in its very definition requires a stance at odds with the usual, upheld values which Eugene Ionesco describes as 'opposition and rupture . . . While most writers, artists and thinkers believe they belong to their time, the revolutionary . . . feels he is running counter to his time' (cited in Calinescu 1987: 119).

Robert Adlington defines the term *avant-garde* as 'a regularly utilized denomination in the 1930s and 1940s [which] became a more fashionable designation for innovative and experimental movements in the arts even later, in the 1950s and 1960s' (2009: 15). On stage in avant-garde performances there is a recognition of the power of the body as a locus for such ideas. After all, 'the history of the theatre is the history of the transformation of the human form' (Schlemmer 1961: 17). Thus, the focus on the visual image in progressive rock and in subsequent performances that place the body, artistic expression and performance at the forefront may—though music critics have often identified conservatism and an emptiness of meaning—have radical potential.

The Black Parade was perhaps in itself not revolutionary. Yet much symbolism was located here despite the attempts of critics and writers to find little or no meaning in the way rock musicians looked. In turn, such symbolism has played a part in shaping and changing cultural ideas, ideals and stereotypes. It is the power of physical image—with the body at the fore—to affect change and to perform resistance that forms the locus of this chapter.

The notion of resistance of different kinds, as embodied through fashion and style, has underpinned discussions in many of the chapters in this book. The importance of stylistic inventions which present the body not as *fashioned*, but instead more clearly as *costumed,* are first emphasized here. More specifically, the importance of the visual presentation of the body in challenging ways for performers representing marginalized groups is considered through an analysis of the carnivalesque qualities identifiable in the stylistic constructions of queer music performers.

Thus, this chapter argues that the body is an important location for the making of resistances, and it is the very marginalization of the body in music that gives it a natural congruence for challenging resistances in some of the examples that will be discussed here. It will be argued that the satirization and exaggeration of conventional and, later, the display of unconventional bodies by queer performers, in particular, aims to reveal and ridicule mainstream notions of gender, performance and physicality. This flight from rational, mainstream representations of the body allows a break into symbolic emancipation for groups marginalized or underrepresented within the music industry and the media more generally.

BOWIE, BODIES, GENDER AND SEXUALITY

We have considered issues of gender in relation to fashion and clothing throughout this book. In chapters 3, 4 and 5, we examined some of the different ways that bodies are constructed along seemingly fixed, definitely normalized models of appropriate behaviour. Such notions remain important when ideas around sexuality and the body come into consideration. As Stephen Whittle notes, 'gender was irrevocably connected to [the] biological construction of sex difference' (2005: 118), and much queer performance and, indeed, the body of ideas organized as 'queer theory' aims to question this 'hegemony of gendering' (116).

This way of thinking endeavours to work towards the 'deconstruction and the refusal of labels of personal sexual activity . . . [alongside] . . . the removal of pathologies of sexuality and gendered behaviour' (Whittle 2005: 117). The body is a natural site for such questions to be posited since it is through the body as a biological object that gender and, in relation to this, sexuality are established and made visible.

In writings on music, one of the few performers who has been discussed in terms of fashioned image without losing any of his value as a musician is David Bowie. In particular, his attempts to rewrite gender boundaries and, indeed, his own and others' perceptions of sexuality in the 1970s have been of interest to writers. Alongside this, there has been an acknowledgement by writers like Simon Frith (1988) that, in the case of Bowie, the measured artifice with which he approached the task of being a musician is part of the musical point. This seems to have justified a discussion of his body and clothing to a degree that is not seen for many other performers.

As part of the glam rock movement, Bowie used clothing as a challenge to existing forms of countercultural signification—in particular, the kind of anti-glamour, anti-fashion dress-down stylistic conventions of hippy (see Auslander 2006). Thus, Bowie's 'emphasis has always been on art as the invention of self' (Frith 1988: 132). The fact that Bowie seemed to utilize himself as an artwork has validated his use of clothing and fashion as authentic. As Frith argues, 'to appreciate Bowie was not just to like his music or his shows or his looks, but also to enjoy the way he set himself up as a commercial image' (132). The fact that he appeared to be using himself as a lens through which an audience might question their own values was a worthy and cerebral use of a body. His manifestation of different characters and of new ways of conceptualizing gender identities demonstrated other possible ways of thinking. He experimented with roles, playing parts rather than trying to reveal his true self, thus proposing new methods of identity construction. This demonstrated Bowie's complex understanding of human identities and subjectivities, alongside his ability to appreciate and 'posit identity as something entirely malleable and open to radical redefinition, a principle on which Bowie built his entire career' (Auslander 2006: 71).

Thus, David Bowie revealed the artifice lurking behind the veneer of authenticity in identities of all kinds, both on and off stage. This was seen to be an authentic creative act. The most important justification for this was that he was stage-managing himself. As such, he got away with what, in other contexts, might have seemed a much more cynical manipulation. Still, this had implications for the audience's understanding of Bowie as they searched for the authentic identity expected from music stars. Philip Auslander (2006) notes that the audience for Ziggy's last gig at the Hammersmith Odeon, 3 July 1979, could not separate the end of Ziggy from the end of Bowie. As far as they were concerned, Bowie was Ziggy. The ideology of music that shaped audience engagement did not allow for role-playing of this kind.

Bowie was at the heart of a period in music that began to establish the possibilities of mutable identities and the joy of dressing up for musicians. This has come to be adopted in a number of ways, not least in marketing ploys that demand changes of image to both keep audiences interested and money being spent in the demonstration of allegiance (a little like the sports teams who change their strip every season so their fans must constantly keep up to date). But in his earlier incarnations he also provided a model for resistance on the grounds of sexuality via representations of the self that dealt in ambiguities of gender. These were amplified thanks to his declaration of bisexuality in the 1970s. Michael Bronski (2007) made the following comments:

> If the Rolling Stones shocked middle-class sensibilities with their rough, thrusting swagger, it was Ziggy Stardust—David Bowie—who in 1972 singlehandedly invented glam rock, making androgyny, glitter, face paint, and ambi-sexual postur-

ing the newest threat to red-blooded American youth, spawning artists such as KISS and Boy George. Bowie claimed in 1972 that he was bisexual and then ten years later claimed that he did that just to get attention—more attention than cross-dressing, wearing make-up, kissing men on stage, and singing about alien sex? But it didn't really matter, for millions of young listeners Bowie's image and message was that imagination and sexual desire mattered more than gender and sexual orientation.

QUEER THEORY, QUEER IDENTITIES

In many ways, these messages which seek to reject fixed notions of gender and definitions of sexuality echo the concerns of many queer artists, writers and thinkers. Queer theory is a body of work which endeavours to question the fixed models of human sexual behaviour, linked to gender, that form mainstream social relations. These fixed models tend to oscillate around the notion of heterosexuality as normal, so that much of culture is subsequently shaped around heteronormative notions of sexual desire and human relationships. Indeed, the very adoption of the nomenclature *queer* for this body of thinking and for groups of individuals who do not understand themselves to be heterosexual in itself represents a resistance where 'queer does not indicate the biological sex or gender of the subject. More importantly, the term indicates an ontological challenge to dominant labelling philosophies, especially the medicalization of the subject implied by the word "homosexual"' (Meyer 1994: 2).

By stepping away from categorizations of sexual desire as fixed and opposing—hetero/homosexual—the term *queer* aims to break down our very reliance on such organizational models. Equally, in refusing to make *queer* a gendered term more applicable to men than women, the aim is to give 'a challenge to discrete gender categories embedded in the divided phrase "gay and lesbian"' (Meyer 1994). Here we see *queer* as a construction which aims to dispute a number of social power hierarchies around both gender and sexuality which have embedded within them discourses which aim to make normal and acceptable only certain types of behaviour.

The feminist writer Judith Butler argues that 'gender is . . . a construction that regularly conceals its genesis' (Butler and Salih 2004: 114). By this, she attempts to encourage us to understand gender as nothing more than a performance grounded, perhaps, in a long social history, but having little to do with any natural behaviours relating to the biological difference between men and women (something we explored, to some degree, in chapter 3). The constructed nature of gender becomes masked from us as gender norms become socialized, dominant and habitual. Butler (1999) has used the term *performativity* to describe the kinds of daily performance that, whilst they may be unconscious, are no less a construction of an identity than the actions taken by an actor in a film.

For example, Butler sees social gender norms as something embedded in language, arguing that the declaration at birth 'It's a girl! is not a constative utterance but a performative one in which the girl, rather than being described in "neutral" terms, is interpellated as and therefore "becomes" a sexed and gendered subject' (Butler and Salih 2004:140). Thus, 'performativity theory, in its attempt to demonstrate the artifice of human social interactions and identities in their entirety, argues that *all* acts, including those rendered entirely normative, are a form of performance or are performative' (Edwards 2006: 100).

Here, we are encouraged to understand our lives, as they are played out, as shaped by a dialogue with a society that places upon our bodies and our selves expectations to which we must adhere in order to thrive. These performances are not something that we choose to participate in only when in view of others, but are instead internalized within our understanding of ourselves and our own identities. Therefore, 'performativity theory refutes any . . . separation' (Edwards 2006: 99) between the way in which we act behind closed doors and in public: a woman does not merely perform femininity in some situations but instead continues this identity as her natural one, unquestioningly. Thus, her feminine identity is performative, not performed. Consequently, then, Butler encourages us to see gender as 'the repeated stylization of the body, as a set of repeated acts within a highly regulatory frame that congeal over time to produce the appearance of substance, of a natural sort of being' (1999: 43).

In presenting an ambiguous representation of gender and in refusing to be pinned down on the question of sexuality—in the 1970s, at least—David Bowie is one of the first in a long line of performers who have used dress and the body to question gender ideals. By refusing to conform and in revealing the artificial and performative nature of gender through an embodiment that will not fit within proscribed gendered definitions, we see, too, a challenge to notions of sexuality as something that can be organized and understood along gendered lines. Embodying such points has been extremely important for many queer musicians.

DRESS, DRAG AND THE PERFORMANCE OF QUEER IDENTITIES

On the cover of their 2004 album *This Island,* American electro punk band Le Tigre appear in cocktail wear. Kathleen Hanna and Johanna Fateman wear black, with glossy hair; they seem the epitome of femininity. They flank their band mate, J. D. Samson, who takes centre stage in the image sporting a dinner jacket and bowtie, a buttonhole and what appears to be an eight-o'clock shadow on the top lip. It is, of course, not unusual to see a band made up of a variety of gendered identities or dressed to the nines for an album cover. What is unusual in the case of Le Tigre is that J. D. Samson is a woman.

As a queer woman, Samson had made a series of creative choices that articulate a queer identity. First, her name was structured to be ambiguously gendered, and second, her body failed to conform to the gender ideals socialized as fitting to her biological sex. Neither of these devices were, by 2004, particularly groundbreaking. Indeed, there is much about her refusal to gender her image as female that is obviously reminiscent of one of the most well-known queer female performers, k.d. lang, who, in August 1993, appeared on the cover of *Vanity Fair* in a barber's chair apparently being shaved by supermodel-of-the-time Cindy Crawford. Nonetheless, such choices demonstrate what Moe Meyer argues is the kind of 'queer identity' articulated 'as self-consciousness of one's gay and lesbian performativity sets in' (1994: 4).

For Judith Butler, 'trans-gender', 'cross-gender' or drag representations act to provide us with 'a clue to the way in which . . . gender experience might be reframed' (2002: 49). When there is a disjuncture between the perceived gender of a body and the gender being played out on that body through dress, gesture, movement and other forms of adornment, then we see how 'the performance of drag plays upon the distinction between the anatomy of the performer and the gender that is being performed' (Butler 1999: 175). This, for Butler, reveals a dissonance in our most strongly held understanding of the relationship between biological sex and gender, where 'in the place of the law of heterosexual coherence, we see sex and gender denaturalized by means of a performance which avows their distinctness and dramatizes the cultural mechanism of their fabricated unity' (Butler 1999). Thus, for Butler, whose work on gender and performativity has provided an important framework for 'queer' thinkers, any sense of a logical, normal and natural tie between gender, biological sex and sexual practices is the link that needs to be broken through queer resistances.

QUEER RESISTANCE AND SOCIAL CLASS

For many theorists, queer resistances have the potential to not only be shaped by gender, but also by notions of social class. This related to the kinds of ideals and behaviour which signal an adherence to the status quo: the kinds of middle-class or bourgeois values that dominate in most industrial societies.

> Queerness can be seen as an oppositional stance not simply to essentialist for-
> mations of gay and lesbian identities, but to a much wider application of the depth
> model of identity which underwrites the epistemology deployed by the bourgeoisie
> in their ascendancy to and maintenance of dominant power. (Meyer 1994: 3)

The bourgeois ideal of work and heterosexual relationships centring on mar-
riage and childbearing grows to a great extent out of a notion of the nuclear
family as an economically logical method of organizing a capitalist, business-
oriented society. It has also, as we saw in chapter 3, historically positioned
white masculinity at the top of its inherent power systems. Thus, it marginal-
izes behaviours which do not adhere to such ideals through what Thomas A.
King describes as a 'bourgeois morality . . . [which] aimed to close culture
off' (1994: 28).

In considering issues of sexuality, Michel Foucault argued that in attempting to outlaw or at least manage homosexuality as perverse, such bourgeois
ideals 'made possible the formation of a "reverse" discourse: homosexuality
began to speak in its own behalf, to demand that its legitimacy or "naturality"
be acknowledged . . . There is not on the one side, a discourse of power, and
opposite it, another discourse that runs counter to it. Discourses are tactical
elements or blocks, generating in the field of force relations' (1990: 101–2).
Foucault's work argues, then, that when homosexuality is repressed or pathol-
ogized by a society, the result will always be a greater desire for resistance of
such repression and a more urgent requirement for expression.

That class-ridden ideologies played a significant role in the repression of
queer identities makes it understandable that, consequently, it is via representations of class identity that queer resistances often symbolize and are
made visible. We saw in chapter 4 how the bourgeois middle classes rose to
dominance thanks to the industrial revolution, which changed the economic
power base of industrializing societies, primarily in the West, and the French
Revolution, which destabilized centuries of aristocratic rule as the organizational model for social order in such societies. In emphasizing their power as
the new dominant class, by the nineteenth century, 'aristocratic self-display
[had become] resistantly represented by the bourgeoisie as empty shows,
dissimilations concealing a lack of social being' (King 1994: 26). This was
coupled with an emphasis on the interior of the self as the defining facet
of 'deep', meaningful identity, which 'held that consciousness was political,
while the surfaces of the body were not' (King 1994).

Thus, style, surface and appearance were marginalized parts of human
identity, and there was an increasing tendency, into the twentieth century, to
present a rational body as the most desirable one. As we saw in chapter 3,
style and appearance were relegated to the feminine domain, where they were
seen to be in concert with a natural lack of depth from which the female sex

suffered. Yet in twentieth-century modernity, rationality of even this female body became a requirement, something we will examine in greater detail later in this chapter.

Such class relations came to be the way in which queer identity played itself out. As King argues, 'the effeminate man [challenged] the legitimacy of bourgeois morality' (1994: 28). This acted as a dangerous reminder of an alternative social order since effeminacy was linked to not only homosexual men, but also to aristocratic behaviour and identity. For writers like Moe Meyer (1994) and Thomas A. King (1994), the affectations of aristocratic life, like a certain kind of nonchalance, alongside an understanding of the power of style and appearances, have been retained as a method of resistance to dominant bourgeois ideals. Labelled 'camp', such postures have come to form an important facet of queer identity.

In music, elements of camp are everywhere and have been extremely visible, certainly since the 1970s, thanks to the glam rock poses and gender ambiguity that made up the performances of David Bowie and his contemporaries: Marc Bolan, Freddie Mercury, the New York Dolls, Mott the Hoople and Elton John. This is true to some extent, whatever the actual sexual preferences of these performers. But it is in the way that camp is used by outwardly queer performers to make queerness visible that we might locate true the resistance of fixed notions around sexuality.

SCISSOR SISTERS: CAMP AND COSTUME

The Scissor Sisters enjoyed significant mainstream success in the United Kingdom with their self-titled first album. The band members argued that they enjoyed less success on their home turf—the United States—because 'the genre-stratified US record industry . . . just wouldn't know what to do with them. Britain, it seems, was much more welcoming to their kaleidoscopic sound and image' (see McLean, 2004).

When Scissor Sisters opened the UK's most high-profile music awards, 'The Brits', in 2005, their performance epitomized their camp aesthetic. On a stage set with a soft, amorphous barn and a line of giant watermelons, an oversized pink puppet bird sits on its two eggs as the music begins. The setting resembles a kind of surrealist version of the Midwest farm from the Wizard of Oz, and three members of the band are already on stage in costumes which variously evoke cowboys and farmers: denim dungarees, embroidered check shirts and straw hats.

From the eggs emerge Jake Shears and Ana Matronic, the lead singers. Shears wears dark tan leather trousers and braces and reveals a bare, smooth chest. The leather trousers are embellished with a feather tail. Matronic is in a cocktail dress of bright yellow feathers: a colour partly evocative of Sesame Street's Big Bird, making the whole scene reminiscent of a Jim Henson TV special. The watermelons sing backup, the barn sings along, too, more eggs enter the stage and perform formation dances and the pink bird (their mama) joins them to party. At the end of the song, giant gold wings spring up behind Shears, and, like the song, which tells the story of coming out to mama, the transformation into fully fledged and visible queerness is symbolized in this four-minute performance.

This could be argued to be the epitome of camp if, as Richard Dyer argues, 'camp is a way of being human, witty and vital, without conforming to the drabness and rigidity of the heterosexual male role' (2002: 94). For Dyer, camp is about 'a certain taste in art and entertainment, a certain sensibility' (49). Here, he echoes some of the definitions suggested by Susan Sontag (2000). Primarily, for many writers, camp is about presenting 'a vision of the world in terms of style—but a particular kind of style. It is the love of the exaggerated, the "off", of things-being-what-they-are-not' (291; see also Dyer 2002). It is also concerned with making queer identity visible (see for example Meyer 1994) and 'drawing attention to the artifices employed by artists' (Dyer 2002: 60). This results in an unabashed celebration of the surface and the artificial that defines camp aesthetics of the kind employed by Scissor Sisters. Richard Dyer would argue that appearances are the natural place for queer identity to rest:

> Because we had to hide what we really felt (gayness) for so much of the time, we had to master the façade of whatever social set-up we found ourselves in—we couldn't afford to stand out in any way, for it might give the game away about our gayness. So we have developed an eye and an ear for surfaces, appearances, forms: style. Small wonder then that when we came to develop our own culture, the habit of style should have remained so dominant in it. (2002: 59)

In fashion terms, a female performer like Kylie Minogue may be understood to be engaging with the aesthetics of camp as strongly as a band like Scissor Sisters which is populated by a number of queer performers. Indeed, this relationship was somewhat cemented when the band collaborated with Minogue on the 2004 single 'I Believe in You'. With a visual and dramaturgical emphasis to her live shows and—with the help of her stylist, William Baker—the attainment of camp fashion-icon status, 'Kylie as a performer, like most pop performers, is about spectacle' (Brennan 2007: 182).

For Minogue's Showgirl tour in 2007, British designer John Galliano created a Swarovski crystal–encrusted leotard: 500,000 crystals, according to the Victoria and Albert Museum, which exhibited Kylie's costumes and a re-creation of her dressing room in London in 2007. As Sheila Whiteley (2005) notes, Minogue has become a queer icon. She herself 'admits that her appeal to gay men is that they love to brush her hair and dress her up' (Whiteley 2005: 63). The manner in which she costumes her body to camp tastes is part and parcel of this appeal. As Susan Sontag argued, the very idea of camp 'rests on innocence' (2000: 294). Minogue's camp credentials are thus reinforced by 'the degree to which she is portrayed as having fun in her performances. It is this that in turn signifies a sense of innocence' (Brennan 2007: 182).

In 1964, Susan Sontag declared that camp was 'apolitical' (see Sontag 2000). There have been criticisms of camp aesthetics 'suggesting that [it] is potentially misogynistic, sometimes celebrating restrictive cliches of femininity: not egalitarian but elitist, as a sensibility shared only by those with the requisite "queer eye", seduced by consumer culture; and desexualising—engaged with eroticism and desire, but not linking then to any particular sexual practices' (Allain and Harvie 2006: 137). These are controversial views since, for Richard Dyer, 'camp has a radical/progressive potential' (2002: 49) which must therefore have some political basis. For many writers, camp is a deeply political activity and aesthetic not least because it is part of 'the total body of performative practices and strategies used to enact a queer identity, with enactment defined as the production of social visibility' (Meyer 1994: 5). That camp may collude in consumer culture's stranglehold in capitalist societies may have some truth. But it is in the resistance to long-maintained links between particular identities to fixed gender ideals and sexual practices that the basis for queer resistance lies—its power is its fluidity; its emphasis on surfaces and style which make it hard to pin down. Dyer (2002) does suggest that there is always a danger that with its emphasis on fun, camp may mask more serious issues. Nonetheless, in making marginalized identities visible, camp strategies must, therefore, always be in some way political. When embodied, they are examples of symbolic resistances.

However, it would not be true to say that all examples of camp are political, and Kylie Minogue is a case in point. Despite her appeal for the queer community, the adoption of camp aesthetics by a female, heterosexual performer like Minogue cannot be understood to be 'an activist strategy' (Meyer 1994: 1) as it might be for queer performers. For Moe Meyer, this is an example of what she terms 'queer praxis': the adoption of the stylistics of camp by the mainstream. For Meyer, this threatens to undermine the potential for political and social resistances embedded in camp practices of bodily presentation and other expressions of style. Here, camp becomes assimilated into mainstream culture, and in such contexts it '(re)assures its audience of the ultimate harmlessness of its play, its palatability for bourgeois sensibilities' (Davy 1994: 145).

MUSIC, THE MAINSTREAM AND QUEER FEMALE IDENTITIES

As many writers have demonstrated (see for example Halberstam 1994; Davy 1994), specifically lesbian queer identities have been a great deal less palatable to these sensibilities. Kate Davy has forcefully argued that lesbian identities lack positive representations in the media and that those that exist are largely marginalized. High-profile and out lesbian performers in the music industry, with few exceptions—k.d. lang, who has already been mentioned here, and Beth Ditto, who will come into focus later in the chapter—enjoy limited mainstream success.

Davy (1994) argues that 'butch-femme artifice is so much more a part of lesbian discourse than camp' (145), and yet such representations are rarely seen in mainstream popular culture. For Judith Halberstam, the figuration of lesbian identity has been haunted by 'assumptions about the essential masculinity of the lesbian [which have] resulted in the production of stereotypes of the masculine lesbian, turning her into a site for lesbian disidentification' (1994: 57–8). Halberstam (1994, 1998) has argued that this has resulted in a lack of discussion of both the complexity of the butch-femme paradigm and all that lies between it in lesbian identity constructions. To better describe butch identities, she has coined the term 'female masculinity' (see Halberstam 1998).

As Diane Griffin Crowder argues, 'When a woman becomes aware of her lesbianism, she must choose whether to conform to, or revolt against' what she terms the 'female body practices intended to orient behaviour (if not desire) toward heterosexuality' (1998: 47). Griffin Crowder's work aims to 'begin a discussion of how sexualities intersect with the body in social discourse' (47), a notion which is perhaps not entirely absent in fashion studies, but which, overall, has failed to give sustained attention to this intersection in relation to queer women. She examines the feminist debates of the 1970s (see also Nestle 1981), which explored the inexorable gender bind in which queer women find themselves where, just as 'butch' seems too 'male-identified', 'the femme look—feminine clothing and hair, jewellery etc.—became identified as a politically incorrect imitation of heterosexual women' (Griffin Crowder 1998: 56). Thus, despite concerns that butch, lesbian identities may produce 'new versions of sexism, of reproducing a mainstream obsession with masculinity and dismissal of femininity and of conflating, once again, masculinity and lesbian embodiment' (Halberstam 1998: 58), the adoption of some degree of masculine embodiment and dress has been a popular device for making lesbian identity material.

The American hip-hop band Yo Majesty are operating within a music genre where many writers have identified some inherent misogyny (see Arnold 2001; Caracino and Scott 2008). As Haider writes, 'Yo Majesty sound like a violent reaction to everything from gangsta posturing to religious bigotry and fawning pop "babes"' (2008). Despite undergoing changes of membership in 2009, as hip-hop artists, Yo Majesty's stage look relies on sportswear, denim and oversized, baggy, printed T-shirts. As such, their look is primarily unisex, neither entirely butch, nor very feminine.

Playing at the Camden Barfly on 17 November 2008, then members Shunda K and Jwl B refute most of the usual representational symbols of femininity, and it is through the correlation of gender-ambiguous hip-hop looks, gesture and posture that a certain butch sensibility comes into play for this queer female band. With legs open, arms hanging at their sides, beer slugged back from a bottle throughout the performance and, in the case of Jwl B, the microphone used to represent the male phallus, they take something of an aggressive, even confrontational stance which runs counter to mainstream feminine ideals. Griffin Crowder would understand this performance as part and parcel of queer identities:

> Lesbians often cultivate movements (gestures, strides, motions of arms, and legs) that, unlike the circumscribed movements of most women, occupy the full volume of space around the body. Although often read as 'masculine' or even 'aggressive' by straights, such motor movements instead should be understood as a refusal to constrain the body in conformity with social norms. (1998: 59)

Such postures extend to the clothing worn by queer women, reinforcing, also, the dynamic between body and dress that makes material queer identities because 'one of the most frequent reasons lesbian give for choosing "unfeminine" clothing is the need for clothes in which one can move freely, extending the limbs fully and forcefully' (Griffin Crowder 1998).

Thus, queer female bodies speak loudly when their embodiment adopts masculine styles of dressing, adornment and gesture. But it should also be remembered that this is to a great extent fed by a culture that imprints certain expectations with regard to the body upon women of all kinds. Thus, as Kate Davy agues, such knowing resistances on the part of women are confrontational. When queer women refuse to conform to feminine ideals in a way suggestive of a knowingness almost reminiscent of camp, but fundamentally different in its butch-femme aesthetics, 'phallocentric culture is not reassured' (1994: 145). This would account for the lack of representation of lesbian identity in many areas of the mainstream media (see for example Davy 1994).

LESBIAN IDENTITIES, 'NATURAL' BODIES AND FEMALE BODY IMAGE

Alongside embodiment and adornment, the very body involved in such identity constructions can have as much to say. Yo Majesty's Jwl B is famous for revealing her naked torso on stage. This is the antithesis of the kinds of half-naked display that make up many of the more objectifying images in the media (see Berger 1972). As such, she contravenes what Jacqueline Urla and Alan C Swedlund describe as the 'conundrum of somatic femininity' (1995: 277) because she refuses to conform both in her body type and in her willingness to reveal it.

In such contexts, 'female bodies are never feminine enough . . . they must be deliberately and oftentimes painfully remade to be what "nature" intended—a condition dramatically accentuated under consumer capitalism' (Urla and Swedlund 1995: 277). This means that consumer culture and, in relation to it, popular culture have a tendency to present limited types of aspirational bodies for women. In contrast, Jwl B has a real body: in fact, a large body, much larger than the contemporary fashionable feminine ideal, and she uses her position as music performer to unabashedly display this body.

As many writers have demonstrated (see Entwistle 2000; Thesander 1997; Tseelon 1995 and others), bodies themselves are as open to shifts in fashion as the clothing which envelops them. This has applied much more to the female than male body, in part because 'all those bodily spontaneities—hunger, sexuality, the emotions—seen as needful of containment and control have been culturally constructed and coded as female' (Bordo 1995: 206). This is just one of the many ways fashion is implicated in social control as much as it is in personal expression, something we looked at in relation to women in chapter 3. Bodies share a relationship to the culture which surrounds them, and we find 'in the human body the prototype of society, the nation-state and the city' (Russo 1994: 58). Thus, bodies internalize the values of this society and are formed by them. In industrialized societies, where 'making a spectacle of oneself seemed a specifically feminine danger' (53), fleshy bodies came to signify 'uncontained desire, unrestrained hunger, uncontrolled impulse' (Bordo 1995: 189).

As such, bodies had to symbolize the controls necessary in modernity, and 'the slender body codes the tantalizing ideal of a well-managed self in which all is kept in order despite the contradictions of consumer culture' (Bordo 1995: 201). More specifically, the fleshy *female* body also has an unassailable link to 'psychic resonances with maternal power' (208). The maternal is a power base inherently female and thus threatening to male power and domination. This, too, requires containment (see also Nead 1992).

Despite Jwl B's revelation of a larger body, for queer women, issues of body image pertain just as strongly as for heterosexual women. Atkins (1998) has argued that this is the result of the internalization of social attitudes to women's bodies generally, from which queerness does not automatically make them immune. Writers like Dawn Atkins have considered the relationship between fatness and queer sexual identities. Whilst much of this research suggests it would be untrue to say that fatness was entirely embraced amongst queer women, Griffin Crowder has argued that what she describes as 'a "naturalist" ideology explicitly or implicitly underlies many aspects of lesbian thinking about the body'. This aims towards an 'eliminat[ion of] those social interventions deemed harmful . . . [placing] strong values on traits it considers "natural" to women' (1998: 59). Griffin Crowder enforces the fat liberation movement as 'part of an overall feminist and lesbian tendency to fight negative attitudes to the body . . . ingrained in a heterosexual society that imposes an ideal of increasing thinness on women' (59–60).

Susan Bordo (1995) argues that since the 1980s, the emphasis on thinness has moved from an emphasis on weight to accentuate, instead, the creation of a smooth, sleek and modern body: eradicating the lumps and bumps that are in actuality characteristic of the natural female body. Thus, for Bordo, 'cellulite management, like liposuction, has nothing to do with weight loss, and everything to do with the quest for firm bodily margins' (191). Intertwined social and bodily ideals like these are created and reinforced through the kinds of images that circulate in the media. As such, most of the material bodies inhabiting media spaces are forced to conform to such ideals and, moreover, to provide images of bodies that, via image manipulation, may in fact be difficult if not impossible to attain.

This makes the image of a naked Beth Ditto, lead singer of the band the Gossip, on the front cover of *NME* (she had previously posed naked for *Love* magazine) on 2 June 2007 startlingly different to the other covers on the newsstand found at the same time. Ditto is argued to be anything between a British size twenty to twenty-eight, and, at only five feet tall, she displays anything but the idealized firm, defined body. Standing sideways on, Ditto displays mounds of undulating, soft, pale flesh. Her body is a flawless landscape except for the imprints of a tattoo on her upper arm and, for the image, a set of red lips on her right hip with the tagline 'Kiss my arse': an appropriately punk sentiment for the lead singer in a punk band. On 31 May 2007, Germaine Greer wrote in praise of both Ditto and the magazine *NME* for being brave enough to circulate this image. As a feminist, Greer gave recognition to the political as well as sensational dimensions of the image, noting that '[Ditto's] intention is to force acceptance of her body type, 5ft tall and 15 stone, and by this strategy to challenge the conventional imagery of women' (2007).

The bravery necessary to accept and present a female body that fails to adhere to the contemporary ideal may come from the fact that Ditto is a queer woman. Fatness has long been contested ground when understood in relation to the female body—a great deal more of an unacceptable body type for women than for men: 'The Fat woman has been an important figure of spectacularized womanhood in the west since the nineteenth century. In our own days, feminist performance artists have played upon the variations of fleshly display and exaggeration associated with femaleness as a tactic of counter-pornography' (Russo 1994: 24).

Whilst lesbianism and feminism should not and must not be seen to go hand in hand, there has certainly been a shared understanding of the female body as being at the locus of women's lives and of the cultural politics that shape them. Ditto's body might thus be understood as an example of a deeply politicized body in a deeply politicized image. It could be understood to resist 'modernity and its stylistic effects as a radical diminishment of the possibilities of human freedom' (Russo 1994: 61) here in relation to the female body.

Here, Mary Russo is drawing on the ideas of Mikhail Bakhtin, who used the notion of carnival and, within this, the unmanaged body as a metaphor to understand the social effects of and limitations enforced by modernist ideologies. He attempts to remind the reader about the negatives of a social system that was, contemporary to his writings, becoming the norm. As such, he argues that with modernity comes a 'new bodily canon', where 'that which protrudes, bulges, sprouts or branches off is eliminated' and is replaced by 'the individual, strictly limited mass, the impenetrable façade' (Bakhtin 1984: 320). This is a rational and functional body whose machine-like economy echoes modernist concerns. To represent a body like Ditto's can subsequently be understood to be a political act that destabilizes the stranglehold of such fixed ideologies.

FASHION, FATNESS AND MUSIC

This image of Ditto appeared right in the middle of the so-called 'size zero' debates that seized much popular media attention in 2007 and beyond. David Gauntlett (2008) recounts the various ways in which thinness has been reinforced through the popular media as an ideal for women. He also notes some criticism of any simplistic link between images of thinness and the actual cultural manifestation of it: eating disorders and body dysmorphia, for example. At the same time, in considering how the fashion industry has for decades relied on increasingly thin models, some culpability for reinforcing a desire for extreme thinness clearly rests with it. In September 2005, Andre Leon Talley, editor at large of US *Vogue*, surprised no one by confessing that 'most of the *Vogue* girls are so thin, tremendously thin, because Miss Anna [Wintour] don't like fat people' (see bigfatblog.com n.d..) The 2009 documentary film *The September Issue* demonstrated the kinds of power Wintour exerts in a variety of areas of the fashion industry. She can clearly determine who gets a break in the first place and who is successful. She also has critical input in the work of the most high-profile designers and plays an integral part in the complex relationship between creativity and commerce that exists within this industry.

BETH DITTO—FASHION ICON?

Beth Ditto, however, has managed to navigate all these inherent prejudices, in the process becoming something of a fashion icon despite her less than industry-friendly size. In an article in the British newspaper the *Times* in June 2009, she doesn't deny these prejudices. Nor does she feign ignorance at the hypocrisy of an industry where 'one year Karl Lagerfeld was refusing to make clothes for women of a certain size, and the next year he was asking me to play the Fendi party . . . What a contradiction they are! But they're probably just as big victims of not being able to see beyond the ends of their noses as all the people complaining about it. You have to get in there, shake it up' (Hattersley 2009).

Like the fashion industry, much of the press coverage of Ditto's style is unsure and ambivalent. On 11 March 2009, Sarah Vine *half*-admiringly describes Ditto's appearance at Paris Fashion Week in a Herve Leger 'bandage' dress. Vine describes Ditto as a 'little American Boule de Suif in Paris, all chubby cheeks and cheeky smile' (2009) but then goes on to make clear the requisite concerns for Ditto's health that go hand in hand with most discussions of body weight. On the one hand, Vine seems to congratulate Ditto for being brave enough to go out looking like this, but on the other makes suggestions of how larger women can best dress: 'No one demonstrates more amply the maxim that big girls need tailoring. Covering up generous curves with shapeless tops and trousers promotes an image of dreary embarrassment. Ditto's look is all about contouring, hence the bandage dress' (2009).

Underpinning this article, which seems broadly admiring, is, in contrast, a need to chide both Ditto and the fashion industry. Vine makes it clear that she, like many other things in fashion, is not 'normal' but an extreme, arguing that 'it is interesting that Ditto has been so wholeheartedly embraced by the fashion pack, a group of people who seem pathologically incapable of identifying with ordinary women, preferring to gravitate to the extremes of the weight scales' (2009).

For Vine, Ditto's unique ability to carry this off is all down to 'chutzpah'. For Ditto, it's all about creativity: 'A piece of clothing can't talk—it can't tell you that you can't have it—so really, you're just telling yourself that. You make yourself the victim, because if you want clothes that bad, then make them yourself. You have to get creative if you're fat' (Hattersley 2009). Of course, Ditto's solution is not without its problems. She certainly takes a tough line with a group of women whose self-esteem may have been negatively affected by the internalization of a set of cultural requirements for themselves and their bodies that they feel they may have failed to attain.

Ultimately, Ditto did not leave all ordinary fat women to the vagaries of their own creativity, but instead, in June 2009, she launched a clothing range at the high street, plus-size retailer Evans. According to fashion journalist Hilary Alexander (2009b), the collection has diverse inspirations from other female music icons like Debbie Harry and Grace Jones as well as from art movements and club scenes. It would be a brave plus-size woman who would wear many of the clothes because they seem the antithesis of prior ideas of appropriate dressing for a larger body; many are extremely body 'conscious', made from fitted lycra in psychedelic and geometric prints and metallic fabrics. But, as Alexander recounts, Ditto has also included 'tamer items like LBDs, denim, high-waist pencil skirts and black, cotton biker jackets— because not all big girls are as brave as me.' More practical concerns for dressing a larger body are also taken into account with 'leggings [which] feature a high-waist that keeps rolls of flesh under control and prevents the dreaded muffin top' (2009).

It would thus be a mistake to believe that Ditto's induction into *fashionability*, sanctioned by industry power brokers, symbolizes a seismic shift in the ideal fashionable body or industry attitudes to dressing it, as Ditto herself recognizes:

> Some fat girl blogger was saying, 'It's cool that all these famous designers are making clothes for her, but they're not going to make them for everyone.' And the truth is, yes, they're not going to make them for everyone. They make only a few pieces just to fit me . . . For the rest, I have to make it work my own way. Maybe it wasn't supposed to go round my shoulders because it was a skirt, but that's how I wear it. (Hattersley 2009)

Her fairly unforgiving stance and toughness on the subject might be explained in part by her argument that 'if you think fashion is snobby, go hang out with some punks . . . They are beyond elitist' (Hattersley 2009). But that her treatment demonstrates something of an acceptance of an alternative to extreme thinness in the fashion industry must only be a positive, even if it is a mere blip. It may be, too, that it is in Ditto's queerness that we find some explanation for the allowance of this kind of body—she is forgiven by mainstream fashion for her fatness because she is not straight. This, alongside her status as musician, may have allowed her to slip under fashion's radar. As such, the revelation of fat, queer bodies of performers like Ditto and Jwl B provides 'the figure of the female transgressor as public spectacle', one which is 'powerfully resonant' (Russo 1994: 61). Ditto's assimilation into the fashion elite may not signal a seismic shift in attitudes to bodies in the industry, but nonetheless, it does demonstrate the potential of queer lesbian culture to 'resist, exaggerate and destabilise the distinction and boundaries that mark and maintain high culture and organised society' (62).

CONCLUSION

It is thus the melding of music and fashion together that facilitates such resistances. The numerous unwritten rules that surround music—many focused on appropriate behaviours—established, too, the boundaries for transgression. As such, to self-consciously and actively celebrate artifice in a music industry that has an ambivalent relationship to the role of appearance can only command attention. The furore around Lady Gaga's on- and off-stage costumes and the uncertainty about how to value her attests to that. This is not to say that the music industry and those inhabiting it have failed to recognize the importance of physical image, but in most cases the *creation* of these images—their unnaturalness—is in denial.

Many queer performers can be understood to be entering into such practices as an expression of their own cultural identity, by displaying unconventional bodies or dressing them in unconventional ways. Since ideals of gender and sexuality are written through the body as inhabited, then it is natural that alternative views of how that body can be inhabited and subsequently how it can and should look are articulated through it. At the same time, the acceptance of a performer like Beth Ditto into mainstream fashion, despite an appearance so at odds with the fashionable ideal, may be sanctioned because of her queerness. The fashion industry may be populated by many queer men, but queer women are arguably underrepresented in this industry. As such, Ditto is exotic other, and a fascination with her sexual difference may legitimate her physical difference. Thus, while a body such as hers is unusual in its inclusion in the image-obsessed music and fashion industries, its presence may not represent a permanent sea change in attitudes. Nonetheless, bodily presentations which are at odds with most other representations in these areas of cultural life should not be surprising. Queer performers are compelled to break the rules of fashion and of music performance because the rules were not written with them in mind.

Conclusion: Music, Fashion, Image

THE MUSICIAN AS CELEBRITY

The notion of authenticity has been a texture running throughout this book. As I argued in the introduction and in chapters 1 and 2, music stars and their audiences are always reaching for an experience that resonates with the deeper aspects of the self. Thus, the relationship between music performer and audience is rooted in the emotions. This experience is often made all the more powerful because of a variety of aspects of performance, including embodiment. This is despite the fact that to focus on the visual aspects of music has been seen to betray its imagined authenticity. Style, in particular, is always tinged with the history of fashion, replete with accusations of superficiality.

The music star inhabits a liminal space between the authentic and the constructed—as does every person who gets dressed in the morning. But like the fashioned identities of most everyday people, being conscious of this ambiguity sits uncomfortably with the more steady sense of self we often prefer to believe in. All well-known people enact a 'star personality'. As Simon Frith argues, 'A star is also . . . an act; performance is not as self-revealing as it may seem' (1996: 211–12). Music stars are most often involved in what Firth calls 'a process of double enactment . . . both a star personality (their image) and a song personality, the role that each lyric requires' (212).

This notion of authenticity has been central to the way the figure of the musician has been considered both historically and theoretically and is also implicated in some of the ways in which it has *not* been considered in very much detail. These discourses mark out the musician as a particular kind of performing body. In the analysis of celebrity culture, any discussion of music stars falls well short of that of the film and TV personalities who have taken centre stage in such work. For example, the work of Jackie Stacey (1991, 1994) has been key to our understanding of the film star as a specific kind of 'star body' which has played an influential role in the shaping of—in the case of Stacey's work—female audiences, through a process of identification. Focusing, in particular, on the golden age of Hollywood in the 1940s and 1950s, Stacey examines the processes of identification and recognition with the star as 'expressive of resistance' (1991: 148) and as a method by which identities are produced and shaped; a route to personal empowerment. Key to notions of identification are the consumption habits that make this material. These are mostly focused on fashion and appearance.

In much discussion of film stars as star bodies of this kind, it is this dual identity—the star both off and on screen—and a melding of the two, that seems primarily to shape a specific understanding of the way in which they operate as cultural figures. There is thus always the suggestion that a real person lies behind the identity enacted on screen or stage. This is part of the tantalizing appeal of celebrity culture to which the glut of celebrity magazines—*Heat, Star, Closer, OK* and *Hello,* to name but a few—testify. In contrast, the audience's relationship to the music star is complicated by the fact that what is seen on stage and screen is most often understood to *be* the music star.

Whilst writers such as Graeme Turner (2004) acknowledge that musicians play a part in the celebrity system, the construction of a star image seems to be implicitly understood as something that only happens through interventions from those managing and marketing music stars. The manipulation of identity and image is assumed to be either an accident that befalls the talented—a difficult path to be trodden whilst maintaining artistic integrity—or the main point in the case of the most manufactured of music performances. In much writing on celebrity culture, the spotlight falls on TV and film stars. When music stars are discussed, the focus is often on manufactured groups. This seems to reflect the way in which the word *celebrity* has come to be more suggestive of someone who 'develops their capacity for fame, not by achieving great things, but by differentiating their own personality from those of their competition' (5). This is at odds with music stars, who *seem* to portray an *authentic* identity, and may help to explain the absence of a full discussion of how they work as part of a larger celebrity culture. This, in turn, fails to acknowledge that in contemporary culture, even the most gifted must also mark themselves out within their market. Musicians are always understood to be 'not like a film character where there is a limited and original text. It is a presentation of the self for public consumption which accommodates something private and personal' (Marshall 2000: 163).

The nature of what it means to be a music star is, therefore, never clear cut, and 'the pop singer's enactment of the pop star . . . is also a site of desire . . . In performance then . . . instead of "forgetting who they are" singers are continuously registering their presence' (Frith 1996: 212). The construction of a viable stage image thus becomes the means of differentiation for all musicians—an essential part of stamping themselves out within the music community. Thus, perhaps the enactment of the music star would be better understood as a more complex construct of identity with elements of both self and artifice. It is always in some measure performative, as all identities are. It is never wholly a presentation of the self as a cohesive and stable reality, but neither is it an entirely false image to be applied and removed at will. It would be interesting to see how these ambiguities could be better situated in a more sustained debate within studies of celebrity culture.

LADY GAGA

This is important because, as I hope this book has demonstrated, the role of the musician in shaping the tastes, ideas, beliefs and behaviours of the audience for music is significant: perhaps more so than that of the film star in the contemporary period. The landscape which is the product of the involvement of these two areas of culture is in a state of constant change. In the time between conceptualizing and producing this book, Lady Gaga has become one of the most significant figures not only in global pop but also for the way in which she vociferously connects fashion and music (and art) in all performances and representations. In April 2010, she was included in *Time* magazine's Top 100 Most Influential People. Cyndi Lauper, a similarly kooky American pop star of an earlier generation, writes a tribute in the same issue, describing Gaga as 'a performance artist. She herself is the art. She is the sculpture' (see Lauper 2010).

In an article entitled 'Lady Gaga Is a Creation, but an Authentic One' (see Spectrum News 2009), Lady Gaga forcefully argues that though she only 'became' Gaga five years previously, this embodiment perfectly reflected who she has always been. Just like The Misshapes in chapter 1, she is undoubtedly a product of New York. She often recounts the influence of Warhol and the contemporary New York party scene in the creation of 'Lady Gaga'. She says that 'I'm self manufactured . . . (I look) at it not as poison or lowbrow, but . . . in a very highbrow way, and self making myself to be a powerful visionary and say something that will generally speak to people [*sic*]' (Moody 2009). Just like David Bowie, Gaga's authenticity, then, is her acknowledged 'inauthenticity' or, perhaps more accurately, her acknowledgement that neither word quite describes the fashioned identities of any of us.

This emphasis on the visual should mean that it comes as no surprise that her influence is best evidenced by her video and online presence. The *Guardian* newspaper's 'Digital Content Blog' reported that, alongside the release of her single 'Telephone' in early 2010, she was the first artist to reach one billion video views online. The blog argues that it is Gaga's consistency in producing must-see videos that makes her such a success online and that 'some way down the line, those 1bn views must translate to music sales and justify Universal's strategy' (see *Guardian* n.d). Thus, she is first and foremost a visual experience, and though many of her videos, particularly 'Telephone', have filmic narratives, like many music videos, they primarily attempt to 'tell an image, rather than to tell a story' (Hebdige 1988: 237), and place Gaga's persona centre stage.

This central position of style undoubtedly overshadows her music. The question is—does this matter? It certainly makes it somehow surprising that she can play piano extremely well and has a powerful, almost pitch-perfect voice. In an article in the *Guardian* newspaper on 12 December 2009, Bryony Gordon acknowledges this, but ultimately decides that 'Lady Gaga is the ultimate triumph of style over substance.' Interestingly, she wonders 'what the clothes are hiding, rather than expressing' (Gordon 2009). This makes clear a pervasive belief that dress is expected to make visible on the outside of the body something truthful from inside.

Yet as we have seen throughout this book, style arguably inhabits the gap between these two spaces. Dressing down can be no more a true expression of a real, stable, inner self than dressing up. Lady Gaga's style is no different from any other fashioned identity. It only becomes worthy of comment because she makes its construction visible and, in doing so, blurs our understanding of what a performance is and where it happens because she takes great care to live out this persona always. The general suspicion all of this arouses converged on a great deal of new media chatter about the possibility that Gaga was a hermaphrodite.

Nonetheless, in 2010, Lady Gaga has clearly captured the imagination of her fans and holds a great deal of influence over other participants in the music industry. She is surrounded by a creative team, the Haus of Gaga, who help her develop and maintain her persona. There is also much speculation that this will develop into a full-blown fashion range. At the time of writing, the only products available seem to be some very conventional and uninspiring merchandise: printed T-shirts, sunglasses, wristbands and some very ordinary-looking sequinned masks. It is doubtful that any of this would sate the appetites of diehard Lady Gaga wannabes. As we saw in chapter 2, it is the do-it-yourself inventiveness of the Gaga look that seems be most persuasive. *Time* magazine (see *Time* n.d.) photographed fans arriving for a gig at the Landmark Theatre in Richmond, Virginia, and this spirit of improvization is in evidence everywhere. Girls and boys in hats and masks, painted faces and pink wigs dance and blow bubbles as they arrive. A boy wears feathers and a homemade tinfoil hat seemingly inspired by the Nasir Mazhar orbit hat worn by Gaga on the cover of *V* magazine in August 2009. A girl has playing cards pinned into her hair.

The performative potential of style for fan cultures is well realized, as we saw in chapter 2, but Gaga's success in this regard has infiltrated the music industry itself. Dressing up to outrageous degree is increasingly becoming a requirement for pop music, and evoking the kind of art and club life purportedly lived out by Gaga is part and parcel of such representations. In the video for her single 'All Night Long', British *X Factor* 2008 winner Alexandra Burke populates just such a nightlife. Partygoers wearing silver, feathers, fake fur and thick theatrical makeup feature alongside Burke, a platinum blonde reminiscent of Gaga herself and a man wearing goggles made from crayons and formed in a similar shape to those made from cigarettes and worn by Gaga in the 'Telephone' video. The idea of a do-it-yourself lifestyle that has captured an audience and a lucrative market is clearly something that those promoting other performers are keen to tap into.

This brief analysis of Lady Gaga returns to many of the themes discussed in this book. In particular, the part that fans play in making a star successful, the performative potential of star styles for fan identities and the intertextual reach of her imagery across the industry all echo ideas already presented here. No book on fashion and music could ignore her. As her career progresses, it will be interesting to see what long-term implications this might have for how popular music and its stars are conceived.

MICHAEL JACKSON

Also during the process of writing this book, Michael Jackson died. His death was surrounded by fervent outpourings of grief from his fans, with vigils held all over the world. Twenty-four-hour news coverage allowed a global audience to watch as his death was confirmed and the murky details surrounding it unfolded. In the following months, numerous performers paid tribute, including Beyoncé in Melbourne in 2009 (Figure 15). Prior to his death, Jackson had been represented by the mass media as at best a tragic figure and at worst a deviant one. His creative and significant career had come to be overshadowed by accusations of child abuse, court cases and excessive plastic surgery that made him almost unrecognizable. Michael Jackson was a master of what Frith calls 'rootless self-invention' (1989: 173), but the excessive cosmetic surgery suggested a deeper, psychological aspect to this mutability.

The influence of Jackson on mainstream men's dressing is debatable, but he undoubtedly enjoyed a loyal following, and his style was a defining bridge between audience and performer. We have seen the significance of this throughout this book. Most interestingly, after his death, fashion became a form of rehabilitation for Jackson's image, a way of sidelining the darker facets of his public image and focusing instead on a celebration of its more positive aspects. In September 2009, the magazine *Harper's Bazaar* paid homage to Jackson's style as a tribute. British model Agyness Deyn adopted a number of styles from Jackson's career—the tuxedo from the *Off the Wall* era, the

Figure 15   Beyoncé pays tribute to Michael Jackson, Melbourne, September 2009. © arvdix, 2010, used under license from shutterstock.com

red leather jacket from 'Thriller', and a variety of military-inspired looks worn throughout his career.

The visual impact of Jackson's style was made striking by the inclusion of details and accessories—from a trilby hat to trousers at half mast worn with white socks to draw attention to his ankles and thus his dance moves, black loafers and, arguably most iconic, one bejewelled white glove. Costume designer Deborah Nadoolman Landis discusses the part she played in creating some of Jackson's key looks, most notably the red jacket for the 'Thriller' video in 1983. Here, she notes the influence of Fred Astaire (and some would identify Gene Kelly, too) on a number of aspects of Jackson's style. The embodiment of his identity as dancer was clearly a motivating factor for much of what he wore. She describes him as 'one of the most naturally and intuitively elegant men on this (or any other) planet' (Landis n.d.).

Like many performers, Jackson's style was informed by his role as both fan (of Astaire and Kelly) and star. The creation of style for contemporary music stars is always part of a complex set of discourses: 'a web of significance', to return to Jansson's (2002) term. In order to trace this, a number of enduring ideas about how some aspects of music performance are privileged over others have to be disabused. Equally, some of the lasting notions about fashion which see it as superficial and insincere must be unpicked. This book aims to suggest some of the ways in which this might happen. It is clear that the music star has great cultural significance to fashion and vice versa. Consequently, the way in which music performers perform, via fashion, has wider cultural implications on their audiences, whether ardent fans or more casual consumers.

Bibliography

AARP, The Magazine (2008), May/June, <http://www.aarpmagazine.org/table_of_contents_may__june_2008.html> accessed 14 November 2009.

Adlington, R. (2009), *Sound Commitments: Avant-Garde Music and the Sixties*, New York: Oxford University Press.

Alexander, H. (2009a), 'David Koma on His New Collection,' *Telegraph* [online], 6 November, <http://www.telegraph.co.uk/fashion/fashionnews/6515130/David-Koma-on-his-new-collection.html> accessed 13 March 2010.

Alexander, H. (2009b), 'Beth Ditto's Collection for Evans,' *Telegraph* [online], 6 July, <http://www.telegraph.co.uk/fashion/style/5734946/Beth-Dittos-collection-for-Evans.html> accessed 30 December 2009.

Allain, P., and Harvie, J. (2006), *The Routledge Companion to Theatre and Performance*, Abingdon: Routledge.

Allison, A. (2009), 'The Cool Brand, Affective Activism and Japanese Youth', *Theory, Culture and Society*, 26/2–3: 89–111.

Americana Music Association (n.d.), 'What Is Americana', <http://americanamusic.org/index.htm?id=18376&sid=18345> accessed 3 December 2009.

Anderson, B. (1991), *Imagined Communities: Reflections on the Origins and Spread of Nationalism*, London: Verso.

Apple Bottoms shop (n.d.), <http://www.applebottoms.com/shop.php> accessed 12 December 2009.

Arlidge, J. (2008), 'My Sporting Life', *Guardian* [online], 23 November, <http://www.guardian.co.uk/sport/2008/nov/23/pharrell-williams-neptunes-sport> accessed 26 September 2010.

Arnold, R. (2001), *Fashion, Desire and Anxiety: Image and Morality in the Twentieth Century*, London: I.B. Tauris.

Atkins, D. (1998), 'Looking Queer: Body Image and Identity', in *Lesbian, Bisexual, Gay and Transgender Communities*, New York: Haworth Press.

Atolliver, G., and Ossé, R. (2006), *Bling: The Hip-Hop Jewellery Book*, London: Bloomsbury.

Auslander, P. (2006), 'Watch That Man David Bowie: Hammersmith Odeon, London, July 3, 1973', in I. Inglis (ed), *Performance and Popular Music: History, Place and Time*, Aldershot: Ashgate.

Bakhtin, M. (1984), *Rabelais and His World*, Bloomington and Indianapolis: Indiana University Press.

Barker, C. (2000), *Cultural Studies: Theory and Practice*, London: Sage.

Barthes, R. (1990), *The Fashion System,* Berkley and Los Angeles: University of California Press.

Barthes, R. (2000), *Mythologies,* London: Vintage.

Baudrillard, J. (1994), *Simulacra and Simulation*, Ann Arbor, Michigan: University of Michigan Press.

Bayton, M. (1990), 'How Women Become Musicians', in S. Frith (ed.), *On Record: Rock, Pop and the Written Word*, London: Routledge.

BBC (2010), *Something for the Weekend* [TV programme], BBC2, 2 May 2010.

Beale, C. (2007), 'Why the High Street Is Being Swamped by Celebrity Clothing Ranges', *Independent* [online], 8 April, <http://www.independent.co.uk/news/uk/this-britain/why-the-high-street-is-being-swamped-by-celebrity-clothing-ranges-443467.html> accessed 8 February 2009.

Belfast Telegraph (2010), 'Fury over Primark's Padded Bikinis for Children', 14 April, <http://www.belfasttelegraph.co.uk/news/local-national/fury-over-primarks-padded—bikinis-for-children-14766514.html> accessed 15 April 2010.

Bennett, A. (2000), *Popular Music and Youth Culture: Music, Identity and Place*, Basingstoke: Palgrave.

Bennett, A. (2001), *Cultures of Popular Music*, Maidenhead: Oxford University Press.

Benyon, J. (2002), *Masculinities and Culture*, Buckingham: Open University Press.

Berg, M. (2005), *Luxury and Pleasure in Eighteenth Century Britain,* Oxford: Oxford University Press.

Berger, J. (1972), *Ways of Seeing*, London: Penguin.

bigfatblog.com (n.d.), 'Vogue Picks Its Battles', <http://www.bigfatblog.com/node/1111> accessed 1 January 2010.

Bitten and Bound (2009), 'Miley Cyrus Covers ELLE August 2009 (PHOTOS)', 8 July, <http://www.bittenandbound.com/2009/07/08/miley-cyrus-covers-elle-august-2009-photos> accessed 20 February 2010.

Bocock, R. (1993), *Consumption*, London: Routledge.

Booboo (2006), 'Shock . . . Horror', musicbanter.com [online], 30 June, <http://www.musicbanter.com/general-music/4475-shock-horror-27.html#ixzz0av2KhMMi> accessed 12 August 2009.

Bordo, S. (1995), *Unbearable Weight: Feminism, Western Culture and the Body*, Berkley: University of California Press.

Bourdieu, P. (1984), *Distinction: A Social Critique of the Judgment of Taste*, London: Routledge.

Brennan, M. (2007), 'The Best Pop Princess: Kylie Minogue', in A. McKee (ed.), *Beautiful Things in Popular Culture,* London: Blackwell.

Breward, C. (1999), *The Hidden Consumer: Masculinities, Fashion and City Life 1860–1914*, Manchester: Manchester University Press.

Bronski, M. (2007), 'Winning Queer Culture Wars', *Z Magazine* [online], July, <http://www.zmag.org/zmag/viewArticle/19455> accessed 18 December 2009.

Brown, R. (1965), *Social Psychology*, London/New York: Macmillan.

Bruzzi, S., and Church Gibson, P., eds. (2000), *Fashion Cultures: Theories, Explorations and Analysis*, London: Routledge.

Butler, J. (1999), *Gender Trouble: Feminism and the Subversion of Identity*, London: Routledge.

Butler, J. (2002), 'Performative Subversions', in S. Jackson and S. Scott (eds), *Gender: A Sociological Reader*, London: Routledge.

Butler, J. and Salih, S. (2004), *The Judith Butler Reader*, Oxford: Blackwell.

Buxton, D. (1990), 'Rock Music, the Star System and the Rise of Consumerism', in S. Frith (ed.), *On Record: Rock, Pop and the Written Word*, London: Routledge.

Bytheway, B. (2003), 'Visual Representations of Late Life', in C. Faircloth (ed.), *Aging Bodies: Images and Everyday Experience*, Walnut Creek, CA: AltaMira.

Calefato, P. (2004), *The Clothed Body*. Oxford: Berg.

Calinescu, M. (1987), *Five Faces of Modernity: Modernism, Avant-Garde, Decadence, Kitsch, Postmodernsim*, Durham, NC: Duke University Press.

Callan, J. (2004), 'I've Been Happily Unmarried to the Same Girl for 20 Years . . . But I've Slept with 4,600', *Daily Mirror* [online], 7 April, <http://www.kissinuk.com/kissmags16.htm> accessed 12 January 2010.

Cameron, K. (1999), 'Introduction', in K. Cameron (ed.), *National Identity*, Exeter: Intellect Books.

Caracino, C., and Scott, K. (2008), *The Porning of America: The Rise of Porn Culture, What It Means, and Where We Go from Here*, Boston: Beacon.

Cashmore, E. (1990), *Making Sense of Sports*, Abingdon: Routledge.

Cavallaro, D. (2006), *French Feminist Theory: An Introduction*, London: Continuum.

Chandler, R. M., and Chandler-Smith, N. (2005), 'Flava in Ya Gear: Transgressive Politics and the Influence of Hip Hop on Contemporary Fashion', in L. Welters and P. Cunningham (eds), *Twentieth Century American Fashion*, Oxford: Berg.

Charlton, K. (1998), *Rock Music Styles: A History*, Boston: McGraw Hill.

Chen, K. H. (1998), 'MTV: The Disappearance of Postmodern Semiosis, or the Cultural Politics of Resistance', in A.S.A. Berger (ed.), *The Postmodern Presence: Readings on Postmodernism in American Culture and Society*, Walnut Creek, California: AltaMira.

Chernilo, D. (2007), *A Social Theory of the Nation State: The Political Forms of Modernity beyond Methodological Nationalism*, Abingdon: Routledge.

Church Gibson, P. (2000), 'No One Expects Me Anywhere: Invisible Women, Ageing and the Fashion Industry', in S. Bruzzi and P. Church Gibson (eds), *Fashion Cultures: Theories, Explorations and Analysis,* London: Routledge.

Church Gibson, P. (2006), 'Analysing Fashion', in T. Jackson and D. Shaw (eds), *The Fashion Handbook,* Oxford: Routledge.

Cixous, H., and Sellers, S. (1994), *The Hélène Cixous Reader,* London: Routledge.

Clampin, F. (1999), '"Those Blue Remembered Hills . . .", National Identity in English Music (1900–1930)', in K. Cameron (ed.), *National Identity,* Exeter: Intellect Books.

Clarke, G (2005), 'Defending Ski Jumpers: A Critique of Theories of Youth Subcultures', in K. Gelder and S. Thornton, *The Subcultures Reader,* Abingdon: Routledge.

Clifford, T. (2002), 'Gene Simmons: *Kiss and Make-up—The Autobiography of Gene Simmons*' [review], *Rock's Backpages,* March, <http://www.rocksbackpages.com/article.html?ArticleID=2640> accessed 8 February 2009.

Cohen, S. (2002), *Folk Devils and Moral Panics,* 3rd ed., Abingdon: Routledge.

Cook, D. T. (2004), *The Commodification of Childhood: The Children's Clothing Industry and the Rise of the Child Consumer,* Durham, NC: Duke University Press.

Cosgrove, S. (1988), 'The Zoot Suit and Style Warfare', in A. McRobbie (ed.), *Zoot Suits and Second-Hand Dresses,* Basingstoke: Macmillan.

Craik, J. (1994), *The Face of Fashion,* London: Routledge.

Craik, J. (2005), *Uniforms Exposed: From Conformity to Transgression,* Oxford: Berg.

Cranny-Francis, A., Waring, W., Stavropoulos, P., and Kirkby, J. (2003), *Gender Studies: Terms and Debates,* Basingstoke: Palgrave Macmillan.

Cullen, J. (2005), *Born in the U.S.A.: Bruce Springsteen and the American Tradition,* Middletown, CT: Wesleyan University Press.

Currid, E. (2007), *The Warhol Economy: How Fashion, Art and Music Drive New York City,* Princeton, NY: Princeton University Press.

Daily Mail (2008), 'Rolling Stone Keith Richards Takes Time Out from Rock 'n' Roll to Model for Louis Vuitton', 3 March, <http://www.dailymail.co.uk/tvshowbiz/article-525069/Rolling-Stone-Keith-Richards-takes-time-rock-n-roll-model-Louis-Vuitton.html> accessed 20 December 2009.

dailyfix.com (n.d.), 'Sharon Stone Is 50, Topless and Likely Photoshopped to Hell!', <http://thedailyfix.com/2009/08/06/sharon-stone-is-50-topless-and-likely-photoshopped-to-hell> accessed 1 February 2010.

Davis, F. (1992), *Fashion, Culture and Identity,* Chicago: University of Chicago Press.

Davy, K. (1994), 'Fe/male Impersonation. The Discourse of Camp', in M. Meyer (ed.), *The Politics and Poetics of Camp,* London: Routledge.

De Beauvoir, S. (1953), *The Second Sex*, New York: Alfred A Knopf.

Deleuze, G. (2006), *The Fold: Leibniz and the Baroque*, London/New York: Continuum.

Douglas, M. (2002), *Purity and Danger*, London: Routledge.

Dovey, J., Lister, M., Giddings, S., Grant, I., and Kelly, K. (2009), *New Media: A Critical Introduction*, Abingdon: Routledge.

Dyer, R. (1979), *Stars*, London: British Film Institute.

Dyer, R. (2002), *The Culture of Queers*, London: Routledge.

Eckert, C. (1996), *The Carole Lombard in Macy's Window*, London: Athlone Press.

Edensor, T. (2002), *National Identity, Popular Culture and Everyday Life*, Oxford: Berg.

Edgar, A., Sedgwick, P., and Sedgwick, P.R. (1999), *Key Concepts in Cultural Theory*, London: Routledge.

Edwards, T. (2006), *Cultures of Masculinity*, London: Routledge.

Ehrenreich, B., Hess, E., and Jacobs, G. (1992), 'Beatlemania: Girls Just Want to Have Fun', in L. Lewis (ed.), *The Adoring Audience: Fan Culture and Popular Media*, London: Routledge.

Entwistle, J. (2000), *The Fashioned Body: Fashion, Dress and Modern Social Theory*, Cambridge: Polity Press.

EW.com (n.d.), '20 Best Boybands Ever!' *Entertainment Weekly* [online], <http://www.ew.com/ew/gallery/0,,20218514_2,00.html> accessed 12 January 2010.

Faircloth, C. (2003), 'Introduction. Different Bodies and the Paradox of Aging: Locating Aging Bodies in Images and Everyday Experience', in C. Faircloth (ed.), *Aging Bodies: Images and Everyday Experience*, Walnut Creek, California: AltaMira.

fanforum.com (n.d.), 'Zac Efron—Style Section—Zac's Clothes', Fan Forum, <http://www.fanforum.com/f251/style-section-zac-s-clothes-62796819/index5.html> accessed 20 February 2010.

Featherstone, M. (2007), *Consumer Culture and Postmodernism*, 2nd ed., London: Sage.

Featherstone, M., and Hepworth, M. (1991), *The Body: Social Process and Cultural Theory*, London: Sage.

Featherstone, M., and Hepworth, M. (2005), 'Images of Ageing: Cultural Representations of Later Life', in M. Lewis Johnson, V. L. Bengston, P.G. Coleman and T.B.L. Kirkwood (eds), *The Cambridge Handbook of Age and Ageing*, Cambridge: Cambridge University Press.

Fenton, S. (1999), *Ethnicity, Racism, Class and Culture*, London: Macmillan.

Finkelstein, J. (1991), *The Fashioned Self*, Cambridge: Polity Press.

Finkelstein, J. (1996), *After a Fashion,* Melbourne: Melbourne University Press.

Fiske, J. (1989), *Reading the Popular*, London: Unwin Hyman.

Fiske, J. (1992), 'The Cultural Economy of Fandom', in L. Lewis (ed.), *The Adoring Audience: Fan Culture and Popular Media*, London: Routledge.

Fiske, J. (1998), 'MTV: Post-Structural, Post-Modern', in A.S.A Berger (ed.), *The Postmodern Presence: Readings on Postmodernism in American Culture and Society,* California: AltaMira.

Flügel, J. C. (1930), *The Psychology of Clothes*, London: Hogarth Press.

Forman, M. (2002), 'Keeping It Real? African Youth Identities and Hip-Hop', in R. Young (ed.) *Music, Popular Culture, Identities*, Critical Studies 19, Amsterdam/New York: Rodopi.

Foucault, M. (1990), *The History of Sexuality: An Introduction, Volume I*, New York: Vintage.

Foucault, M. (2003), *The Birth of the Clinic*, London: Routledge.

Foucault, M., and Boulez, P. (2000), 'On Music and Its Reception', in D. B. Scott (ed.), *Music, Culture and Society: A Reader,* Maidenhead: Oxford University Press.

The Fox (n.d.), 'The Fox: An Elton John Fan Page', <http://www.wonka.nl/elton/index.php?option=content&task=view&id=42&Itemid=33> accessed 20 February 2010.

Fox, A. A. (2004), *Real Country: Music and Language in Working-Class Culture,* Durham, NC: Duke University Press.

freshnessmag.com (2008), 'Pharrell x Louis Vuitton—Blason Jewelry Collection', Freshness [online], 6 January, <http://www.freshnessmag.com/2008/01/06/pharrell-x-louis-vuitton-blason-jewelry-collection> accessed 6 June 2009.

Frith, S. (1978), *The Sociology of Rock*, London: Constable & Co.

Frith, S. (1988), 'Only Dancing: David Bowie Flirts with the Issues', in A. McRobbie (ed.), *Zoot Suits and Second-Hand Dresses,* Basingstoke: Macmillan.

Frith, S. (1989), 'Euro Pop', *Cultural Studies*, 3/2: 166–72.

Frith, S., ed. (1990), *On Record: Rock, Pop and the Written Word*, London: Routledge.

Frith, S. (1996), *Performing Rites*, Oxford: Oxford University Press.

Frith, S., and McRobbie, A. (1990), 'Rock and Sexuality', in S. Frith (ed.), *On Record: Rock, Pop and the Written Word*, London: Routledge.

Gauntlett, D. (2008), *Media, Gender and Identity: An Introduction*, Abingdon: Routledge.

Giddens, A. (1991), *Modernity and Self Identity: Self and Society in the Late Modern Age,* Stanford, California: Stanford University Press.

Gilbert, J., and Pearson, E. (1999), *Discographies: Dance Music, Culture and the Politics of Sound*, London: Routledge.

Gilroy, P. (1993), *The Black Atlantic: Modernity and Double Consciousness*, London: Verso.

Gledhill, C., ed. (1991), *Stardom: Industry of Desire,* London: Routledge.

Glennon, J. (2009), 'Miley Cyrus Clothing Line', suite101.com [online], 2 August, <http://childrensteenfashion.suite101.com/article.cfm/miley_cyrus_clothing_line> accessed 20 February 2010.

Gordon, B. (2009), 'Lady Gaga: An Overhyped Star for the 21st Century', *Guardian* [online], 12 December, <http://www.telegraph.co.uk/comment/columnists/bryonygordon/6795324/Lady-Gaga-an-over-hyped-star-for-the-21st-century.html> accessed 3 May 2010.

Gould, S. J. (1985), 'The Hottentot Venus', in *The Flamingo's Smile*, New York: W. W. Norton.

Greer, G. (2007), 'Well Done, Beth Ditto. Now Let It All Hang Out', *Guardian* [online], 31 May, <http://www.guardian.co.uk/music/2007/may/31/news.germainegreer> accessed 22 April 2010.

Griffin Crowder, D. (1998), 'Lesbians and the (Re/De)Construction of the Female Body', in D. Atkins (ed.), *Looking Queer: Body Image and Identity in Lesbian, Bisexual, Gay and Transgender Communities*, New York: Haworth Press.

Gross, M. (1977), 'Kiss: Where No Band Has Tread Before', *Marvel Comics,* <http://www.rocksbackpages.com/article.html?ArticleID=8556> accessed 26 February 2010.

Grossberg, L. (1999), Same As It Ever Was? Rock Culture. Same As It Ever Was? Rock Theory', in K. Kelly and E. McDonnell (eds), *Stars Don't Stand Still in the Sky: Music and Myth*, New York: New York University Press.

Grosz, E. (1994), *Volatile Bodies: Toward a Corporeal Feminism*, Bloomington and Indianapolis: Indiana University Press.

Guardian (2010), 'Amy Winehouse to Unveil Fashion Collection', 11 March, <http://www.guardian.co.uk/music/2010/mar/11/amy-winehouse-fred-perry-fashion> accessed 12 March 2010.

Guardian (n.d.), 'Digital Content Blog' [online], <http://www.guardian.co.uk/media/pda/2010/mar/25/lady-gaga-video> accessed 15 April 2010.

Haider, A. (2008), 'Yo Majesty: Futuristically Speaking, Never Be Afraid', *Metro* [online], 28 September, <http://www.metro.co.uk/metrolife/328670-yo-majesty-futuristically-speaking-never-be-afraid> accessed 29 December 2010.

Halberstam, J. (1994), 'Between Butches', in S. Munt and C. Smyth, *Butch/Femme: Inside Lesbian Gender,* London: Casell.

Halberstam, J. (1998), *Female Masculinity*, Durham, NC: Duke University Press.

Hall, S. (1997), *Representation: Cultural Representations and Signifying Practices,* London: Sage.

Hallam, E., and Hockey, J. (2001), *Death, Memory and Material Culture*, Oxford: Berg.

Hamilton, J. (2010), 'Paedo Heaven on Our High Street', *Sun* [online], 15 April, <http://www.thesun.co.uk/sol/homepage/news/2933105/High-Street-

stores-are-selling-sexually-provocative-clothes-for-children.html> accessed 16 April 2010.

Harkins, A. (2004), *Hillybilly: A Cultural History of an American Icon,* New York: Oxford University Press.

Harmsworth, A. (2009), 'Stone Reveals Breasts in Bondage Shoot at 51', *Metro* [online], 10 August, <http://www.metro.co.uk/showbiz/717078-stone-reveals-breasts-in-bondage-shoot-at-51> accessed 8 February 2010.

Harris, S. (2007), 'Grand Designs: A Brief History of Fashion Endorsement', *Independent* [online], 8 April, <http://www.independent.co.uk/news/uk/this-britain/why-the-high-street-is-being-swamped-by-celebrity-clothing-ranges-443467.html> accessed 8 February 2009.

Harrison, D. (2009), 'Out of the Closet: Elton John Wardrobe of Crazy Costumes in Charity Sale', *Telegraph* [online], 12 December, <http://www.telegraph.co.uk/news/newstopics/celebritynews/6796946/Out-of-the-closet-Elton-John-wardrobe-of-crazy-costumes-in-charity-sale.html> accessed 29 December 2009.

Harvey, D. (1990), *The Condition of Postmodernity,* Oxford: Blackwell.

Hatch, D., and Millward, S. (2000), 'On Black Music and Authenticity', in D. B. Scott (ed.), *Music, Culture and Society: A Reader,* Maidenhead: Oxford University Press.

Hattersley, G. (2009), 'The Brilliance of Beth Ditto', *Times* [online], 14 June, <http://women.timesonline.co.uk/tol/life_and_style/women/fashion/article6462773.ece> accessed 29 December 2009.

Hayward, S. (1999), 'Questions of National Cinema', in K. Cameron (ed.), *National Identity,* Exeter: Intellect Books.

Hebdige, D. (1979), *Subculture: The Meaning of Style,* London: Routledge.

Hebdige, D. (1988), *Hiding in the Light,* London: Routledge.

Hegarty, P. (2004), *Jean Baudrillard: Live Theory,* London: Continuum.

Hills, M. (2002), *Fan Cultures,* London: Routledge.

Hobson, J. (2003), 'The Batty Politic: Toward an Aesthetic of the Black Female Body', *Hypatia,* 18/4: 87–105.

Hollander, A. (1993), *Seeing through Clothes,* Berkley and Los Angeles: University of California Press.

Hollander, A. (1994), *Sex and Suits: The Evolution of Modern Dress,* New York: Alfred A. Knopf.

Holm Hudson, K. (2002), 'Introduction', in K. Holm Hudson (ed.), *Progressive Rock Reconsidered,* London: Routledge.

Holt, D. B. (2004), *How Brands Became Icons: The Principles of Cultural Branding,* Boston: Harvard Business School Press.

Holt, D. B. (2006), 'Towards a Sociology of Branding', *Journal of Consumer Culture,* 6/3: 299–302.

Horne, S. (2009), 'Party Monsters', *Page Six Magazine, New York Post,* 8 February.

Horyn, C. (2006), 'Cool, at Least for a Few Minutes', *New York Times*, 14 September.

Hudson, P. (2009), 'Put It Away, Granny Madonna—You're Too Old to be Flashing Your Crotch', *Daily Mirror* [online], 7 January, <http://www.mirror.co.uk/celebs/columnists/polly/2009/01/07/put-it-away-granny-madonna-youre-too-old-to-be-flashing-your-crotch-115875-21021971> accessed 8 February 2010.

insider.com (n.d.), '50 Cent Thinks Jay-Z Too Old for Tour', Insider [online], <http://www.theinsider.com/news/1869133_50_Cent_Thinks_Jay_Z_Too_Old_To_Tour> accessed 12 November 2010.

Irigaray, L., and Whitford, M. (1991), *The Irigaray Reader*, Oxford: Blackwell.

Jameson, F. (1991), *Postmodernism, or the Cultural Logic of Late Capitalism*. Durham, NC: Duke University Press.

Jansson, A. (2002), 'The Mediatization of Consumption: Towards an Analytical Framework of Image Culture', *Journal of Consumer Culture*, 2/1: 5–31.

Jenkins, H. (1992), 'Afterword: The Future of Fandom', in Lewis, L. (ed.), *The Adoring Audience: Fan Culture and Popular Media*, London: Routledge.

Jensen, J. (1992), 'Fandom as Pathology: The Consequences of Characterization', in L. Lewis (ed.), *The Adoring Audience: Fan Culture and Popular Media*, London: Routledge.

Jones L. (2009), 'Liz Jones Moans: A Dustbin Lid Dress and Trousers That Made Her Thighs Look Chunky . . . Cheryl Cole's Disastrous *X Factor* Wardrobe', *Daily Mail* [online], 5 November, <http://www.dailymail.co.uk/femail/article-1225226/Cheryl-Coles-disastrous-X-Factor-wardrobe-trousers-thighs-look-chunky.html> accessed 1 March 2010.

Jones, T. (2008), 'Cheryl Cole: Style Icon', *Sun* [online], 10 September, <http://www.thesun.co.uk/sol/homepage/woman/fashion/article1667350.ece> accessed 26 February 2010.

Julier, G. (2000), *The Culture of Design*, London: Sage.

Katz, S. (1996), *Disciplining Old Age: The Formation of Gerontological Knowledge*, Charlottesville: University of Virginia.

King, T. A. (1994), 'Performing Akimbo: Queer Pride and Epistemological Prejudice', in M. Meyer (ed.), *The Politics and Poetics of Camp*, London: Routledge.

Kiss Fan Site (n.d.), 'Kiss Collectibles and Comics: Black Rhino Kiss Hoodie by Marc Ecko', <http://kissfansite.yuku.com/topic/18755> accessed 9 March 2011.

kisscostumes.com (n.d.), 'Adult KISS Costumes', <http://www.kisscostumes.com/adult-kiss-costumes.html> accessed 19 February 2010.

kissfanshop.com (n.d.), 'Paul's Costumes', Kiss Fan Shop [online], <http://www.kissfanshop.de/PaulStanley/costumesPaulFirehouseHelmetsUSA.htm> accessed 19 February 2010.

Kratz, C., and Reimer, B. (1998), 'Fashion in the Face of Postmodernity', in A.S.A Berger (ed.), *The Postmodern Presence: Readings on Postmodernism in American Culture and Society,* California: AltaMira.

Kristeva, J., and Moi, T. (1986), *The Kristeva Reader*, New York: Columbia University Press.

Lady-Gaga.net (n.d.), 'GaGallery', <http://www.lady-gaga.net/gallery/display image.php?album=496&pos=2> accessed 20 February 2010.

Laing, D. (1990), 'Making Popular Music: The Consumer as Producer', in A. Tomlinson (ed.), *Consumption, Identity and Style: Marketing, Meanings and the Packaging of Pleasure*, London: Routledge.

Lauper, C. (2010), 'Lady Gaga', *Time* [online], 29 April, <http://www.time.com/time/specials/packages/article/0,28804,1984685_1984940_1984943,00.html> accessed 1 May 2010.

Laver, J. (1969), *A Concise History of Costume*, London: Thames and Hudson.

Lewis, L., ed. (1992), *The Adoring Audience: Fan Culture and Popular Media*, London: Routledge.

Lister, M., and Wells, L. (2000), 'Seeing Beyond Belief: Cultural Studies as an Approach to Analysing the Visual', in Y. van Leeuwen and C. Jewitt (eds), *The Handbook of Visual Analysis*, London: Sage.

Longhurst, B. (1995), *Popular Music and Society,* Cambridge: Polity Press.

Longhurst, B. (2007), *Popular Music and Society,* 2nd ed., Cambridge: Polity Press.

Lurie, A. (1981), *The Language of Clothes*, London: Random House.

Lury, C. (1996), *Consumer Culture*, Cambridge: Polity Press.

Lury, C. (2004), *Brands: the Logos of the Global Economy*, London: Routledge.

Marie Claire (2009), 'Cheryl Cole Plans Her Own Fashion Line', *Marie Claire* [online], October, <http://www.marieclaire.co.uk/news/427770/cheryl-cole-plans-her-own-fashion-line.html> accessed 15 April 2010.

Marshall, P. David (1997), *Celebrity and Power: Fame in Contemporary Culture*, Minneapolis: University of Minnesota Press.

Marshall, P. David (2000), 'The Celebrity Legacy of the Beatles', in I. Inglis (ed.), *The Beatles, Popular Music and Society: A Thousand Voices*, New York: St Martin's Press.

Maultby, P. (2000), 'On Africanisms', in D.B. Scott (ed.), *Music, Culture and Society: A Reader,* Maidenhead: Oxford University Press.

Mazor, B. (2009), 'Americana by Any Other Name', *No Depression* [online], February, <http://archives.nodepression.com/2009/02/americana-by-any-other-name> accessed 1 December 2009.

McCarthy, K. (2006), 'Not Pretty Girls? Sexuality, Spirituality, and Gender Construction in Women's Rock Music', *Journal of Popular Culture*, 39/1: 69–94.

McCracken, G. C. (1990), *Culture and Consumption: New Approaches to the Symbolic Character of Consumer Goods and Activities*, Bloomington and Indianapolis: Indiana University Press.

McLean, C. (2004), 'Cutting Edge of Camp', *Telegraph* [online], 22 January, <http://www.telegraph.co.uk/culture/3610651/Cutting-edge-of-camp.html> accessed 29 December 2009.

McLoughlin, N. (2000), 'Rock, Fashion and Performativity', in S. Bruzzi and P. Church Gibson (eds), *Fashion Cultures: Theories, Explorations and Analysis*, London: Routledge.

Meagher, S. (2008), *Philosophy and the City: Classic to Contemporary Writings*, Albany: State University of New York Press.

Meyer, M. (1994), 'Introduction', in M. Meyer (ed.), *The Politics and Poetics of Camp*, London: Routledge.

Miley Fashion (n.d.), 'MILEY FASHION: Your #1 Source for Miley Cyrus' Style', <http://dresslikemiley.net> accessed 20 February 2010.

Mills, S. (2008), 'Rapped up in Tweed', *Guardian* [online], 23 September, <http://www.guardian.co.uk/lifeandstyle/2008/sep/23/fashion.outkast> accessed 26 September 2009.

Moir, J. (2008), 'Madonna Sups Deep at the Fountain of Youth', *Telegraph* [online], 26 March, <http://www.telegraph.co.uk/comment/columnists/janmoir/3556572/Madonna-sups-deep-at-the-fountain-of-youth.html> accessed 9 February 2009.

Moody, N. K. (2009), 'Going Gaga for Pop's "It" Girl', *Jakarta Globe* [online], 26 June, <http://www.thejakartaglobe.com/artsandentertainment/going-gaga-for-pops-it-girl/314585> accessed 12 April 2010.

Moore, A. F. (2001), *Rock: The Primary Text*, Aldershot: Ashgate.

Morales, A. (2009), '*X Factor* Judge Cheryl Cole's Dress Was a Horror Show', *Daily Mirror* [online], 2 November, <http://www.mirror.co.uk/celebs/news/2009/11/02/x-factor-judge-cheryl-cole-s-dress-was-a-horror-show-115875-21791576> accessed 1 March 2010.

Mort, F. (1996), *Cultures of Consumption: Masculinities and Social Space in Late Twentieth Century Britain*, London: Routledge.

Muggleton, D. (2000), *Inside Subculture: The Postmodern Meaning of Style*, Oxford: Berg.

Nadoolman Landis, D. (n.d.), 'Michael Jackson: Costume Icon, part 1', Frocktalk [online], <http://frocktalk.com/?p=940> accessed 15 April 2010.

Ndalianis, A., and Henry, C. (2002), *Stars in Our Eyes: The Star Phenomenon in the Contemporary Era*, Westport, CT: Praeger.

Nead, L. (1992), *The Female Nude: Art Obscenity and Sexuality*. London: Routledge.

Negus, K. (1996), *Popular Music in Theory: An Introduction*, Hanover, NH, and London: Wesleyan University Press.

Negus, K. (1997), 'Sinead O'Connor—Musical Mother', in S. Whiteley, *Sexing the Groove: Popular Music and Gender,* London: Routledge.

Nestle, J. (1981), 'Butch-Femme Relationships: Sexual Courage in the 1950s', *Heresies,* 12: 21–4.

Nicol, G. (2007), *Misshapes,* New York: PowerHouse.

Nixon, S. (1996), *Hard Looks: Masculinities, Spectatorship and Contemporary Consumption,* London: University College London Press.

Odell, A. (2009), 'LVMH Targets Danity Kane in Trademark Suit', *New York Magazine* [online], 3 June, <http://nymag.com/daily/fashion/2009/03/lvmhs_targets_danity_kane_in_t.html> accessed 12 November 2009.

Odih, P. (2007), *Advertising in Modern and Postmodern Times,* London: Sage

Ogbar, J. (2007), *Hip Hop Revolution: The Culture and Politics of Rap,* Lawrence: University Press of Kansas.

Pajaczkowska, C. (2005), 'On Stuff and Nonsense: The Complexity of Cloth', *Textile,* 3/3 (Fall): 220–49.

Parker, R. (n.d.), 'Mod: Then and Now', Modculture.com [online], <http://www.modculture.co.uk/culture/culture.php?id=43> accessed 3 January 2010.

perezhilton.com (n.d.), 'Sharon Stone Bares It All!,' <http://perezhilton.com/category/sharon-stone/page/2> accessed 2 February 2010.

Phillips, D. (n.d.), 'Mods Will Always Be with Us', Modculture.com [online], <http://www.modculture.co.uk/culture/culture.php?id=40> accessed 2 February 2010.

Pink, S. (2008), 'Analysing Visual Experience', in M. Pickering, *Research Methods for Cultural Studies,* Edinburgh: Edinburgh University Press.

Polhemus, T. (1994), *Streetstyle: From Sidewalk to Catwalk,* London: Thames and Hudson.

Powell, J. (2004), *Rethinking Gerontology: Foucault, Surveillance and the Positioning of Old Age,* Sincronia [online], <http://sincronia.cucsh.udg.mx/powell04.htm> accessed 8 February 2010.

Quick, H (2009), 'Hail the Return of Rock Chic', *Daily Telegraph* [online], 14 April, <http://www.telegraph.co.uk/fashion/5154575/Hail-the-return-of-rock-chic.html> accessed 1 May 2010.

Rabinow, P., ed. (1991), *The Foucault Reader,* New York: Penguin Books.

Russo, M. (1986), 'Female Grotesques: Carnival and Theory', in T. De Lauretis (ed.), *Feminist Studies/Critical Studies,* Bloomington: Indiana University Press.

Russo, M. (1994), *The Female Grotesque: Risk, Excess and Modernity,* Oxford: Routledge.

Sands, S. (2006), 'EMO Cult Warning for Parents', *Daily Mail* [online], 16 August, <http://www.dailymail.co.uk/news/article-400953/EMO-cult-warning-parents.html> accessed 29 December 2009.

Sandvoss, C. (2005), *Fans,* Cambridge: Polity Press.

Sawyer, M. (2009), 'Different Class, the Pair of Them', *Observer Music Monthly* [online], 19 April, <http://www.guardian.co.uk/music/2009/apr/19/art-and-music> accessed 29 December 2009.

Schlemmer, O. (1961), 'Man and Art Figure', in W. Gropius and A. Wensinger (eds), *Theatre of the Bauhaus*, Middletown, CT: Wesleyan University Press.

Sennett, R. (2003), 'Resistance', in M. Bull and L. Back (eds), *The Auditory Culture Reader*, Oxford: Berg.

Sheinbaum, J. (2002), 'Progressive Rock and the Inversion of Musical Values', in K. Holm Hudson (ed.), *Progressive Rock Reconsidered,* London: Routledge.

Siegel, C. (2005), *Goth's Dark Empire*, Bloomington and Indianapolis: Indiana University Press.

Simpson, R. (2006), 'Madonna Can't Hold Back the Hands of Time, *Daily Mail* [online], 4 May, <http://www.dailymail.co.uk/tvshowbiz/article-385059/Madonna-hold-hands-time.html> accessed 14 November 2009.

Sims, J. (1999), *Rock/Fashion*, London: Omnibus Press.

Singh, A. (2008), 'Miley Cyrus *Vanity Fair* Photo: Annie Leibovitz Defends Her Portrait', *Telegraph* [online], 29 April, <http://www.telegraph.co.uk/news/1906675/Miley-Cyrus-Vanity-Fair-photo-Annie-Leibovitz-defends-her-portrait.html> accessed 11 January 2009.

Slater, D. (1997), *Consumer Culture and Modernity*, Cambridge: Polity Press.

Sontag, S. (1972), 'Double Standard of Ageing', *Sunday Review* [online], <http://www.mediawatch.com/wordpress/?p=33> accessed 23 September 2009.

Sontag, S. (2000), 'Notes on Camp', in J. C. Oates and R. Atwan (ed.), *The Best American Essays of the Century*, New York: Houghton Mifflin.

Spectrum News (2009), 'Lady Gaga Is a Creation, but an Authentic One', *Kuwait Times* [online], 29 June, <http://www.kuwaittimes.net/read_news.php?newsid=MTEwNTk5NjIzNQ> accessed 12 April 2010.

Stacey, J. (1991), 'Feminine Fascination: Forms of Identification in Star Audience Relations', in C. Gledhill (ed.), *Stardom: Industry of Desire,* London: Routledge.

Stacey, J. (1994), *Stargazing: Hollywood Cinema and Female Identification*, London: Routledge.

Steele, V. (2001), *The Corset: A Cultural History*, New Haven/London: Yale University Press.

Stokes, M., ed. (1994), *Ethnicity, Identity and Music: The Musical Construction of Place*, Oxford: Berg.

Straw, W. (2002), 'Music as Commodity and Material Culture', *Repercussions* [online], 7–8 (Spring–Fall 1999–2000, published 2002), <http://strawresearch.mcgill.ca/strawrepercussions.pdf> accessed 25 June 2009.

Strinati, D. (1995), *An Introduction to Theories of Popular Culture*, London: Routledge.

Summers, L. (2001), *Bound to Please: A History of the Victorian Corset*, Oxford: Berg.

Tankel, J. D., and Murphy, B. K. (1998), 'Collecting Comic Books: A Study of the Fan and Curatorial Consumption', in C. Harris and A. Alexander (eds), *Theorizing Fandom*, Cresskill, NJ: Hampton Press.

Thesander, M. (1997), *The Feminine Ideal*, London: Reaktion.

Thornton, S. (2005), 'The Social Logic of Subcultural Capital', in K. Gelder (ed.), *The Subcultures Reader*, London: Routledge.

Thornton, S. (2006), 'Understanding Hipness: "Subcultural Capital" as a Feminist Tool', in A. Bennett, B. Shank and J. Toynbee (eds), *The Popular Music Studies Reader*, London: Routledge.

Time (n.d.), 'The World Goes Lady Gaga' [online], <http://www.time.com/time/photogallery/0,29307,1957589_2030488,00.html> accessed 15 April 2010.

Toynbee, J. (2006), 'Making Up and Showing Off: What Musicians Do', in A. Bennett, B. Shank and J. Toynbee (eds), *The Popular Music Studies Reader*, London: Routledge.

Triggs, T. (1992), 'Framing Masculinity', in J. Ash and E. Wilson (eds), *Chic Thrills: A Fashion Reader*, London: Pandora.

Tseelon, E. (1995), *The Masque of Femininity: The Presentation of Women in Everyday Life*, London: Sage.

Tulloch, C. (1992), 'Rebel without a Pause: Black Street Style and Black Designers', in J. Ash and E. Wilson (eds), *Chic Thrills: A Fashion Reader*, London: Pandora.

Turner, G. (2004), *Understanding Celebrity*, London: Sage.

Urla, J., and Swedlund, A. C. (1995), 'The Anthropology of Barbie: Unsettling Ideals of the Feminine Body in Popular Culture', in J. Terry and J. Urla (eds), *Deviant Bodies*, Bloomington and Indianapolis: Indiana University Press.

Vale, M. (2001), *The Princely Court: Medieval Courts and Culture in North-West Europe 1270–1380*, Oxford: Oxford University Press.

Veblen, T. (1994), *The Theory of the Leisure Class*, London: Penguin Classics.

Vine, S. (2009), 'Get the Beth Ditto Bandage Dress Look', *Times* [online], 11 March, <http://women.timesonline.co.uk/tol/life_and_style/women/fashion/article5883058.ece> accessed 29 December 2009.

virginmedia.com (n.d.), 'Too Old for Pop?', Virgin Media [online], <http://www.virginmedia.com/music/pictures/toptens/too-old-for-pop.php?ssid=10> accessed 29 December 2009.

Vogue (n.d.), 'Cheryl Cole: Style File', <http://www.vogue.co.uk/celebrity-photos/091021-cheryl-cole-x-factor-fashion-and-st/gallery.aspx?Page=3> accessed 16 April 2010.

Wallace, A. (2002), 'Jamie Lee Curtis: True Thighs', *More* [online], September, <http://www.more.com/2049/2464-jamie-lee-curtis-true-thighs> accessed 8 February 2010.

Walsh, J. (2008), 'The Mod Couple: Sir Paul Smith Interviews Paul Weller', *Independent* [online], 7 June, <http://www.independent.co.uk/arts-entertainment/music/features/the-mod-couple-sir-paul-smith-interviews-paul-weller-841567.html> accessed 12 January 2009.

Warwick, J. (2007), *Girl Groups, Girl Culture: Popular Music and Identity in the 1960s*, London: Routledge.

Waugh, P. (2006), *Literary Theory and Criticism: An Oxford Guide*, Oxford: Oxford University Press.

Wazir, B. (2002), 'Still the Boss', *Guardian* [online], 27 October, <http://www.guardian.co.uk/music/2002/oct/27/artsfeatures.popandrock> accessed 14 January 2009.

Weedon, C. (1997), *Feminist Practice and Poststructuralist Theory*, Oxford: Blackwell.

Whiteley, S. (1997), *Sexing the Groove: Popular Music and Gender,* London: Routledge.

Whiteley, S. (2000), *Women and Popular Music: Sexuality, Identity and Subjectivity*, London: Routledge.

Whiteley, S. (2005), *Too Much Too Young: Poplar Music, Age and Gender*, Abingdon: Routledge.

Whittle, S. (2005), 'Gender Fucking or Fucking Gender', in I. Morland and A. Willox (ed.), *Queer Theory*, Basingstoke: Palgrave.

Wicke, P. (1999), *Rock Music: Culture, Aesthetics and Sociology*, Cambridge: Cambridge University Press.

Wilbekin, E. (2008), 'The Return of the Prepster', *Giant* [online], 28 December, <http://giantmag.com/style/emil-wilbekin/the-return-of-the-prepster> accessed 12 September 2009.

Wilkes, D. (2008), 'Have Age and Stress Launched a Shocking Attack on Madonna's Face?' *Daily Mail* [online], 28 July, <http://www.dailymail.co.uk/tvshowbiz/article-1038955/Have-age-stress-launched-shocking-attack-Madonnas-face.html> accessed 8 February 2010.

Williams, L. (1999), 'National Identity and the Nation State: Construction, Reconstruction and Contradiction', in K. Cameron (ed.), *National Identity*, Exeter: Intellect Books.

Williams, R. (1971), *Culture and Society: 1780–1950*, London: Pelican.

Williamson, J. (1978), *Decoding Advertisements: Ideology and Meaning in Advertising,* London: Marion Boyars.

Wilson, E. (1985), *Adorned in Dreams*, London: Virago.

Wilson, E. (1992), 'Fashion and the Postmodern Body', in J. Ash and E. Wilson (ed.), *Chic Thrills: A Fashion Reader*, London: Pandora.

Wilson, E. (1999), 'The Bohemianization of Mass Culture', *International Journal of Cultural Studies*, 2/1: 11–32.

Wilson, E. (2003), *Bohemians: The Glamorous Outcasts*, London: I.B. Tauris.

Wiseman, E. (2009), 'Today I'm Wearing . . . Style Blogger Susie Lau Is Headed for Fashion's Front Row', *Guardian* [online], 8 February, <http://www.guardian.co.uk/lifeandstyle/2009/feb/08/susie-lau-fashion-blogs> accessed 3 April 2010.

World Entertainment News Network (2008), 'Topless Jamie Lee Curtis Promotes Ageing Beautifully', Starpulse.com [online], 22 March, <http://www.starpulse.com/news/index.php/2008/03/22/topless_jamie_lee_curtis_promotes_aging_> accessed 12 January 2010.

Index